Random Excess

The Wild Ride of
Michael Cowpland
and Corel

ROSS LAVER

VIKING

VIKING
Published by the Penguin Group
Penguin Books Canada Ltd, 10 Alcorn Avenue, Toronto, Ontario,
Canada M4V 3B2
Penguin Books Ltd, 27 Wrights Lane, London w8 5TZ, England
Penguin Putnam Inc., 375 Hudson Street, New York, New York 10014, U.S.A.
Penguin Books Australia Ltd, Ringwood, Victoria, Australia
Penguin Books (NZ) Ltd, cnr Rosedale and Airborne Roads, Albany,
Auckland 1310, New Zealand

Penguin Books Ltd, Registered Offices: Harmondsworth, Middlesex, England

First published 1998
1 3 5 7 9 10 8 6 4 2

Printed and bound in Canada on acid free paper ∞

CANADIAN CATALOGUING IN PUBLICATION DATA

Laver, Ross
    Random excess: the wild ride of Michael Cowpland and Corel

ISBN 0-670-87972-X

1. Cowpland, Michael C.J. 2. Corel Corporation. 3. Chief executive officers –
Canada – Biography. I. Title

HD9696.63.C34C67 1998   338.7´610053´092   C98-931553-3

Visit Penguin Canada's website at **www.penguin.ca**

To Kathy
for her love and patience

Prologue

On a Saturday night in 1990, several thousand men and women gathered in the cavernous, dimly lit interior of Houston's George R. Brown Convention Center to witness a shootout. Happily for the many pacifists in the crowd, the event had nothing whatsoever to do with firearms. Instead, the duellists—one a thirty-nine-year-old self-made millionaire, the other a thirty-eight-year-old former advertising art director—were packing laptop computers loaded with competing brands of graphics software. Their host was the Houston Area League of PC Users (HAL-PC), a 12,000-member club that was, and is, one of the largest community-based groups of personal computer users and hobbyists anywhere in the world.

Several times a year, the directors of HAL-PC organized these head-to-head product demonstrations so that members could stay informed about the constantly expanding universe of PC software. Thanks to the shootout format—a kind of "battle of the bands" for computer geeks—the events were often both educational and, by software industry standards at least, entertaining. For the combatants, however, it was serious business. A properly executed demo could easily spur hundreds or thousands of sales to the sorts of people marketing experts call "early adopters"—consumers who rush to get their hands on the latest technology and, through word of mouth, can make or break a product in the mainstream marketplace.

As they warmed up in the VIP room behind the main convention hall, the two high-tech gunslingers looked anything but evenly matched. J. Paul Grayson, the millionaire, was chairman and chief executive officer of Micrografx Inc., a company he and his brother

George co-founded in 1982, barely a year after the introduction of the IBM PC. Launched in a Dallas garage on the strength of a $5,000 Visa card advance, Micrografx struck it rich by becoming the first independent software company to recognize the enormous potential of Microsoft's Windows operating system. Months before Microsoft chairman Bill Gates unveiled Version 1.0 of Windows in November 1985, Micrografx was selling a Windows-compatible program called In★A★Vision that allowed computer users to draw simple images on the screen. That product eventually gave way to a much more sophisticated one, Micrografx Designer. By 1990, Paul and George Grayson were sitting atop a $60-million company with a stellar reputation and a long list of glowing reviews. Paul Grayson, a tireless promoter with close-cropped brown hair and a thin moustache, was about as blue-chip as it is possible to get in the highly unstable PC software industry. A director of the U.S. Software Publishers Association, he had been honoured as "Emerging Business Entrepreneur of the Year" in 1989 by *Inc.* magazine and the international accounting firm of Ernst and Young.

Grayson's opponent in the Houston shootout was Susan Wimmer, a self-described "road warrior" from a small Canadian software company called Corel Systems Corp. A native of Connecticut who had moved to Ottawa so her husband could do postgraduate work at Carleton University, Wimmer fell into a fascination with computers and desktop publishing while designing ads for the Wrangler jean company in Greensboro, North Carolina. Now she was one of three product specialists whose job was to travel around the United States showing off Corel's main product—a graphics application called CorelDRAW—to software dealers and potential customers.

On this night, Wimmer was well cast as David to Grayson's Goliath. True, Micrografx was the larger and more established company, and Grayson himself was, for Texans, something of a homegrown hero. But it was the Ottawa outfit that had momentum—which, in the software business more than any other, is what matters most. Even before CorelDRAW's release in 1989, trade magazines had been raving about it and drawing comparisons that were unfavourable to Grayson's product, which was $100 more expensive and geared primarily to technical artists and graphics professionals. CorelDRAW, which was easier to use and boasted a number of innovative features, appealed to beginners as well as pros. In no time it had begun to slice deeply into Micrografx's sales.

Grayson, to put it politely, was steamed. His arms tightly folded across his chest, his thin lips tightly pursed, he paced back and forth in the backstage area while, out front, the master of ceremonies delivered a few introductory remarks. Wimmer, eager to break the tension, wandered over to the Micrografx chairman at one point and cheerfully introduced herself. To her surprise, he turned away and refused to shake her hand.

Minutes later, the emcee summoned Grayson to the stage. Smiling and waving to the crowd, he strolled over to the podium, plugged his laptop into the overhead video-projection system and launched into a well-rehearsed, flawless demo of his firm's product. When he finished thirty minutes later, the audience responded with warm applause.

Wimmer was still thinking about Grayson's refusal to shake her hand when she took his place on the dais and strapped the miniature microphone around her neck. *If that's the way you want to be*, she thought to herself, *so be it—but you asked for it.* Above and behind her, the video screen glowed brightly with an image of the CorelDRAW opening screen, ready to respond to every movement of the cursor.

Almost from the start, it was obvious that the crowd preferred the upstart CorelDRAW over its more entrenched competitor. The special effects were faster and more polished, the colour-handling and text-manipulation functions far more impressive. In every way, the product seemed smoother and more powerful. As Wimmer ran through her routine, seamlessly moving from one feature to the next, the crowd oohed and aahed, interrupting frequently with bursts of applause. Several dozen of the more rambunctious members of the audience cheered or shouted out accolades—"Yeah!" and "All right!"

Hearing all the commotion, a visitor standing outside the hall might have been forgiven for wondering whether Elvis Stojko himself were performing triple Axels on stage. Here was the software industry's equivalent of a gold-medal performance: a lone woman behind a podium, clutching a computer mouse in her left hand and creating imaginative, colourful designs on a computer screen. And when the demo was over, several thousand boisterous technology nuts took to their feet in a sustained standing ovation.

Susan Wimmer will never forget that night in Texas, just as she will never forget the exhilaration of working for what, at the time, was the fastest-growing consumer software company on the planet. In less than five years, Corel went from being a money-losing unknown to the world's second-largest producer of software for the consumer market, with a stock market capitalization of $1.2 billion. Its programs were routinely judged the best in their class by leading computer magazines. At trade shows across North America, CorelDRAW drew standing ovations and wild applause from computer users, who fell in love with the company's main product the moment they saw it. More than a dozen of Corel's senior employees—including Wimmer, who resigned in 1994 to return to the United States—became multi-millionaires thanks to one of the industry's most generous employee stock option plans.

And then, suddenly, the roof fell in.

The story of how and why Corel scaled the ladder of the PC software industry, and then tumbled back to earth again, is ultimately the story of its flamboyant founder and CEO, Michael Cowpland. At once one of the most audacious, admired and ridiculed entrepreneurs in Canada, Cowpland helped to create not one but two of the country's best-known technology companies, the other being Mitel Corp., a Kanata, Ontario-based producer of telephone equipment that soared to great heights in the 1970s before running into trouble in the early 1980s.

If, as former *InfoWorld* columnist Robert X. Cringely has suggested,

Bill Gates is the Henry Ford of the personal computer industry, Mike Cowpland is its Lee Iacocca—an engineer whose greatest talent is in marketing, a born salesman and inveterate hype-spinner whose failures are every bit as memorable as his successes.

More than that, Cowpland is an extravagant hedonist in an industry heavily populated with shy, inward-looking nerds. While his employees sit hunched over their keyboards, sometimes for twenty-four hours at a stretch, in hopes of overcoming some arcane programming problem, Cowpland can often be found scampering around a tennis court, jetting off to his Florida retreat or skiing in the Swiss Alps. His taste in cars runs to Porsches and Lamborghinis; his taste in women is embodied by his second wife, Marlen, a platinum-blond knockout who enjoys scandalizing the more sober inhabitants of Canada's capital by parading in public in outfits that leave remarkably little—certainly not her diamond-pierced navel—to the imagination. Their garish, $10-million mansion in Ottawa's staid Rockcliffe Park is a sensualists' wonderland, with a 4,000-square-foot master bedroom, twin squash courts, an outdoor hot tub and swimming pool ringed by white Roman columns, a fully equipped gym and a circular wine cellar stocked with Dom Perignon.

Cowpland's ostentatious lifestyle has earned him the enmity of Ottawa's self-appointed guardians of taste and morality, but their criticism is nothing compared to the abuse he has taken from Corel's own shareholders. From a high of $26.25 a share in 1995, the stock slid to $2 in early 1998, taking with it more than a billion dollars of investors' money. Rubbing salt in their wounds, Cowpland himself sold $20 million worth of stock, a third of his stake, in August 1997, mere weeks before the company reported a huge third-quarter loss. By spring of 1998, the once high-flying Corel had been abandoned by every major pension and mutual fund manager in the country. The dwindling band of investment analysts who continued to follow the company spent most of their time trying to forecast how much money Corel would lose in the next quarter. Added to that was a growing list of legal difficulties, including an Ontario Securities

Commission investigation into Cowpland's stock sales and a U.S. class-action suit that accused the company of deliberately misleading shareholders about its financial position. There was even a lawsuit from former Hollywood screen star Hedy Lamarr, who was incensed that Corel had used her image as the centrepiece of a marketing campaign for the newest version of CorelDRAW.

As one problem piled on top of another, Cowpland kept up a brave front. Whenever a reporter or investor got within hearing range, he'd launch into a frenetic song and dance about the fabulous new products Corel supposedly had in the pipeline, the whiz-bang applications that were sure to revolutionize the industry. "Watch this space," he'd say, his eyes sparkling with the promise of technological breakthroughs still to come. At the company's annual meeting in April 1998, he brushed aside calls for his resignation, brashly telling shareholders that within a year they would be cheering his performance.

Yet the truth was that Cowpland had no idea how he would, or even if he could, turn Corel around. The industry was evolving so rapidly that it was impossible for anyone to know where things were heading next. From as far back as the early days of Mitel, Cowpland's style has always been to ride as many new technology waves as possible, on the theory that one of them will surely turn out to be the Big Kahuna—the one that breaks though the technological clutter and becomes a mainstream hit. CorelDRAW emerged from that process, and the hundreds of millions of dollars it generated eventually gave Cowpland the resources to buy the world's number-two word-processing application, WordPerfect. But now both of those markets are saturated, which means that Cowpland is under increasing pressure to find some new wave to keep his company afloat.

Like any good salesman, Cowpland understands the importance of keeping up appearances. He'll turn fifty-six in the fall of 1998, and nothing worries him more than the fear that others might suspect he is slowing down. Tennis and squash are part of his regular regimen, not simply because he relishes the competition but because, out there on the court, he can wage daily war against the aging process. At the office, in his desk drawer, Cowpland keeps dozens of small pill bottles: vitamins, health supplements and every manner of herbal concoction that might help combat the ravages of time. He cultivates the lean and hungry look, in part because it epitomizes his preferred way of doing business.

In a way, Cowpland's whole life is an act of self-promotion. When he talks to reporters, he never fails to mention his recent athletic exploits: the celebrity tennis matches in Florida, the daredevil bob-sledding in St. Moritz, the karate and kick-boxing lessons with Marlen. Is there another man in Canada—or anywhere else for that matter—who would dare send out Christmas cards adorned with a photograph of his wife posing seductively in a form-fitting Santa suit, complete with red stiletto heels?

The irony is that Cowpland is fundamentally a shy, insecure man, a man who craves approval and is determined to convince others that he knows what he's doing, even when he doesn't. "He comes across as flashy and loud, but he really isn't," says Aili Kurtis, a graphic artist who worked at Corel for seven years and designed CorelDRAW's ubiquitous hot-air balloon logo. "He's actually a very quiet, sensitive guy. It's as though he's consciously taken on this persona, this image of the millionaire with his fancy wife and these fancy cars and the fancy house. And it's all just a cover-up by somebody who's really very sensitive and very private." Merri Lemmex, another former employee, calls Cowpland "a painfully shy person. In the four years I spent at Corel, I think I talked to him every day and yet you never actually had a conversation with him. He tends not to look you in the eye, and he always looks like he's just about to walk out the door, like his mind is racing ahead to another meeting."

In person, those insecurities make Cowpland an easy man to like. Even when you suspect he isn't telling the whole truth—about his negotiations with a potential business partner, for example, or the reason why he sold a third of his stake in Corel in advance of disastrous financial results—he comes across not as a liar or a con man but as someone who is simply afraid that others will think less of him. Picture an embarrassed schoolboy who wants to avoid being sent to the principal's office. The high-tech world is full of people who consider Cowpland reckless and unpredictable, yet in a quarter century of tumultuous business dealings he has acquired remarkably few enemies. The break-up of his first marriage was prolonged and extremely messy, according to friends, but, in public at least, even Darlene Cowpland has nothing but good things to say about her former husband.

Cowpland spends so much time trying to please and impress people that it's easy to forgive his impulsive behaviour and his tendency to exaggerate his own accomplishments. Even many of the people who have been fired from Corel over the years find it hard to bear a grudge. Robert Lendvai, a former sales manager who lost his job in 1993 after seven years with the company, is a good example. Looking back on the episode, his main complaint is not that he was terminated without warning, but that afterwards Cowpland declined to take his calls or meet him face to face. "I tried to speak to him a couple of times, but Mike wasn't comfortable dealing with that shit. The funny thing is, I just wanted to tell him it was a good ride, I did well with the stock options, and no hard feelings."

The doorbell rings and Mike Cowpland, his slender frame visible through a frosted glass panel beside the entranceway, bounds over to answer it. As he ushers me into the house with a handshake and a hurried "How ya doing?" four impeccably groomed dogs erupt in a canine frenzy, tails wagging furiously, wet noses burrowing into pant legs. The dogs belong more to Marlen than to Mike, a fact deduced from their cutesy names. The largest, an Afghan hound, is Chanel; there is also a golden retriever called Blondie and a furry little Maltese that answers to Bunny. The only exception to the naming convention is Java, a three-year-old white German shepherd that is quite possibly the only dog in Ottawa named for a computer programming language. Being part wolf, Java "tends to be a bit unstable," Cowpland jokes. "Just like the language."

It is late June 1998, a few days after Corel's latest bombshell. Slipped in almost as an afterthought in a press release announcing yet another money-losing fiscal quarter was the revelation that the company—after repeated denials that it was planning to cut staff—is shutting down its Utah engineering centre, a facility it acquired in 1996 with the takeover of WordPerfect. Five hundred and thirty employees, a third of Corel's payroll, are being let go, along with two high-ranking executives, Eid Eid and Paul Skillen, who have been with the company for eight and six years respectively. A few weeks earlier, Cowpland had been full of praise for the two executives. Now, suddenly, they are "empire-builders" who talk a good game but rarely deliver. "Between us, Eid wasn't a leader," he says dismissively. Referring to Skillen, whom Cowpland put in charge of the Utah operation at the time of the acquisition, he says, "Basically, it's very easy to be fooled by him because this guy could impress a team of New York analysts twenty deep. But in terms of getting the job done, it wasn't happening."

If Cowpland is feeling any more sorry for the 530 Utah engineers and customer service employees who have just lost their jobs, he isn't letting on. "The fact of the matter is, it's a heck of lot more efficient to run the whole thing out of Ottawa," he says, sipping champagne and puffing on a Cuban cigar. Curled up next to him on one of several S-shaped modular white leather sofas in the Rockcliffe Park living room, Marlen is attired in a spandex body suit, a Harlequinesque number with rectangular patches of red, white and gold set against a black background. Donna Karan's name is printed in large letters across her chest. When she gets up to answer the phone, the letters do not jiggle.

Cowpland is keen to talk about Corel's latest comeback plan, but first he pulls out a cartoon from *PC Week* magazine. It shows Marlen at a recent computer industry gathering in New York City, dressed in a slinky black cat-suit and preening next to Michael Dell, the billionaire founder of Dell Computer. She hadn't planned to attend the dinner, but one of Corel's top salesmen talked her into it in hopes of generating some much-needed publicity for Corel. It worked.

"It's kind of neat because Michael Dell was there and they didn't pay him any attention," Cowpland says. "She was pushing the envelope, but what's great about it is she pulls it off."

"Michael always says we have so much fun, the government is going to start taxing it," Marlen says, laughing.

But surely they aren't having much fun now, with Corel having lost money for six straight quarters?

"That's the interesting thing," Cowpland says. "The way I look at it, business is like a sport, and you don't win all the time. But if you keep on playing hard you're going to do well eventually. The neat thing is, everybody's super-pumped and this is the highest morale we've had in ages."

It sounds convincing, but Cowpland is known for his unrelenting optimism. For more than a year, the news out of Corel has been disastrous, yet Cowpland has never stopped promising that the company is on the brink of a major breakthrough. He has done it so many times that most people who follow the company just roll their eyes and smirk when they hear it. And yet in some ways all that bravado is more than just an act. Cowpland himself seems genuinely to believe what he is saying, as though all that is required to restore Corel to the pantheon of high-tech greatness is to keep trusting in his own ability to make it happen.

Doesn't he ever have moments of self-doubt?

"Oh yes, but he doesn't show it," Marlen says. She launches into an anecdote about the most recent CorelDRAW gala, an annual, company-wide extravaganza. "Michael gives speeches all the time but he was very, very stressed about the gala. You know, the shares had gone down so far."

Cowpland looks uneasy at the direction of the conversation. "Trying to organize a celebration with all that going on, that was hard work. But, you know, there's always the challenges ahead. And as long as you're continuously pushing forward it's going to happen."

Marlen is nodding vigorously in agreement.

"When we met, in 1986, Corel was just starting out, and it was really not going well," she says. "At one point, Michael was so sick for three days. It was stress—gastroenteritis. At that point he almost did not believe in Corel, but he kept on going and kept on pushing, and five years later Corel was a tremendous success. Now he believes in Corel, and the shares are down, and he knows how much he can bring them back up. He did it before and he can do it again, only better."

I glance across at Cowpland. He is beaming. He and Marlen have many things in common, but the most important is this: they both believe in Mike Cowpland.

Chapter One

For all its worldwide influence, the microcomputer industry has always been a remarkably compact and tightly knit community, founded by young, middle- and upper-middle class males who grew up in suburban U.S. West Coast homes. Think of Bill Gates, the quintessential techno-nerd—privileged son of a successful corporate attorney and his socialite wife, a childhood computer whiz who attended an elite private school in Seattle and might have graduated from Harvard had he not chosen to drop out in his sophomore year and become the world's richest man. Or Steve Jobs, the wise-ass megalomaniac with rock star good looks who co-founded Apple Computer in the garage of his parents' home in Los Altos, California. Or Larry Ellison, the legendary Silicon Valley playboy and chairman of Oracle Systems, a giant maker of database software. Smart, entrepreneurial and burning with ambition, these pioneers of computing grew up in a country where opportunity was—or at least seemed to be—boundless, in a culture that nurtured innovation, refused to recognize limitations and took for granted that the future would be brighter and more exciting than the past.

To say that Mike Cowpland was raised in different circumstances is an understatement. True, his father's family did have money once, but by the time young Michael appeared on the scene the fortune was long gone. More to the point, perhaps, the faded "resort" town of Bexhill-on-Sea in southeastern England, where Cowpland was born and went to school, has about as much in common with sun-splashed Silicon Valley as a pint of lukewarm British ale has with a bottle of oak-aged California chardonnay.

I

The local tourism bureau generously describes Bexhill as "a town in East Sussex that combines the best of both worlds, the 'olde worlde' charm of the Edwardian era—when good personal service wasn't just a marketing gimmick—and enough modern facilities to keep even the most restless and energetic holiday-maker more than satisfied." Restless and energetic tourists would be wise not to believe everything they read. In fact, like many English seaside communities, Bexhill forfeited its status as a holiday destination the moment inexpensive air travel and all-inclusive package tours made it possible for middle-class Britons to escape to the sunny Mediterranean on their once-a-year getaways. More recently the town has attempted to promote itself as a weekend retreat for Londoners, but the task is made more difficult by the shortage of significant local historical attractions. About the best the local boosters can come up with is the oft-repeated assertion that it was the first British resort to allow mixed bathing on its beaches, in 1901.

The whiff of raciness imparted by that landmark event has, it must be said, long since dissipated. For decades, Bexhill-on-Sea has been a community of geriatrics—the sort of place people retire to and then wait to die. The result is a kind of quiet solemnity. With its neatly trimmed hedges, well-tended rose bushes, whitewashed tea shops and narrow streets leading down to a stony beach, Bexhill is peaceful and reserved where many other English seaside communities are merely tacky and depressing. In *The Kingdom by the Sea*, a book he wrote after journeying on foot and by rail around the British coast, the novelist and travel writer Paul Theroux remarked on the town's "dull comforts and warm rooms and large windows and busy churches. . . . There were no youths at all in sight; every human I saw there was elderly, and most of them were attached to a leash and being pulled along by a dog, and even the dogs looked senile." Theroux added, "It seemed clear to me that once an English person had reached Bexhill-on-Sea he had no intention of going any farther. This was, so to speak, the edge of the cliff."

Apart from having broken the taboo against mixed bathing,

Bexhill's other major claim to fame is that, in 1902, it played host to Britain's first automobile races. Sponsored by the eighth Earl De La Warr, a local notable, the trials began at the top of Gallery Hill so as to give the participants an opportunity to gather speed. From there the cars headed downhill to the Earl's private bicycle course, a flat, kilometre-long stretch of dirt track that was later opened to the public as a seafront promenade. "The curves of the course are easy enough," a British motoring correspondent wrote after attending the races, "and if there is one drawback it is the length of the runoff, perhaps, the biggest cars attaining their fastest speed and having to apply their brakes with rather unpleasant force."

Since 1990, the races have been commemorated on the first weekend of every May by an antique auto festival—antique being a relative term, given that many of the Bexhill residents who show up for the festivities are considerably older than most of the vehicles on display.

As it happens, cars and engines of all sorts were among the abiding passions of the young Mike Cowpland, along with mathematics. He came by those interests honestly. Although he spent most of his childhood in a three-storey Victorian house a stone's throw from the Earl's old bicycle track, his father's family's roots were in the county of Herefordshire, 270 kilometres to the northwest. His paternal grandmother, Ethel Morgan, was the sister of Henry Morgan, founder of the company that makes classic two-seater sports cars. (In a nod to the family history, Cowpland keeps a blue Morgan in the ten-car garage under his sprawling Rockcliffe mansion.) Her father was the Reverend H.G. Morgan, an Oxford University graduate and brilliant mathematician who raised his family in a stone rectory in the village of Stoke Lacy, not far from the county seat of Hereford.

In her twenties, Ethel married Willie Cowpland, an Anglican minister's son who played the organ for many years at Hereford Cathedral. After the ceremony the couple moved into a large estate in the nearby village of Ullingswick and had four children: Betty (who died at an early age), Audrey, Ronald and Douglas. Like Ethel Morgan,

Willie Cowpland came from a well-to-do family, but he was a gambler and lost most of his money betting on horses. "My mother would say that he was lazy," says Douglas Cowpland, Ethel Morgan's younger son and Michael's uncle. "I recall her indicating that the only job he ever did was to rake the driveway."

Ethel, on the other hand, was both adventuresome and highly self-assured, known throughout Herefordshire as a skilled huntswoman and tennis player. "We had quite a large property with two tennis courts," says Ronald Cowpland, Michael's father. "Growing up, I used to watch my mother play tennis all the time. She served underhand but she was very good—played for the county, in fact. She always put a lot of spin on the ball."

Willie Cowpland didn't play tennis, but his wife adored the game and played at every opportunity—in part, one suspects, to steal time away from her husband. For it wasn't just tennis that she had grown to love. One of her occasional partners was a dashing army captain turned professional artist named Jack Kilgour, who was married with five children. For an active young mother living a sheltered life in rural England, Kilgour, still fit and handsome in his late thirties, was difficult to resist: a decorated First World War veteran, a painter whose canvases had been exhibited in the Royal Academy in London, a skilled tennis and field hockey player and a racer of motorcycles.

In light of her unhappy marriage, it was perhaps to be expected that Ethel would begin to have strong affections for her frequent tennis partner. But that hardly lessened the shock for all concerned when she and Kilgour ran off together in 1931, taking with them her three surviving children.

"They played tennis together and then they eloped—wasn't that awful?" says Ronald, who was sixteen at the time. "And that created the scandal of Herefordshire. Today they wouldn't wink an eyelid, but in those days when you ran off and left your husband it wasn't too good, was it? Especially in Herefordshire. My mother's sister never spoke to her again. And my cousins wouldn't talk to me for the longest time. We were the black sheep after that performance."

Unfortunately, Ethel Cowpland's taste in men wasn't much better the second time than the first. She and Jack Kilgour were together for little more than a year before he kissed her goodbye and returned to his wife, leaving his former lover pregnant with another girl, whom she named Heather. Ethel was devastated, both because of Kilgour's decision to leave and because she had lent him a substantial sum of money, which he never repaid. "Have you heard of 'Dynasty'?" Ronald Cowpland says. "That's what it was like, really, because my mother lost out and my poor old dad would have nothing to do with us after that. Eventually he lost the house in Herefordshire and went to live as a lodger with my old nanny. So it was bad all around, really."

Ethel, however, soon bounced back from her grief. With what remained of her inheritance, she purchased a small hotel in Folkestone on the southeast coast of England, near Dover. For additional income, she ran a small kennel in which she bred Pugs. A peppy, outgoing woman who rarely hesitated to speak her mind, Ethel grew to value her independence. From time to time Kilgour would drop by and suggest that they pick up where they had left off, but she would have none of it. "As I got older I recall overhearing conversations where he was keen to get back together with her and she didn't want much to do with him," Douglas Cowpland says. "I remember pretending to be asleep once when they were talking in the sitting room and it was quite revealing. I really don't know if she wanted to marry him in the early years, but by that point she was quite independent. I think she just wanted to be left alone with her dogs."

After the evacuation of Dunkirk in June 1940, she called her staff together and announced that she was closing the hotel to join the Women's Royal Naval Service (the Wrens), a division of Britain's Royal Marines. She spent the rest of the war based in Dover, helping to feed and look after the naval squadrons that rescued pilots whose planes had been shot down over the English Channel. According to family lore, she once cooked for Winston Churchill during one of the prime minister's wartime visits to Dover.

Ronald Cowpland, Ethel's older son, was every bit as energetic and free-spirited as his mother. He was fortunate as a young man to be able to draw on a small trust fund that had been set up in his name by the Cowpland family before it split apart. The money relieved him of the obligation to find work and left him free to socialize and play tennis; to his mother's delight, he became tennis champion of Dover and surrounding Kent County in his early twenties. Only when war broke out in 1939 did he decide to settle down and marry Marjorie Plackett, the cleverest and prettiest of the young women who had worked in his mother's hotel. "I had to move quickly because all the women were getting taken—the Canadians were coming over and marrying all the good-looking girls, so you had to act fast or you wouldn't have a chance," said Ronald.

A few months later he joined the army signal corps as a private. The young couple spent their first few years together living in a succession of military camps in southern England. Their first son, Geoffrey, was born on August 4, 1940. Michael followed on April 23, 1943.

After the invasion of Normandy in June 1944, Ronald endured six months bogged down with his unit in Caen, France, "living on dry biscuits, which was very good for the waistline." His army pay amounted to seven shillings a week, of which two were required to be saved, but on the side he ran a popular football betting pool among his fellow soldiers. "He's always been what the British call a punter," Mike Cowpland says. "He and his buddies liked to place bets on who was going to win that week's football matches back in England, so he would collect the money and whoever guessed the most winners would get the prize. Lo and behold he won the first one, which was highly embarrassing, even though you can't really fix who's going to win. Then he won the second one, which was even more embarrassing. When it came to the third one he actually won that, too, but he pretended he didn't because he thought it would be way too controversial. The real problem was just that he knew the teams so well. Sport has always been a big part of his life, and he passed that on to me."

For the record, Ronald insists that his knowledge of each team's strengths and weaknesses was cursory at best, and that his back-to-back victories in the betting pool were "complete luck." His friends, however, suspected otherwise. "For a while, they were all sharpening their bayonets to take me out to the woods."

Like many people born in Britain during the war, Michael and Geoffrey Cowpland had very little contact with their father while they were small children. The young family's first opportunity to live together under one roof came in 1946 when Ronald returned to civilian life. Casting about for something to do, he heard about a small tennis club that was for sale in Bexhill, about 60 kilometres west of Dover. He promptly made arrangements to buy it and then set himself up as a travelling tennis instructor. "He loved tennis, so he turned it into a career," Mike says, admiring his father's resourcefulness. "He used to get contracts from private girls' schools through southeast England. He'd drive around to them during the day, giving lessons, and then come back at night."

Money was still tight, so Marjorie Cowpland opened a small café and homemade cake shop called Sugar and Spice on the ground floor of the family's small, three-bedroom house at 25A Weston Road in Bexhill. Managing the shop and keeping its shelves supplied with freshly baked cakes, muffins and scones was no simple task for a mother of two small boys, and it was made even more difficult by the fact that staples such as flour and sugar were still being rationed in Britain several years after the war. "My mother and father worked together as a team," Mike Cowpland said. "My brother and I learned a lot about business from them. You could see how you earned your money by selling things and making things and doing things, instead of waiting around for someone else to give you a job."

When Mike was about seven or eight, his mother closed the cake shop and the family moved to a more spacious terraced house at 32 Wilton Road, two blocks from the seafront in a part of the town centre that is now a designated conservation area because of its high concentration of well-preserved Victorian buildings. The subject wasn't much discussed in front of the children, but Geoffrey Cowpland believes that one of the reasons for the move was that his mother was beginning to have trouble contending with the physical demands of running a café. It would be several more years before she was diagnosed with Hodgkin's disease, a disorder of the lymphatic system whose symptoms include fever and progressive enlargement of the lymph nodes. According to Michael, it was only ten years or so later that the rest of the family realized she was fatally ill. "We knew she was going up to London for medical treatment, but she didn't tell anyone what she had, not even my dad. She was used to being the pillar of strength, and probably didn't want to bother anyone."

Far from feeling sorry for herself, Marjorie Cowpland decided to start another business—albeit one that required less physical exertion. She and her husband were fanatical about bridge, so together they opened a bridge club in their new home. The members played five afternoons a week, gathering around card tables set up in two large rooms off the front hall. Marjorie and Ronald organized tournaments, collected membership fees and charged players for tea and other light refreshments. The Wilton Road Bridge Club soon became the most popular such organization in Bexhill, a town where people have always taken their bridge seriously.

To this day, son Michael is convinced that his father would have made a great software developer because bridge, like computer programming, demands excellent short-term memory. "I've got more technical and formal training than he had, but at the same time he's obviously got super-intelligence because at one point he played bridge for England. He and my mother had a fabulous time. They'd go off to Europe playing in tournaments with people like Omar Sharif, and my dad sometimes played at this big gaming club in London called Crawford's where they played for big money. I remember they would come back from four-day weekends in France where in a typical day they'd play probably twenty sets of hands, and a week later they'd still be discussing in detail the card play of one particular hand. There'd be comments like, 'No, no—you shouldn't have played the four of clubs, you should have played the three, because that would have signalled me to play the ace of hearts,' and on and on. I used to think, Jeez, how can they remember one hand in such detail out of maybe sixty hands?"

Being the only two children in the household, Michael and Geoffrey naturally spent much of their time in each other's company. Yet their personalities were like day and night. Geoffrey was a thoughtful, cautious boy, while Michael was effervescent and impulsive, constantly seeking out new experiences. "I'm a quieter person than he is, I suppose," says Geoffrey, now a chartered accountant in southern England. Looking back, Geoffrey thinks the difference in their characters owed something to timing. He was born near the beginning of the war, at a time of great uncertainty and deprivation for Britain, while Michael came along toward the end of the conflict, and had scarcely begun to talk by VE-Day in May 1945.

As the older boy, Geoffrey was raised to feel a stronger sense of duty and responsibility than his younger brother. "When you go through life as the first-born son, you tend to be perhaps not quite so much the live wire as the younger one, who hasn't got so many responsibilities," he says. "The fact is that our folks were pretty busy most of the time, and Mike and I were often thrown together to look after ourselves. Being the older boy, I was always the one who was put in charge." Ronald Cowpland offers a similar explanation: "I was working about eighty hours a week, with four or five schools, and I was the Sussex County tennis coach, so Geoffrey looked after Michael more than me, really. You could even say Geoffrey was more like his dad."

From the age of about six or seven until the time he left Bexhill-on-Sea to go to university, Geoffrey Cowpland's best friend was a boy his own age named Tony Carr. Geoffrey and Tony were in the same class at school and played together constantly—often with Michael tagging along, eager to join in. Carr, who emigrated to Canada in 1986 and is now a psychiatrist in Hamilton, Ontario, remembers Geoffrey as a sensitive, considerate young man, while Michael was fun-loving and not afraid to take risks. "If Michael was a girl, you would say he was vivacious," Carr says. "He was a very participating person, interested in everything that came along. If you happened to mention that you were going to a new place or to try a new sport, he would always want to come along. . . . If you wanted to be nasty you could call him distractible. He was certainly attracted to all sorts of new things as they went past him."

Given that their father's income depended to a large extent on his reputation as a tennis instructor, Cowpland and his brother felt pressure to play the game well. The two boys began taking lessons from their dad when Michael was six. Away from the court, they practised for hours by hitting a tennis ball against a high brick wall in the back yard of the house on Weston Road.

The dedication paid off, because in their teens both boys won Sussex County championships in their respective age groups. "As a tennis teacher your dream obviously is to have a Pete Sampras, you know?" Michael says. "So [my father] was very keen and competitive—he definitely wanted us to win." Even so, Cowpland says his father was a supportive coach who encouraged his progeny but never pushed them hard in pursuit of victory. "It was always very positive, not like some parents," says Cowpland. For several years, after he'd made his fortune in Canada, Mike Cowpland provided sponsorship money to Andrew Schneider, six-time Canadian men's champion in the late 1980s and early 1990s. "When Andrew's dad was around he'd be screaming from the sidelines, even when Andrew was twenty-two or twenty-three. That's the eastern European style and I guess it works because there's an awful lot of eastern European champs. But in England you don't get driven that hard because there's this underlying belief that competing is the important thing, not necessarily winning."

When Tony Carr was about twelve, he began taking tennis lessons from Ronald Cowpland too. His recollection is of a serious, somewhat irritable man who had no tolerance for kids who wasted time. "He was a nice guy and a good teacher, but he could get quite irritated if you messed about or were late," Carr says. "My memory is very much that Michael's father was not someone you messed about with. One treated his father with great respect."

Cowpland's least favourite childhood memories tend to revolve around school. He was a bright pupil who generally enjoyed school-work, but he detested the bullying that was so much a part of the English educational system in those days. He vividly recalls being chased by a pack of older boys and hurled into the gorse bushes on his first day at Harewood Prep School, a local private boys' school he attended from the age of six until he was nine.

The tuition fees at Harewood, even for day students, were the equivalent of several thousand dollars a year in today's currency, a considerable stretch for a full-time tennis instructor and bridge club co-manager. But the Cowplands had lofty expectations for their two sons. "They definitely had to dig deep into their pockets, but they wanted us to have every opportunity," Geoffrey says. And Harewood certainly seemed like an excellent choice. Surrounded by several acres of well-tended green lawn, the school occupied a three-storey, red-brick Victorian building less than a kilometre west of the town centre near the community of Cooden Beach. In total there were no more than about seventy pupils, each of whom was required to wear grey flannel slacks (shorts in warmer weather), a white shirt and tie and a jacket with wide vertical stripes of red, white and green, with a cap to match.

There were two things in particular students tended to dislike about Harewood. One was the uniform: the other young people in Bexhill made fun of it and called the boys who wore it "zebras." The other was the headmaster, a sour Anglican reverend named Noel Woodruff who couldn't seem to go a day without thrashing the living daylights out of some hapless charge. Indeed, Woodruff dispensed corporate punishment so frequently and with such obvious enthusiasm that eventually some of the parents protested. "He was very strict—quite an unpleasant character, really," Geoffrey Cowpland recalls. "He used to cane people at the drop of a hat." At school, the two brothers were known as Cowpland Major and Cowpland Minor, but the headmaster called young Michael "Harum Scarum." He apparently considered the boy disorderly and untidy, more interested in amusing himself than in following the rules.

Despite that, Cowpland rarely got into serious trouble. Yet even he acknowledges that he found elementary school physically intimidating and, in the early years, he couldn't wait to go home every afternoon. One teacher, he recalls, routinely punished the student who happened to receive the lowest mark on any test, regardless of how well he might have done. Another instructor would clobber boys with a shoe for the slightest mistake in math. "I guess we learned a lot because of the pressure to learn, but it wasn't a positive experience. A major incident would be leaving your cap off. You'd get caned at least once a week, and of course people who boarded [at the school] would get caned every day. It was considered to be normal."

When Michael was nine, his father pulled him out of Harewood and enrolled him in a new local prep school called Pendragon, while Geoffrey moved on to Bexhill Grammar School. Pendragon's founder, Alexander Everett, had been the deputy headmaster at Harewood but quit after he discovered that Reverend Woodruff was sexually molesting some of the students. Popular with the boys and a respected coach of cricket and soccer, Everett believed in pushing boys to achieve their potential but not at the expense of their emotional well-being. In 1962, twelve years after setting up Pendragon, he emigrated to the United States and helped to establish a private boarding school in Texas. A few years after that, he combined his theories of education and his interest in Eastern religion in a San Francisco–based organization he called Mind Dynamics Incorporated, which was the precursor to the 1970s' human potential movement that spread throughout California and around the world. One of Everett's best-known disciples was Werner Erhard, the founder of est, who began his career as a Mind Dynamics instructor.

After two years at Pendragon, Cowpland was old enough to join his brother at Bexhill Grammar School, a state-run institution for academically oriented students whose parents could not afford to send their children to a private boarding school. It was there that his natural abilities in math and science really began to shine. He was usually among the top three or four students in his year, and could have done better had he worked harder. Instead, he tended to coast, perhaps because things came too easily for him. He loved subjects that required him to figure out the solutions to complex problems. History and Latin, on the other hand, were dry and boring. What was the point of memorizing all those dates and phrases when they were of no practical use in the modern world?

More than anything, young Michael loved tinkering with mechanical gadgets and electric motors. By the age of eight he was seriously hooked on Meccano, the metal construction sets that can be used to make small motors, cars and other devices. "He used to amaze us with the things he'd create," said Geoffrey. "Once he built this enormous mechanical robot, with no plans or anything. We couldn't believe it when he actually got it to walk around." He also loved taking apart radios and other household appliances, figuring out how they worked and then putting them back together. Later on, he volunteered to set up the hi-fi equipment for the weekly dances in a local church basement, one of the few organized social activities for young people in the area.

Cowpland's hero in those years was Tony Carr, whom he describes as "the ultimate gadget guy." At school, the boys put their scientific talents to work dreaming up imaginative pranks for which they were rarely caught. Perhaps the most notorious was the time they mixed iodine and a concentrated ammonia solution to produce a liquid solution called nitrogen tri-iodide, which dries to form small black crystals that are explosive on contact. "One morning we painted some of the liquid on the floor of the classroom near the door," Carr says. "It wasn't dry when the teacher walked in, so nothing happened. But about ten minutes later he got up from his desk and there was this great, gratifying bang. Then he began to stamp about on the floor and there were more bangs, and there was great anger and fury. The teacher had a screaming fit—I think he felt a little outclassed."

Several of the boys' other pranks involved the use of marbles and ball bearings. Once, they placed a handful of them strategically inside the school piano. "It made a horrendous sound during morning prayers," Cowpland says. On another occasion, Carr showed his mates how to construct elaborate mazes inside their desks, using books, small blocks of wood and Meccano girders. "This was great fun because it meant you could be fiddling with your marble on the desk, and when the teacher demanded to know what was going on you could drop the marble into the ink well, hold up your empty hands and say, 'Nothing, sir.' " Once inside, the marble would roll around the maze for ten or fifteen seconds before dropping out of a hole in the bottom of the desk near the student's knees. "The only problem was that every now and then the marble wouldn't come out, so you'd have to open your desk a crack and peek in. The teachers would see all this furtive activity going on behind desks and wonder what the hell we were doing. They probably thought we were masturbating."

Another great influence in Cowpland's early life was his grandmother Ethel, who moved to Bexhill after the war to be close to her oldest son. Cowpland describes her as "the centre of energy for the whole village" and has vivid memories of his grandmother zipping around town on a small motorbike. After school, he frequently rushed over to her house to play or perform chores. Other boys might have complained about having to cut the grass, but Ethel owned a gasoline-powered lawnmower and Cowpland considered himself fortunate to be allowed to use it. She gave him more responsibility than young men his age were used to having, with the result that he always felt more mature and confident in her presence. When he was thirteen, Ethel offered to let him use her motorbike whenever he wanted in return for taking charge of its maintenance. Cowpland was overjoyed. "It was one of those small British bikes where the motor was actually in the rear wheel. I got a copy of the repair manual and used to take the whole thing apart and put it back together again." More than once Cowpland got into trouble for leaving a pile of engine parts in the kitchen sink, usually just when his mother needed to start cooking Sunday dinner.

Though Cowpland remembers his hometown as "very boring," there was some consolation in the fact that Bexhill was also a popular place for European families to send their children to learn English. When summer rolled around, the place came alive with students from Scandinavia, France, Germany and beyond. "There were very few local girls at that time—or there were but they were scattered thinly. But in the summer you'd get all these attractive foreign girls, really dynamic and peppy, and there'd be fantastic times. My first girlfriend was a girl from Germany. In fact, most of the girls I hung around with were from Europe." Several times as a teenager, Cowpland spent part of the summer on the Continent studying French. He smiles thinking back on those experiences. "It was like a hotbed of activity. I was lucky I got any studying done there."

Although Cowpland says he doesn't remember studying particularly hard in school—"I was just going through the motions and doing what I was told"—it was obvious to everyone else that he was far ahead of most his peers in math and physics. He was also intensely competitive and had a will to succeed, something he demonstrated on the soccer pitch as well as in the classroom. In his final year at grammar school he sent off applications to three universities: Birmingham, Leeds and Imperial College in London. In his mind they were all equal, but when Imperial wrote back and told him that he had been accepted, he quickly packed up and moved to South Kensington, site of the college's main campus.

He didn't know it at the time, but he could hardly have chosen a better place to continue his education. Founded in 1907 with the merger of the Royal College of Science, the Royal School of Mines and the City and Guilds College, the Imperial College of Science, Technology and Medicine is recognized as one of the premier scientific institutions in the world. Esteemed alumni include T.H. Huxley, the great nineteenth-century biologist and philosopher, author H.G. Wells, Sir Alexander Fleming and Sir Ernst Chain, the Nobel

Prize-winning discoverers of penicillin, and Nobel laureate Denis Gabor, the inventor of holography.

Cowpland was eighteen in 1961 when he started in Imperial, and still far from certain about the sort of career he wanted to pursue. His love of machinery had led him to enrol in mechanical engineering, but during his first year he concluded that he had made a mistake. In his view, mechanical engineering was a "fairly static" science in which the pace of change was incremental and the opportunities for innovation were fairly limited. "The next jet engine would have maybe a 1 percent efficiency improvement over the previous generation of jet engine," he said. "It really didn't seem that exciting to me, so I decided to transfer into electronic engineering for my second year."

It was an unusual move, but Cowpland sensed that the field of electronics was on the cusp of an unprecedented period of innovation. Back in the late 1940s, three American scientists working at Bell Labs in Murray Hill, New Jersey, had invented the transistor, a tiny crystal that acted like a switch to control the flow of electricity in circuits. Transistors, or semiconductors as they were later called, were cheap to manufacture, had no moving parts and were far more reliable than the vacuum tubes they replaced.

One of those Bell Lab scientists, a California native and amateur magician named William Shockley, later founded his own company, Shockley Semiconductor, in the Santa Clara Valley south of San Francisco, and hired a group of gifted young scientists and engineers to assist him with his work in solid-state physics, particularly his groundbreaking research into silicon-based semiconductor components. Shockley shared the Nobel Prize for physics in 1956 but by all accounts he was an inept manager with paranoid tendencies (he is remembered today primarily for his theories of racial superiority and for starting a sperm bank for geniuses in the 1970s). Fed up with their boss's eccentricities, several of those promising young scientists deserted Shockley and opened their own lab, Fairchild Semiconductor, a division of Fairchild Camera and Instrument Corporation. In 1959, they hit upon an idea that would change the world. To reduce the cost of manufacturing semiconductors and eliminate the need for large factories full of workers soldering together individual components, they figured out how to put several transistors together on a single insulating wafer of silicon dioxide. Using a photographic process to print thin metal lines on top of the silicon, these integrated circuits, or chips, could be churned out by the thousands, with the cost of production falling rapidly as volume increased.

With the invention of the semiconductor and the integrated circuit, the electronics industry was beginning to explode. Initially used to replace unreliable mechanical relays in telephone exchanges, by the mid-1950s semiconductors had become part of popular culture with the development of the first transistor radio—a device that quickly became the fastest-selling retail item of all time. In 1954, IBM announced that it would no longer use vacuum tubes in its computer systems and the company unveiled the world's first fully transistorized computer. By 1961, the semiconductor industry had surpassed $1 billion in annual revenues. It took several more years before integrated circuits began to be designed into ordinary electronic devices, but by the mid-1960s they, too, were beginning to revolutionize electronics. On its own, a single transistor could act as an on-off switch or amplify the flow of current through a device. Arranged together in large numbers in integrated circuits, switching on and off 100 million times a second or more, they became arithmetic and logic processors that could drive calculators, control watches and perform myriad other complex tasks.

Like many of his contemporaries, Cowpland was fascinated by the possibilities of solid-state physics. At university he read everything he could find on the subject, scouring the Imperial College library for the latest reports from scientists in the United States, where most of the ground-breaking research was taking place. In his spare hours, he played for the college's soccer and tennis teams and competed in university bridge tournaments. He excelled in his studies but was never the sort of student to spend all of his time in the lab or with his nose buried in a book. Instead of hanging around the pub to unwind after a long day of lectures and research, he would change into his shorts and hit the tennis courts. He craved activity. Far from wearing him down or distracting him from academic pursuits, the vigorous work-outs seemed to sharpen him mentally and increase his energy level.

In hindsight, it's easy to see that Cowpland inherited both his passion for physical activity and his entrepreneurial spirit from his father. Ronald Cowpland still plays golf three times a week—he has a 20 handicap—and shoots a game of snooker every Thursday at the local branch of the British Legion. He continued to play tennis regularly until his late sixties. "I think I got the love of competition from him, and also he's very much a believer in fair play, very straightforward. I think that's fairly common in Britain, a non-cheating approach. And also not bad-mouthing people—if you can't say anything good about someone, don't say anything at all." From his mother, Cowpland says he gained an optimistic outlook and a sense of fun. "She was a very positive person, all the time."

Unfortunately, Marjorie Cowpland never lived to see the full extent of her younger son's success. He was only twenty-eight when she died of Hodgkin's disease in 1971. Ronald Cowpland, however, is still fit and spry at the age of eighty-two. In October of 1997 he married his third wife, Mary, seventy-three, whom he met playing bridge at the club he and Marjorie had established forty years ago. (Marlen Cowpland says her father-in-law is a ladies' man who "marries them and wears them out. . . . He was dating three or four women before he decided on Mary.") For their honeymoon they took a twelve-day cruise from Southampton to Madeira, Algiers and Tunisia, playing bridge twice a day while aboard the ship. They won the bridge championship on the cruise and, after returning to England, the regional championship for Sussex and surrounding counties. In late June 1998, they finished fourth in the national championships in Birmingham, narrowly missing out on the grand prize of a cruise worth seven thousand pounds. "It was close," he says. "We had it in our sights, but it was not to be."

Ronald Cowpland freely admits to knowing nothing about computers and precious little about his son's company, yet he isn't at all surprised by his son's success. "I think he gets his personality from my grandfather, H.G. Morgan, who was a senior wrangler at Oxford—that's the highest class of mathematician in England. It's in the blood of our family. A lot of people tell me Michael's a genius. The same goes for my niece—her mother was the dumbest thing, and yet she had the highest degree of mathematics at Sussex University. It's like racehorses—it's all in the breeding, isn't it?"

Chapter Two

In his third and final year at Imperial College, Cowpland received five job offers. Four were from British companies, but the one that interested him most was from the research arm of Canada's Northern Electric, a subsidiary of Bell Canada. Later renamed Bell Northern Research (BNR) and then Nortel Technologies, the facility had been established several years earlier after a 1956 U.S. antitrust decree effectively blocked the free transfer of technology and product designs to Northern Electric from AT&T and its manufacturing firm, Western Electric, in the United States. Back in 1911, Western Electric had purchased a half interest in Northern Electric, with the result that, for half a century, the Canadian company functioned as an offshoot of its American cousin, turning out copies of telephones and switchboards designed in the United States. The consent decree, designed to loosen Western Electric's grip on the supply of telephone equipment, ended that arrangement, much to the eventual benefit of Canada's telecommunications industry.

Forced to come up with its own product designs or else pay the going rate for access to Western's technical plans, Northern decided in 1958 to create its own research and development laboratories in Montreal, Quebec, and Belleville, Ontario with a combined staff of forty-two people. Three years later, the operations were merged and relocated to a 30-hectare site on the western outskirts of Ottawa. The national capital held several attractions for the fledgling operation, not the least of which were the presence of the federal government's own extensive scientific and engineering facilities and close proximity to the politicians and bureaucrats who dispensed federal research money.

Financial considerations also weighed heavily in Cowpland's decision to leave Britain and accept the Northern Electric offer. The job in Canada paid $5,400 a year, far more than British electronics firms were offering at the time for entry-level engineers. "At first I thought there must be some currency conversion mistake, but lo and behold it was true. So I thought, well, that's worthwhile giving it a try for a year or so."

At first, Northern assigned Cowpland to one of its factories in London, Ontario, but after three weeks he was invited to join the research labs in suburban Ottawa. He didn't realize it at the time, but it was an important opportunity for the young engineer—a chance to immerse himself in solid-state electronics at a time when the industry, and his employer, were entering a period of massive growth. By the time Cowpland arrived in Ottawa and found a small one-bedroom apartment in the Algonquin Towers on Lisgar Street, Northern employed several hundred engineers and scientists and was easily Canada's leading facility for industrial electronics research.

Cowpland spent the next four years designing electronic telephones as a replacement for traditional electro-mechanical devices—experience that later proved invaluable when he resolved to strike out on his own. "It got so busy that I never thought about moving back to England," says Cowpland, who was responsible for creating one of the world's first transistorized telephones. He enjoyed the work and relished being on the leading edge of technology, in an environment where originality was both demanded and rewarded. No longer able simply to import new technology from the United States, Northern Electric was trying to give itself a competitive advantage in the marketplace by building up an arsenal of patents. "As an employee, one of the incentives was that you'd get $500 when you applied for a patent and $500 when it was issued. So I thought, super—I'll apply for patents. I think I ended getting the most patents in the company. Not all would be the sort you'd make a fortune on, but we were building a barrier of protection for the company. I've always thought that when companies put incentives in place, people will work for them."

As his income grew, Cowpland began to indulge his boyish enthusiasm for gadgets, particularly sports cars. One of his first big purchases in Canada was a used Triumph two-seater, which he drove all winter, even though the passenger side window was broken and could not be rolled up. He also joined a local tennis club and indulged his passion for competitive sports by playing the game several times a week. Before long he'd acquired a circle of close friends, most of whom he'd met on the tennis court.

A few months after arriving in Ottawa, Cowpland met Darlene McDonald, an attractive blonde who worked as a secretary in "mahogany row," the executive offices at Bell Northern Research. "One of my friends worked in Michael's area of the building and she set us up," Darlene Cowpland says. "On our first date we went to a Christmas dance, and I guess we saw each other steadily after that. He had a great sense of humour, which is what attracted me to him in the first place. I can remember going skiing with him and I'd be sitting next to this open window in his Triumph, laughing and freezing half to death. We always had fun together." After dating for almost four years, the couple married in 1968 and moved into a one-bedroom apartment in Bayshore, a west-end neighbourhood less than two kilometres from BNR's main research campus. Their first daughter, Paula, was born a year later, followed by Christine in 1972. By then they were living in a three-bedroom house in nearby Nepean, purchased for $25,000 with a down payment borrowed from Darlene's mother.

His experience at Bell Northern Research influenced Cowpland in another way, too. Early on, the operation developed its own distinct corporate culture, one that pitted engineers against one another in a competitive race to generate as many new ideas as possible. Some researchers thrived in that environment, while others found it stressful or quit in frustration when their ideas were rejected. It didn't always make for a happy and contented workforce, but it did foster creativity and innovation, essential qualities for any successful high-tech enterprise.

One example of that innovative impulse was the decision to establish Northern Electric's Advanced Devices Centre, a lab-within-a-lab that, in the mid-1960s, set out on an intensive program of research into the potential applications of integrated circuits for both military and civilian purposes. In 1969, prodded by the Canadian government and given $100 million in federal money as seed capital, Northern spun the centre off as a separate corporation, Microsystems International Ltd., which was to be the foundation of a domestic semiconductor industry. Cowpland joined Microsystems right away, and after two years as a chip designer he was promoted to manager of circuit design.

In reality, Northern Electric was never exactly sure what it wanted out of Microsystems, but in its short life the new company nurtured a remarkably talented collection of young engineers, men who in the following decades would launch their own companies—some thirty in all—and help transform a dull government town into a hothouse of high-tech enterprise. Along with Cowpland, they included Dick Foss and Bob Harland, who founded Mosaid Technologies, a semiconductor design firm; Larry O'Brien, who started the satellite communications company Calian Technologies; and David Moore, founder of Siltronics, a designer of custom and specialty microchips that went under in the late 1980s.

"Sometimes in life you get these cocoons that fling out all sorts of amazing things," Cowpland says now. "In music, for example, there was [blues singer] Long John Baldry in Britain. Elton John used to play in his group, and so did Mick Jagger and that Scottish guy, Rod Stewart. It's like there's a bit of magic dust that rubs off on everyone and spawns a lot of creative results. I think at Microsystems we all felt we were pretty capable people, surfing at the leading edge of technology worldwide. We thought, well, there's nothing really more advanced than this. And that's exciting—you know you're breaking new ground."

While all this was going on, Cowpland was furthering his education, determined to keep on top of the rapid advances in the field of electronics. While working at BNR, he had enrolled in the master's program in electrical engineering at Carleton University, attending lectures two evenings a week. Eventually he was awarded a fellowship from the National Research Council, which made it possible to take a leave of absence from work and devote himself full-time to his thesis. As soon as that was out of the way, he applied for another scholarship to pursue his PhD. His boss at Microsystems, Dick Foss, agreed to keep him on as a consultant, working three or four days a week. The subject of his doctoral thesis was the use of a microchip to convert telephone pulses to digital signals that could be understood by computerized switching systems.

Among the other up-and-comers at Microsystems was an ambitious young Welshman named Terry Matthews. Trained in electrical engineering in the United Kingdom, Matthews had immigrated to Canada in 1969, when he was twenty-six, and landed a job in the marketing department of Microsystems. He and Cowpland soon became best friends, drawn together by a shared interest in cars, sports and potential business opportunities, however unlikely they seemed. On weekends they would scour the classified section of *The Ottawa Citizen* for junky old cars that could be fixed up, driven for a while and then resold at a profit.

One night, Cowpland came across an ad for an old Citroen DS21, France's answer to the Rolls Royce. The owner was asking $300. The two engineers immediately drove over to have a look. It was dark, but the car looked fantastic, with fancy interior lights and a hydraulic suspension system that allowed the driver to raise or lower the vehicle at the touch of a button. They paid cash for the car on the spot.

The next morning, they realized they had made a huge mistake— the Citroen was rusted through practically from the waist down. Fortunately, Matthews knew a fair bit about fibreglass, so they immediately hopped in his car and headed to Canadian Tire for some supplies. Over the next few weekends they painstakingly repaired every square centimetre of the body, until it looked practically as good as new. At last it was time to give the car a paint job. But just as they were jacking it up to make it easier to paint the lower body, oil spurted out of a leak in the hydraulic system. The ever-resourceful Matthews again hit upon a solution: he would simply insert a screw in the hole and weld it to the main hydraulic line, plugging the leak. The idea might even have worked had not the flame from the welding torch ignited the oil, setting the entire car on fire. "Eventually we put out the flames. Anyway, it looked magnificent when we finally got it cleaned up and painted. We sold it for $600."

On another occasion, Cowpland and Matthews decided to form their own part-time electronics company, which they immodestly called Advanced Devices Consultants of Canada Ltd. To raise money for research, they made arrangements to import several electric lawn-mowers from England and sell them to friends and acquaintances. The machines resembled old-fashioned push-mowers but were powered by rechargeable batteries, which meant there was no need for a long extension cord. Unfortunately, the first shipment of three machines didn't reach Ottawa until the end of the summer, too late to be of much use. They also turned out to be unsuitable for Canadian grass, which is thicker and heavier than English grass. "It seemed like a great idea, but like a lot of great ideas it wasn't worth the trouble," Cowpland says.

Despite the grandiose name, Advanced Devices Consultants had no paid staff and no office to speak of beyond a dimly lit corner of the basement in Cowpland's suburban home. "The house had quite a big basement, so we had a washer and dryer and next to it was Michael's workbench with a soldering iron and a telephone," says Darlene Cowpland. "Often Michael and Terry would be out doing something and I'd have to run down and answer the phone. Many times there'd be a room full of little children playing down there, all between the ages of one and three, and they'd all be screaming, so I'd have to put my hand over the phone so that whoever was on the other end of the line—some engineering company, for example—wouldn't hear all these kids playing in the background."

Cowpland's career was progressing nicely, but at work he was growing more and more frustrated. He had always believed that Microsystems had huge potential, but the big guns at Northern didn't seem to share his conviction. Early on, Microsystems had paid $1 million to license some proprietary technology from a struggling California start-up named Intel, whose founders—Gordon Moore and Bob Noyce, the former CEO of Fairchild Semiconductor—were destined to become two of the most influential men in the history of Silicon Valley. It was Moore who came up with Moore's Law, which states that the number of transistors that can be superimposed on a given size piece of silicon will double every eighteen months. In 1971, Intel took that idea to its logical conclusion by inventing the microprocessor—a programmable chip no larger than a thumbnail that contained most of the essential elements of a computer. Intel also developed the dynamic random-access memory chip, which, together with the microprocessor, is the foundation of all modern personal computers.

Using Intel's technology, Microsystems was soon producing its own memory chips. But it was a low-margin business in which volume was everything, and Microsystems never managed to turn a profit. The problem, in Cowpland's view, was bad management: he was convinced that the bean-counters at Northern didn't have what it takes to survive in such a high-risk, competitive environment. Culturally, the company was far better suited to making telephone systems, for which it was guaranteed a steady stream of orders from Bell Canada, BNR's parent.

On top of the frustration he felt, Cowpland was itching to make more money. "I'd been in a hothouse environment where the raises were coming in fast and furious—a good raise would be 30 percent in a year. But then we hit a bit of a slowdown and I remember getting a 5 or 6 percent raise. It was like, wow, I'm banging my head against the ceiling here. That was the catalyst. I thought, now is the time to do something."

Matthews was every bit as impatient, so in 1973 the two British expatriates resigned from Microsystems and set up a new company, which they called Mitel Corp. They joked that the name was short for Mike and Terry's Lawnmowers, an explanation that eventually became part of the Cowpland mythology. The truth was that they wanted a name with a technological ring to it that didn't refer to any specific kind of product—a generic name like Intel. To the extent that it meant anything at all, Mitel stood for Mike and Terry's Electronics.

With two young children at home and only a few thousand dollars in savings, Cowpland was taking a substantial risk. Early on, he even traded in his late-model Camaro for a used, $200 Pontiac Acadian in order to raise additional capital. Yet Darlene Cowpland says she never doubted her former husband's decision to quit his job at Micro-systems. "I used to say, 'What's the worst that could happen?' The worst thing was that we would just go back to our little one-bedroom apartment in Bayshore. I always liked a challenge, and Ann [Matthews] was the same way. They lived in Kanata, and at one point Mike and Terry asked us to go to their lawyer's office to sign some documents. I remember the lawyer said, 'Do you girls know what you're signing?' We looked at him and said no, and then he said, 'Well, you're signing away your houses.' But we just sat down and signed the papers. Ann's a pretty easy-going person, and I guess I am, too." She added that her former husband never doubted for a minute that the business would be a success. "He and Terry were similar in the way they were both very enthusiastic, both couldn't be contained, both had so many ideas. They felt constrained by the normal, nine-to-five jobs they were in— they wanted to do more. I remember Terry saying to Michael early on, 'Michael you've got all these ideas—we should do something with them.' And out of that was born Mitel."

Although Cowpland and Matthews had big dreams for their little start-up, the company didn't exactly come flying out of the gates. Mitel's first product was a security intercom system for high-rise apartment buildings. At the time, most apartment projects had fire alarms but no intercoms; a landlord who wanted an intercom system would normally have to install loudspeakers in the ceilings and run separate wires throughout the building, at considerable expense.

Cowpland, however, had figured out how to tap into the existing phone wires in a way that wouldn't interfere with regular calls. To complete the system, it was necessary only to equip each apartment with a telephone that had a built-in speaker. In an emergency, rather than simply triggering an alarm, the fire marshal could broadcast detailed instructions to the building's occupants from a control panel in the lobby.

Cowpland's intercom system was wonderful in theory and worked well at the prototype stage, but there was one flaw. To actually make a sale, Mitel had to secure the approval of not one but three parties: the building's owner, the phone company and the fire department. Unfortunately, getting all three to agree on anything proved close to impossible. After four or five months without a sale, Cowpland and Matthews shelved the idea and went looking for another.

Big idea number two was a product that made it more convenient for people to make conference calls using multi-line business phones. The trouble with most existing phones was that the sound volume would drop off as soon as the user patched in a second call. Cowpland solved that problem by designing a two-way amplifier that boosted the voice signals. Again, the technology was fine, but instead of selling to end-users, Mitel had to convince telephone manufacturers to install the amplifiers as original equipment, which proved tougher than expected. Matthews, who handled the marketing side while Cowpland did most of the technical work, did manage to line up one phone manufacturer, only to have that company run into tough times and shut down. "Our customer effectively disappeared," Cowpland says, "so that was another dead duck."

Optimistic as always, Cowpland immediately went to work on an idea he had first explored while working on his doctoral thesis at Carleton University: a converter that could take musical tones from a push-button phone and convert them into the analog pulses emitted by older, rotary-dial phones. Most large telephone companies at the time were in the process of upgrading their lines to permit the use of touch-tone phones, but the procedure was slow, and in many areas business customers knew they would have to wait several years for touch-tone service. Cowpland's device, built with off-the-shelf electronic components, made it possible for a company to install sleek, modern, push-button phones throughout its offices long before the local phone company got around to upgrading the lines in that neighbourhood.

The tone-to-pulse converter was Mitel's first successful product. As sales picked up, the two men hired three employees and began scouting around for office space; up to that point, they had been working from home. They eventually moved into a small, two-storey building on Leacock Way in Kanata, two blocks from Matthews's house. Mitel's offices were at opposite ends of the second floor, totalling no more than about a hundred square metres. The building's other occupants were the Kanata Junior Chamber of Commerce, a couple of doctors and a dentist. In the evenings, after putting the kids to bed, Darlene Cowpland would drive over to do the typing, "borrowing" one of the other tenants' typewriters because Mitel still hadn't got around to buying one for itself.

Although Mitel was beginning to expand, it was still very much a hands-on business. Cowpland soldered the circuit boards himself, often working late into the night to keep up with orders. Once, he had just finished making a dozen or so tone-to-pulse converters for the U.S. subsidiary of a big Swedish telecommunications firm, Stromberg-Carlson, when Matthews stuck his head in the door and said he didn't feel comfortable shipping them out—the design was so good that somebody might decide to copy it. Cowpland told him not to worry, that by the time anyone figured out how to copy the boards Mitel would probably be on to the next version. Matthews, however, was insistent. He rushed out and bought a tub of thick, black epoxy compound and proceeded to pour the liquid over the circuit boards so as to conceal the inner workings.

That evening Matthews and Cowpland went back into the office to check on the circuit boards, which were due to be shipped the following morning. To their horror, the epoxy compound was still soft and gooey. Matthews quickly reread the instructions, realized that the liquid would set faster above sixty degrees Celsius and rushed home to stick the boards in the oven. He finally got back around midnight, at which point the black coating was nice and hard. Unfortunately, when Cowpland tested the boards he discovered that some of the transistors had failed because of the heat, with the result that the converters no longer worked. "We didn't know whether to laugh or cry," Cowpland says. Matthews, resourceful as always, grabbed a sharp knife and began cutting away the compound. By morning he and Cowpland had managed to find the defective parts and replace them, in time for the boards to be driven down to Stromberg-Carlson's offices in Rochester, New York.

Mitel in those days was a buzzing hive of disorder. Cowpland and Matthews were the ultimate do-it-yourselfers—what they didn't know about running a business, they happily improvised. "I always thought that running a business was pretty straightforward," Cowpland says. "When you take engineering courses—solid-state physics and the like—the sort of math you get involved with is pretty mind-boggling, with incredibly complex equations. Accounting seems awfully easy after that. You're really just adding and subtracting. I never really could understand why people made such a big fuss about it, really."

Down the road, Cowpland's informal, seat-of-the-pants style would drive many of his employees—and shareholders—to distraction. But as far as he was concerned, it was a waste of effort to spend any more time on management issues than was absolutely essential. The money came from selling circuit boards, so what mattered was how quickly Mitel could crank them out. Instead of commissioning a detailed study of the market, he devised a simple formula for deciding how much to charge for the company's products. "In those days I would literally design every component on the board, so I knew how much the parts cost easily enough. Later on there'd be a bunch of people assembling them, so you took the amount they earned per day and divided by the number of boards they produced to get the assembly cost. Now you've got the cost of the board and the cost of the assembly, and then we'd have a rule of thumb—multiply by three for the selling price, because if you do that you're going to get about a 50 percent profit after allowing for some extra costs. If you can get more than that, it's gravy. Anything less and you're getting a little tight."

Mitel was their company, founded with a few thousand dollars of their own money, so Cowpland and Matthews could do what they pleased. But it wasn't long before they started to attract potential investors. One night in 1974, Cowpland and his wife attended a party at their next-door neighbour's house. As the evening progressed, Cowpland struck up a conversation with a man named Kent Plumley, a lawyer at the city's largest and most prestigious law firm, Gowling and Henderson. When Plumley asked him what he did for a living, Cowpland replied that he and a friend had recently started their own company in the telecommunications field and were convinced there was a ton of money to be made by harnessing new technology and getting products to market faster than the big telecom manufacturers. Plumley listened intently and then told Cowpland that he and his partner should give him a call if they ever decided to bring in outside investors

The next day, Cowpland recounted the conversation to Matthews and the two men agreed to take Plumley up on his offer. After a few quick phone calls, Plumley put together a circle of investors consisting of five lawyers at Gowling and Henderson in Ottawa and five others in Toronto, including his brother Don. Each lawyer put up $10,000 for 2.5 percent of the company, for a total of $100,000. To Cowpland and Matthews, it seemed like a fortune—enough to purchase some badly needed equipment and conduct more research on promising new products for the rapidly expanding telephone market.

The story has an interesting postscript. For several months, Cowpland and Matthews worked at selling more circuit boards, while keeping their investors informed of their progress through a series of monthly reports. Before long, however, the Toronto group began to complain that the information they were receiving wasn't detailed enough. Frustrated, they finally struck an agreement to sell their shares to Kent Plumley and the other Ottawa investors for a total of $60,000, which meant they had each made 20 percent after only about six months. It was a handsome return, but not nearly as impressive as the money they would have made had they chosen to hang in. At its peak in the early 1980s, Mitel boasted a market value of roughly $2 billion: 2.5 percent of that would have been $50 million, not bad for an initial investment of $10,000.

Early on, Matthews decided that Mitel's digs weren't impressive enough for a company that was trying to land supply contracts from giant phone companies. More than once he asked the other tenants in the building to wear white lab coats bearing Mitel's logo so as to convince prospective customers that the company had more employees than it did—a kind of high-tech Potemkin village. He even moved his living-room furniture into the office on one occasion to give the offices a classier look.

With money in the bank, twenty-five employees and a growing backlog of orders, Cowpland and Matthews decided it was time to move offices—which was just as well, because the local authorities were by then threatening to kick them out of the building for breaking the zoning by-law. In 1975, Mitel moved into a former hovercraft factory on the outskirts of Kanata. Darlene Cowpland hired a live-in housekeeper and joined the company as purchasing agent, "in charge of buying everything from toilet paper to integrated circuits." She stayed in that job for two years, by which time Mitel was so big it required a full-time director of operations in the person of John McLellan, who, in the mid-1990s, was president of Bell Canada. A second wave of financing, in 1976, resulted in the sale of 10 percent of the company for $100,000 to Toronto-based Helix Investments, whose founder, Ben Webster, soon became one of Cowpland's closest friends. The money was used to finance the purchase of a bankrupt chip factory in Bromont, Quebec, southeast of Montreal. From that point on, Mitel was able to manufacture the integrated circuits for its own products. Today, the Bromont plant is one of Mitel's most profitable operations.

Although Mitel's tone-to-pulse converters continued to sell well for several years, the real breakthrough came when Cowpland turned his engineering skills to the development of a computerized office switchboard to replace the electro-mechanical models that had been in use for many years. Known as private branch exchanges, or PBXs, these software-controlled switches were all the rage by the late-1970s—"the hub of the automated office," as one analyst put it. Mitel introduced its first PBX product, the SX-200, in 1977 and quickly drew a flood of orders from major purchasers, including Bell Canada. Before long, the company dominated the lower end of the market for PBXs with a range of products suitable for small businesses, including the SX-20 and the SX-10.

Suddenly, Cowpland's and Matthew's dream was a reality. As sales took off, the company moved into a sprawling new smoked-glass-and-brown-brick head office in Kanata and added scores of young engineers to its research and development team. Still only in their mid-thirties, the two founders became the darlings of Canada's fledgling high-tech industry, renowned for both their risk-taking instincts and their informal, free-wheeling management style. Decisions were made on the spur of the moment, engineers pursued their own ideas with minimal supervision, and employees who achieved above-average results could look forward to fat bonuses and plenty of perks. In some ways, it was more like a college campus than a working corporation. It wasn't that Mitel was a cushy employer—far from it. Cowpland and Matthews toiled long hours and expected their employees to do the same. But they also believed in rewarding workers who put in extra effort, just as Cowpland himself had earlier been rewarded for the patents he secured on behalf of Northern Electric.

Cowpland and Matthews not only seemed to have boundless energy, they also proved to be masters of motivation. In 1977, when Mitel had about a hundred employees, they flew the entire staff, with spouses, down to Fort Lauderdale, Florida, to celebrate the fact that the company had met a shipping target for the SX-200. On another occasion, they presented a manager named Ernest Childs with a $25,000 stainless-steel DeLorean sports car for winning a contest to recruit new workers. Mitel became famous for the lavish annual bashes it threw for its employees, family members and friends, with entertainment provided by the likes of B.B. King and the Charlie Daniels Band. "People around here are used to the fact that we're really down to earth," Cowpland told writer David Thomas in 1982, summing up his managerial philosophy. "Everything's first names. Nobody's better than anybody else. Which is important, because you want to make sure they don't feel intimidated. If the ideas don't flow, then the whole thing grinds to a halt. Especially in high tech, the people who know the most tend to be at the lower levels with the hands-on jobs. So if you don't get that communication flowing you end up with an ivory tower approach where all the big honchos think they know everything and make the decisions. Then you get into trouble."

In the late 1970s, trouble was the last thing anybody associated with Mitel. The company went public on the Toronto Stock Exchange in 1979, creating instant millionaires of at least half a dozen employees thanks to a company-wide profit-sharing plan. Cowpland and Matthews each held about 20 percent of the equity, although Cowpland sold shares aggressively and borrowed heavily to finance an increasingly lavish lifestyle. By the beginning of the 1980s his portfolio of properties included a sprawling new house in Nepean, a condominium in Florida, two tennis clubs in west-end Ottawa, a racquet-and-fitness centre and a British-themed restaurant called Hunter's Crossing, which he purchased as a favour to the former owner. There was also a collection of cars: a Chevrolet Corvette for everyday use, an Audi Quattro for family trips and a twelve-cylinder Jaguar for weekend excursions in the country. "People knew I had money so I tended to get dragged into bail-outs quite a bit," Cowpland said. "From a business perspective, it was an experimental phase for me. Because I'm a tennis player, people would call me up and say, 'This club's in trouble—it's a good opporunity to buy a piece of the action.' And before you know it I'd have most of the shares, even though I didn't really want to run it."

For a while, it seemed as though everything Cowpland and Matthews touched was destined to turn to gold. Between 1978 and 1983 they opened up at least ten manufacturing plants around the world, a strategy born of necessity, because it was the only way to sidestep the strict local-purchasing rules that were in force in those markets. At its peak, Mitel products were selling in more than eighty countries. The company's workforce reached a peak of 5,791, including 2,200 at head office.

Meanwhile, Cowpland was living the life of a high-tech hedonist. In 1981, he shelled out a million dollars to purchase a ninety-two-hectare country estate on the banks of the Ottawa River in Dunrobin, thirty kilometres northwest of Ottawa, from flamboyant local developer Robert Campeau. (Campeau, whose company had built much of Kanata as well as several large government office buildings in downtown Ottawa, was moving to Toronto to pursue a bigger ambition: a real-estate and retail empire that would span North America. In 1990, after Campeau's ill-timed leveraged buyouts of Allied Stores Corp. and Federated Department Stores Inc., the entire operation collapsed under a mountain of debt.)

The Campeau property, which Cowpland called Stoke Lacy after his grandfather's village in Herefordshire, featured a 2,000-square-metre mansion complete with almost every conceivable luxury. Cowpland, however, wanted more. He immediately spent another million dollars on renovations, including an indoor-outdoor pool with a slide from the rooftop, a $200,000 solarium, a helicopter pad, squash courts and a $25,000 discotheque with a flashing Mitel logo in the centre of the dance floor. He referred to the place as his "weekend retreat," ignoring the inevitable carping in the local papers from gossip columnists for whom Cowpland and his wife seemed the very embodiment of nouveau riche.

Cowpland couldn't care less what the critics said: it was his money and he intended to enjoy every penny of it. In a typical flourish, he threw a Christmas bash at the mansion in 1982 and dispatched a helicopter to pick up the guest of honour, Prime Minister Pierre Trudeau.

Cowpland's parties soon became famous for their surprise guests and worldly pleasures: there were always dozens of beautiful young women, free-flowing champagne and numerous other diversions. "Put it this way—Mike is not afraid to have fun," says his friend Chris Troughton, who lived with Cowpland for several years in the late-1980s and still plays squash with him once a week. "He's a very difficult man to understand, and yet he's really very simple. He works hard, he plays hard. He loves excitement and he is just so inquisitive, always wanting to experience new things. He's not afraid to touch anything or touch anybody—the word 'cannot' is not in his vocabulary."

In some ways, Stoke Lacy was really a bachelor pad for the Mitel president. Visitors to the company's head office were struck by the unusually large number of beautiful women on the payroll, and there were rumours that Cowpland's relationship with one or two of them went beyond the purely professional. What few people outside his small circle of close friends knew was that his marriage to Darlene was gradually disintegrating. Cowpland will not discuss the reasons for the breakup, but current and former friends say he made no secret of his interest in other women. "Mike believes that men are put on earth to be with as many women as possible, and I mean that in the sexual sense," says one longtime friend and former Corel employee. "He used to tell me on the flights we took together or over dinner that the way things should be was the way it was back in the seventeenth or sixteenth century, whereby you had a wife and you had a couple of mistresses on the side. Unfortunately, we live now in the twentieth century and you can't do that without paying a price, which he knows all about."

Not long after Cowpland bought Stoke Lacy, Mitel's good fortune began to run out. Even now, former executives offer conflicting explanations for the company's problems, although most observers agree that Cowpland and Matthews simply bit off more than they could chew. Having carved out a dominant position as a supplier of telephone exchanges for small businesses, they trained their sights on the even more lucrative market for big computerized switchboards. In June 1982, at the company's annual meeting in Ottawa's Chateau Laurier Hotel, Cowpland unveiled a prototype of the SX-2000—a technological marvel that could handle several thousand lines of voice and data communications and would carry a price tag of between $150,000 and $1 million, depending on options. Matthews boasted that the SX-2000 would prove so popular that the company would have to ration delivery. A month later, Mitel announced that it had reached an agreement in principle with IBM to jointly develop and market the SX-2000. Investors took that as a virtual guarantee of success, and bid the stock up as high as $47 a share.

Although the SX-2000 was not scheduled to ship until late 1982 or early 1983, the preliminary reviews were unreservedly glowing. "The 2000 is a tremendous piece of hardware. It's beautifully designed and very powerful," said Ian Angus, an influential telecommunications consultant in Toronto. A communications manager in the Department of National Revenue had nothing but praise for Mitel after trying out one of the prototypes: "It's working fine. Generally speaking, we've been very, very happy with it," Philip Pochallo told *The Globe and Mail*. "There's not much question in my mind that it's marketable and can be produced. I think we can be definitely proud of it."

In reality, Cowpland and Matthews had badly underestimated the time it would take to perfect their new switch. "The silicon was fine, but we had horrible software problems," a former Mitel executive told *Report on Business Magazine* several years after the debacle. "No two SX-2000s came out doing the same thing." To make matters worse, Mitel's decision to go after the market for big computerized switches had put it on a collision course with several deep-pocketed competitors, including NEC Corp. of Japan, Britain's Plessey PLC, Rolm Corp. of Santa Clara, California, and Northen Telecom Ltd., Cowpland's old employer. All four companies were developing similar if slightly less sophisticated digital switches and appeared likely to beat Mitel to market.

By early 1983, Mitel had 120 engineers working overtime to resolve the software glitches. The much-hyped SX-2000 was turning into a financial sinkhole. By the company's own estimate, the ultimate bill for research and development was somewhere between $70 and $100 million. (In 1983, Mitel reported $14.8 million in profits on revenues of $255 million.)

With the project falling further and further behind schedule, IBM, which had not signed a formal contract with Mitel, was growing increasingly impatient. Finally, on June 10, 1983, the computer giant announced that it was buying 15 percent of Rolm for $228 million. Like a jilted husband who wakes up to discover that his wife has moved in with his next-door neighbour, Mitel had no choice but to proclaim loudly that it wanted out of the relationship. The company put out a terse statement that it was "not in the interests of Mitel to continue with its arrangement with IBM"—and then watched as its shares dropped $3.87 to $14.25 in a single day; that day, it was the most heavily traded stock on the New York Stock Exchange.

It was the beginning of a long and painful downward spiral for the former high-tech star. Only a month after the IBM bombshell, Mitel posted a quarterly loss of $4.5 million—the first such shortfall since 1975. In earlier years, Cowpland and Matthews had been celebrated as technological visionaries; now, investors were grumbling that they could no longer be taken at their word, that the SX-2000 had missed so many production deadlines that it was anybody's guess as to when it would finally go on sale. "What's really needed at Mitel is a complete change of management," said Francis McInerney, president of Northern Business Intelligence, a telecommunications research firm. "Matthews and Cowpland are both basically lab guys and the management of the company has got beyond them."

Few people at Mitel would have disagreed with that assessment, although the changes that took place later that year were not as sweeping as many would have liked. In October of 1983, the company that had always prided itself on informality and eschewed professional management advice announced that it had retained McKinsey and

Co., a blue-blood U.S. management consulting firm, "to improve operational effectiveness," in the words of company spokeswoman Diana Daghofer. Simultaneously, Cowpland resigned as president and chief executive and took over as chairman, trading places with Matthews. "Mr. Cowpland has moved into a guiding and directing role," Daghofer said, while Matthews would "focus his energies principally on major strategic issues and decision-making."

But the problems kept getting worse. By the time Mitel began shipping limited quantities of the SX-2000 switch in January 1984, Northern Telecom and NEC were already well ahead in sales in the crucial U.S. market. In Canada, one major distributor, Mid-Canada Phone Systems Ltd. of Sudbury, cancelled its distribution deal for Mitel's unit and opted to carry a competing line of PBXs manufactured by Siemens of Germany. The company blamed "the consistent failure of Mitel Corp. to meet stated delivery dates of this product with its full feature package."

By then, a full-scale retrenchment was underway. In December 1983, Mitel walked away from a $10-million plant in Bouctouche, New Brunswick, that it had built but never occupied. A few months later, the company closed its Irish subsidiary, eliminating about 130 jobs, and sold its manufacturing plant there to local investors. Around the same time, 65 white-collar workers were laid off from the company's headquarters in Kanata. In April 1984, Mitel announced the first yearly loss in its ten-year history—$32.4 million on revenues of $342.6 million. Soon after that, Mitel hired the New York investment house Salomon Brothers to scout around for a new investor, the first sign that Cowpland's and Matthew's hold over the company was beginning to slip.

Chapter Three

To most people who lived in Ottawa in the early 1980s, Michael Cowpland's name stood for conspicuous consumption—the opulent country estate, the tennis clubs, the exotic cars, the annual Mitel blowouts with popular American musicians and all the food you could eat.

Those were just the visible signs of his success. Less well publicized was the degree to which Cowpland was showering money on an array of technology start-ups in the national capital area—small companies with leading-edge ideas that might, just might, make it to the big leagues, like Mitel. Even back then, Cowpland knew that few such enterprises ever live up to their founders' lofty dreams, but he loved playing the elder statesman's role and couldn't resist gambling. In that respect, at least, he was not unusual: the high-tech industry is full of successful entrepreneurs who indulge their passion for technology and appetite for risk by bankrolling new ventures. But Cowpland's new toys were to distract him—in a way that threatened Mitel.

Everywhere you looked in those days, small companies were popping up with promising new ideas. In California, a couple of twenty-something hotshots named Steve Jobs and Steve Wozniak had started a company called Apple Computer, which in 1978 took the world by storm with the first truly usable personal computer, the Apple II. The moment Cowpland saw it, he knew he had to have one for himself. He spent hours playing with the machine and trying out some of the early software, including a spreadsheet program called VisiCalc that had been invented by an MBA student at Harvard Business School. All but forgotten now, VisiCalc was the world's first "killer app"—an application so compelling that it alone justifies the purchase of a computer. Cowpland was amazed by the speed and simplicity of VisiCalc, never realizing that a decade later he would be responsible for introducing a killer app of his own.

Apple's success inspired a legion of competitors—companies such as Tandy, Commodore, Atari and Zenith. Virtually overnight, the personal computer business mushroomed from a hobbyists' playground into a $1-billion industry. What's more, Ottawa was becoming a centre of high-tech innovation, thanks in no small measure to the example set by Cowpland and Matthews at Mitel. "That's often what happens when you try something and it works," Cowpland says. "People knew we didn't walk on water, didn't leap tall buildings. So suddenly they thought, 'If those yo-yos can do it, so can we.'"

By the late 1970s, Ottawa, the former civil service ghetto—a town so famously dull and predictable that columnist Allan Fotheringham dubbed it "Ennui on the Rideau"—was practically crawling with bright young engineers and entrepreneurs. Some saw technology as the road to riches; others were dyed-in-the-wool techies who simply wanted a chance to turn their PhD theses into something real, something they could show their friends. Both groups needed one thing above all to get going: money. And thanks to Mitel, Cowpland had plenty of that.

Cowpland's investment spree started in the late 1970s, when he and a tennis buddy named Glen St. John decided to try their luck in the venture capital business. Born in Regina in 1941, St. John was raised in Ottawa, where he studied political science and quarterbacked the Carleton University Ravens football team. Next he enrolled in law at McGill University in Montreal, playing a year of pro ball for the Montreal Alouettes in 1963 before finishing his degree. For several years he was litigation counsel for the federal Department of Justice, but he found the practice of law boring and decided to return to Carleton to earn a master's degree in public and business administration. "I met Mike at the Rideau Tennis Club in about 1973," St. John recalls. "Right off the bat we seemed to have a lot of things in common in terms of enthusiasm and being competitive. There was a group of about twenty players at the club who were of a competitive nature, so we used to run into each other a lot." Before long, Cowpland and St. John were playing each other once a week and teaming up as doubles partners for tournaments.

St. John, who was still working for the government at the time he met Cowpland, remembers being struck by the fact that Cowpland and Terry Matthews had walked away from secure, well-paying jobs at Microsystems to start their own company. "That was pretty unique in those days, especially in Ottawa. It was intriguing to see two guys who had enough moxie to do that. After a while, of course, I realized it was just Mike's style. He's always taking on the world."

By 1979, armed with his business degree, St. John was operating his own financial planning and tax consulting firm in Ottawa. Whenever he and Cowpland got together for a tennis match, the Mitel co-founder would be brimming with excitement about the emerging opportunities in high technology. Cowpland also had an infectious sense of adventure, so when he approached his tennis partner with the idea of taking a flier on a number of high-tech start-ups in the Ottawa area and beyond, St. John quickly agreed. "He was the dominant investor and I was just learning the technology business," St. John says. "Mike had such an enthusiasm in this area, I just followed along for the ride."

Before long, Cowpland and St. John had their money in at least a dozen promising start-ups. When things started to get unwieldy, they pooled their interests under the umbrella of a venture-capital company they called Bytec—an amalgam of Bytown (Ottawa's original name), the computer term byte and the word technology. Most of the money was Cowpland's, but St. John served as president of Bytec Management Corporation and took responsibility for its day-to-day operations. Another close friend of Cowpland, Ross Tuddenham, the helicopter company owner, was involved on a more informal level. Having earned millions as the owner of a medical lab, Tuddenham was now running a hobby business, a helicopter company, and spending most of his time palling around with Cowpland. He carried no official title but often filled in for Cowpland at meetings when the Mitel co-founder couldn't be there himself. As it grew, Bytec also attracted several outside investors, among them Conrad and Montegu Black and New Brunswick french-fry magnate Harrison McCain, CEO of McCain Foods International Inc.

Bytec's investments were generally in the 10 to 25 percent range. One of the few companies from that period that is still in business is Cognos Corp., an Ottawa-based leader in database-mining software. In 1981, Glen St. John approached Michael Potter, the founder and CEO of Cognos, and offered to put some money in the fledgling company. The arrangement they worked out gave Bytec "something like 10 or 15 percent of the equity" for between $1 and $2 million, Potter says. In addition, St. John got a seat on the Cognos board.

Cowpland recalls the Cognos deal as having been a winner, but Potter's version of events is rather different. About a year after the investment, he says, Cowpland helped to bail out his friend Rod Bryden, the chairman of Systemhouse Ltd., an Ottawa-based developer of customized business software. In the late 1970s, Systemhouse was Canada's biggest software company, but an overly ambitious expansion drive and the 1981-82 recession combined to drive it deep in the red. Systemhouse, moreover, was targeting the same segment of the market as Cognos, so there was a clear conflict of interest. An annoyed Potter talked Cowpland into selling Bytec's interest in Cognos to Noranda Inc. at cost, on the grounds that Cognos had not come very far over the previous twelve months. A couple of years later, Cognos introduced a new line of software and became an international success. Similarly, Cowpland was an important source of seed money for International Semi-Tech Microelectronics Inc., but sold out long before the company and its founder, James Ting, struck it rich.

Many of Bytec's other bets seemed jinxed from the start. One of the more unlikely choices was a company called Imaginamics Inc., which made electronic desk blotters with built-in telephones and calculators. Another prospect that failed to live up to expectations was Data Images Inc., a liquid-crystal display manufacturer that was "a bit ahead of its time" in St. John's estimation, the technology far too expensive to be profitable. Then there was Orcatech Ltd., a short-lived company founded by three researchers from Bell Northern Research who had come up with a sophisticated computer-aided system for designing circuit boards. Bytec also had an interest in a California firm called Magnusson Computers Inc., which folded in 1982.

Arguably the most intriguing of the start-ups Cowpland invested in was NABU Manufacturing Corp., which had devised a system of home computers connected by cable television wires to a central database of computer programs and information. In his 1983 book *Knights of the New Technology*, David Thomas described NABU (named for the Babylonian god of writing) as probably "the most innovative, daring and least-appreciated venture in the Canadian computer and communications industries." The concept was indeed brilliant—in essence, a high-speed Internet long before most Canadians had ever heard of such a thing—but as a commercial proposition NABU proved to be a dud. The company disappeared in the mid-1980s after chewing its way through $50 million for research and development, including $17 million raised in a private placement in 1981 and a further $25 million from a share offering in late 1982.

"It was the classic venture capital portfolio," St. John says of the firms he and Cowpland targeted for investment. "For every ten companies, three die, four wind up as the living dead and the others you hope will be home runs. At one point, we really believed the Hyperion computer would be the home run. If it had been successful, it would have made up for all of the others."

The Hyperion wasn't just a computer, it was one of the very first IBM clones—and Bytec's single most expensive gamble. For a short while, at least, it looked as though it would become a huge Canadian success story. The fact that it is now just a footnote in the history of the PC says a lot about the vicissitudes of the computer industry. Cowpland remembers it as "a great opportunity that was missed," proof that it takes more than brains and good timing to make it into the winner's circle, it also takes a truckload of luck. The Hyperion had some, but not nearly enough.

The story starts with a brilliant and ambitious engineer named Murray Bell, who, like Cowpland, spent his childhood tinkering with motors and building elaborate machines out of Meccano. Born in the late 1940s, the son of an air force officer, he grew up on military bases across Canada and studied engineering physics at Queen's University in Kingston, Ontario, in the mid-1960s, where he won the Governor General's Medal for highest academic average in his graduating year. That brought him a fellowship from the Massachusetts Institute of Technology, where he earned a master's degree in electrical engineering.

After a three-year stint designing weapons for fighter aircraft at National Defence headquarters in Ottawa, Bell decided he could no longer resist the lure of computers. To gain experience, he worked for two computer companies in the city, but he eventually concluded that he could do better on his own. He started a company called Dynalogic Corporation, hired a handful of other engineers and began selling floppy-disk systems. That paid the bills long enough for Bell to pursue his real goal: an advanced microcomputer based on Motorola's 6800 microprocessor, similar to the chip in the original Apple.

So far, so good—or so it seemed. But Bell had committed a strategic error, one that has tripped up many a high-tech entrepreneur over the years. Being an engineer, he went ahead and produced the best machine he knew how, instead of simply adopting someone else's standards. In Bell's case, that meant designing a proprietary operating system based on AT&T's multi-user UNIX system, rather than using an inferior but more popular operating system called C P/M (Control Program for Microcomputers). In the late 1970s, C P/M became a de facto standard among microcomputer makers and consumers, with the result that purchasers of C P/M machines could choose from a much larger selection of software.

By 1981, Dynalogic was in trouble and badly in need of a financial bail-out. Enter Mike Cowpland and Bytec. Cowpland's first step was to propose a merger between Dynalogic and yet another company in which he had invested, a high-tech furniture-maker called Kombi Office Automation Systems. There was talk about producing a futuristic line of furniture with computers actually built right into the desks. Wisely, the idea was dropped before it ever got off the drawing boards. Within a year, Kombi was in receivership, having burned its way through $6 million in five years.

What happened next is the subject of some debate. The way Glen St. John remembers it, he was the one who came up with the idea of manufacturing a portable computer, while Cowpland proposed that it be modelled after the IBM PC, which had just hit the market to great acclaim. An engineer who worked on the project, however, swears that it was Bell's idea to emulate the IBM PC—he knew from bitter experience that it was pointless to design a rogue machine—and that Cowpland simply wanted to build a computer that could be used for e-mail.

In any event, Dynalogic ultimately decided to kill three birds with one stone: it drew up specs for a portable IBM-compatible PC with a built-in modem. Bytec, which had acquired 80 percent of the company from Bell in return for paying off its debts, quickly gave the project the go-ahead.

By all accounts, the Hyperion was a cleverly conceived and beautifully packaged piece of hardware. Cowpland felt strongly that the machine needed to be attractive and not merely functional, so Dynalogic engaged the services of a Silicon Valley designer named David Kelly, who had done a lot of work for Apple. The result was a sleek, cream-coloured, moulded plastic case housing a twelve-centimetre amber monitor, two floppy drives and a separate keyboard that could be stowed in a narrow slot underneath the main processor. Fully assembled, it weighed about nine kilograms—a respectable figure for a portable in those days. "It's a dynamite machine," Cowpland told reporters at the time. "Nicest-looking personal computer in the world."

The architecture inside was pretty impressive too. Today, anyone who wishes to build an IBM clone can do so simply by visiting a local computer hardware store, purchasing the parts and slapping them together on a kitchen table. In 1981, however, things were nowhere near as easy. It took the engineers at Dynalogic many months of four-teen-hour days to figure out how the chips needed to be wired together. Then they had to write their own BIOS (basic input/output system), the special code that links the operating system to the hard-ware. The trick was to come up with a BIOS that performed the same functions as Big Blue's code without in any way infringing on IBM's copyright. The fact that they managed to do so in only a few months, with a development budget of less than a million dollars, remains a source of immense pride for the engineers who worked on the proj-ect. "To this day I think we crafted a BIOS that involved better soft-ware engineering principles than IBM's software," says Donald Bailey, who was in charge of writing the BIOS and is now an instructor in the department of systems and computer engineering at Carleton University. "It might sound a little arrogant to suggest that a small design team with an average age of twenty-three and a half could do a better job than IBM, but certainly there were sparks of ingenuity in what we did."

The rest of the computer world seemed to agree. The first Hype-rion prototypes drew huge crowds when they were exhibited at the 1982 spring Comdex computer trade show in New Jersey. Afterward, a U.S. electronics magazine wrote that "Canada dropped a 20-pound bombshell on Atlantic City." By the time the first Hyperions left the factory in January 1983, with a U.S. retail price of $4,995, there were firm orders for 6,500 machines, enough to warrant a million-dollar advertising blitz in U.S. business magazines.

Behind the scenes, however, there was growing friction between Bell and his financial backers. Despite their similar backgrounds and lifelong love of gadgetry, he and Cowpland were polar opposites when it came to personality. Where Cowpland was brash and impul-sive, Bell was modest, soft-spoken and meticulous. Cowpland had plenty of admirers but only a very few close friends; Bell projected a warmth and innocence that earned him the undying loyalty of the engineers who surrounded him.

At Dynalogic's offices on Colonnade Road in the Ottawa suburb of Nepean, there was an unmistakable atmosphere of "Us" and "Them." The executive suite at the front of the building belonged to St. John, Ross Tuddenham and a handful of other Bytec personnel. The hundred or so engineers and technicians who worked on the Hyperion kept to their own territory in the back, somewhat resentful that their little company had been swallowed up by Cowpland and his cronies. "There really were two separate worlds in that building," says Bailey. "We were the stereotypical techies and Cowpland was the glitz and glamour. He was still at Mitel at the time, but he used to zip in and out to check up on us. He always seemed to be racing from one thing to the next, working on twenty different things at once. He'd ask you a question and before you got the answer out he was asking the next question."

Two memories stand out in Bailey's recollection of those days. The first was that when Cowpland dropped by the Dynalogic building, he invariably left his car in a pedestrian zone right in front of the main entrance rather than use the parking lot—as though he couldn't be bothered to obey the rules that bound mere mortals. The second concerns the time in 1983 when Cowpland hired a crew of workers to tear up the lawn at the far end of the building and construct an asphalt helicopter pad, complete with wind sock. "Every so often a chopper would land in our back yard and out would pop Cowpland and whoever he happened to be showing around that day," Bailey says, laughing at the memory. "It all seems a little bit unbelievable now—real man-on-the-move type stuff, if you know what I mean. As engineers, we all just wanted to design neat products. I guess you could say we were somewhat cynical about the showy stuff, the pomp and circumstance."

Cowpland, as it happened, had his own grievances with the way Bell was running the company, having earlier concluded that the

Dynalogic founder was a skilled scientist but gutless manager. He was particularly annoyed by Bell's constant talk about the need for detailed market research and professional consultants. To Cowpland, any talk of bringing in outside help was tantamount to an admission of failure. Besides, what use was a marketing consultant in an industry in which the key components—microchips—were doubling in speed and capacity every eighteen months? High-tech wasn't like selling soup or laundry detergent, products for which brand image was everything. Victory in the computer business went to the person who managed to get his products to market before the competition. That way, he could scoop up the profits before the field became too crowded and before the technology had a chance to progress to the next level.

The friction led to a confrontation in December 1982, when Tuddenham, acting on orders from Cowpland, informed Bell that he was being kicked upstairs, figuratively speaking, to the position of Dynalogic chairman. Henceforth, St. John would be president. Not long after, Dynalogic became a division of Bytec, and Bell was relegated to the role of vice-president, technology, charged with scouting out new investment opportunities. Stripped of any direct responsibility for the Hyperion, Bell quit in March of 1983. After a brief hiatus he started a computer store in Ottawa called Task Force and set himself up as a consultant.

With Bell out of the way, Cowpland and St. John decided it was time to rethink production of the Hyperion. Orders were flooding in, yet the factory in Nepean could assemble only a few hundred machines a week. Dynalogic had also contracted out some of the manufacturing to an Alabama company called SCI Systems, but it was slow to come on stream. Desperate to break the logjam, Cowpland decided to fold Bytec into a Montreal firm called Comterm, on whose board he had sat since 1982. Consummated on October 24, 1983, the marriage appeared to have been made in heaven: Comterm had loads of experience in high-tech manufacturing, and indeed was already producing a line of terminals that were compatible with IBM mainframe systems. As soon as the paperwork was completed, with

Cowpland owning 21.9 percent of Comterm and serving as its chairman, the company made a public offering worth $25 million. Up to that point, money had been tight and production plagued by bottlenecks. No longer—the Hyperion was ready to take the computer world by storm.

That's when disaster struck.

In order to keep the Hyperion as compact and portable as possible, Dynalogic's engineers had decided early on in the design phase to use a special type of low-profile floppy-disk drive called a half-height drive. At the time, they could find only one supplier, a U.S. company called Remax. What they did not know, however, was that the Remax drives were susceptible to overheating. Some time in late 1983, the phones started ringing off the hook with angry calls from computer dealers across North America. The drives were failing in large numbers, leading consumers to return their computers for a refund and causing sales to dry up.

The engineers scrambled to rectify the problem, but the damage to the Hyperion's credibility had already been done. Comterm eventually found a Japanese supplier for its disk drives, but it took several months to adapt the front panel of the new drive unit to the unique styling of the Hyperion. Meanwhile, suits and countersuits were flying back and forth between Bytec and Remax, which insisted that the problems were not its responsibility.

None of this would have mattered so much were it not for the fact that a lot of other companies were also itching to break into the market for IBM compatibles. The delays caused by the disk-drive failures were all it took for an obscure Houston start-up called Compaq Computer Corp. to establish itself as the primary manufacturer of portable PCs. The first Compaq models weren't as smartly styled as the Hyperion and they weighed significantly more—an arm-wrenching twelve kilograms—but they had one incontestable advantage: they worked. Compaq also had the support of a Louisiana-born venture-capital specialist named Ben Rosen, whose pockets were substantially deeper than Cowpland's. "We were six months ahead of Compaq, but they were much better funded," St. John says. "They were talking in hundreds of millions of dollars while we were talking in tens of millions. So they very quickly closed the loop and the rest is history."

Today, Compaq is the largest computer manufacturer in the world, with revenues of $24.6 billion in 1997.

Comterm struggled on for another year, against insurmountable odds. One other obstacle the company encountered was the reluctance of some major accounts to buy computers from a vendor other than Big Blue. Chief among the holdouts was the Government of Canada. In 1984, Comterm executives complained publicly that federal departments and agencies were purchasing thousands of personal computers a year under tenders that clearly called for IBM products only, contrary to government policies that were intended to favour Canadian suppliers. (Ironically, one public agency that did buy several Hyperion PCs was the U.S. Library of Congress.) "If we can't meet the specifications, fine, then we shouldn't be given the contract," said Chris Coates, Ottawa branch manager for Comterm. "But at least we should be given a chance to compete."

The protests, however, were in vain. That fall, with sales stalled at about 50,000 units, Comterm ceased production of the Hyperion and announced a $37-million write-off. According to St. John, Cowpland's personal loss on the venture was about $3.5 million.

Today, Cowpland shakes his head at the thought of what might have been. "The Hyperion was actually a step ahead of the Compaq at the time, but we ran into some bad luck with those disk drives," he says.

Cowpland also took a sizable hit on his investment in Systemhouse. The business software company was on the verge of collapse in 1982 when Bryden, a former senior civil servant and federal Liberal Party aide, appealed to the Bank of Montreal for permission to restructure its debt.

The bank agreed, but only on condition that the company come up with additional financing. The Systemhouse president immediately thought of Cowpland, who by then was something of a patron saint for the Ottawa high-tech community. "I met with Mike in Ottawa that night," Bryden told *The Ottawa Citizen* years later. "He made the loan directly to me. He just wrote me a cheque for $4 million." Bryden, who was forced out of Systemhouse in 1991 after his personal holding company defaulted on $831 million worth of loans, now owns the Ottawa Senators hockey franchise. He is a close friend of Cowpland's and remains deeply grateful for his help. "If he hadn't done that, I have no doubt the company would have failed in a day or two."

Cowpland's generosity, however, later came back to haunt him. In addition to the $4-million cheque, he apparently also agreed to pledge $23 million worth of his Mitel shares as security for loans to himself and to R.M. Bryden Holdings Ltd., a private holding company that indirectly controlled Systemhouse. In early 1984, as Mitel's continuing problems with the SX-2000 switch drove the value of the company's stock below the level necessary to support the loans, the lenders forced Cowpland to sell the shares. The resulting rash of publicity pushed the stock down even more—from about $15 at the beginning of February to $11 by early March—and drew the ire of analysts and investors, not to mention Cowpland's fellow Mitel executives. "Mike's activities have definitely hurt Mitel and created a negative public perception regarding Mitel stock," Donald Gibbs, the company's former vice-president of finance, later told *The Globe and Mail*. "It created a perception in the marketplace that he was bailing out of Mitel, so many others did, too."

For Cowpland, the fall-out from the share sales marked a significant turning point. Up until then, his media coverage had always been positive, if not downright glowing. Magazine profiles portrayed him as a dashing superhero of the silicon age, a model for aspiring entrepreneurs everywhere. Now, suddenly, he was being painted as an irresponsible gadfly, a modern-day Icarus who had flown too close to the sun and been burned. "High-living, hi-tech exec flying lower," declared *The Globe and Mail* in a front-page headline on January 16,

1985. The story noted that Cowpland's interest in Mitel had fallen to 7 percent from the 23 percent he held at the time of the public offering in 1979. On top of that, he had been forced to put his country estate up for sale to cover his commitments to Comterm. "Although he retains his penchant for the finer things in life," Lawrence Surtees reported, "Mr. Cowpland's personal wealth and his entrepreneurial credentials are greatly diminished. Mitel, once Canada's most remarkable high-technology success story, has tumbled into a struggle for survival—and other companies in which he has invested have also faltered."

What few people outside Mitel knew was that the relationship between Cowpland and some of Mitel's other top officers, including Terry Matthews, had been strained for years. By nature, the two founders were both headstrong and determined to do things their own way, with the result that they were often heading in opposite directions. "There used to be a joke going around that Mike would walk through the plant in the morning and start a dozen projects," a former senior Mitel official says. "Then Terry would walk through in the afternoon, cancel them all and start another dozen. It was as if there were two presidents."

Cowpland readily acknowledges that there were times he and Matthews saw things differently, although he insists that their disagreements were infrequent and rarely serious. "When a company gets that big, you do get occasional situations where you get the push-pull of departments—marketing as opposed to engineering, say—where one side would be using you to promote Opinion A versus Opinion B. But that would happen only once a year or so. There'd be the odd issue that Terry and I would have to sit down and sort out. But once we did that everything would be fine, because we tended to have very similar views. It's just that sometimes people would concoct scenarios as if we didn't."

At times, however, the disagreements clearly were serious. By far the biggest source of discontent—pitting Cowpland not only against Matthews but against a majority of Mitel's board of directors—was

Cowpland's decision to devote so much of his energy to outside investments. Less than a decade after the company's founding, he had all but lost interest in Mitel. It was a pattern of behaviour that would be repeated again and again in Cowpland's life: whenever he feels that he has mastered some innovative technology or overcome a personal challenge, he marches off in search of new thrills and excitement. Mitel, he explained years later, "had almost become too easy and had become big enough to be boring. . . . We had almost six thousand employees worldwide with plants in ten countries, so I tended to spend all my time flying around and discussing generalities, which really didn't turn my crank. I wanted to be involved in daily detail." Part of the problem, he added, was that the big companies that dominate the telecommunications sector tend to move slowly and cautiously, not wanting to embrace new ideas until it is clear they have been widely accepted. The computer business, in contrast, is addicted to change, as is Cowpland himself. In strict financial terms it likely would have made more sense for him to attend to Mitel's internal difficulties, but that was not his style. His friend Chris Troughton sums up Cowpland's motivation this way: "Mike has never chased a dollar in his life. Mike chases dreams."

All of which proved frustrating for those who really did care about Mitel's future. For while the senior engineers there were racking their brains trying to troubleshoot the many software problems that afflicted the SX-2000, Cowpland was buzzing around the countryside in his helicopter like some manic bee in a field of wildflowers, investing his Mitel earnings in every new high-tech company that came along. That he was eventually forced to sell most of his Mitel shares in order to fund those ventures was, in the eyes of many at Mitel, the ultimate indignity. The general feeling around the office was that Cowpland had behaved irresponsibly—and in the process had injured them all by driving down the market price of Mitel's stock.

Matthews himself has never publicly criticized his former partner's actions during this period. But one former member of Mitel's board, who asked not to be named, says it was no secret that Matthews resented the amount of time Cowpland devoted to outside business interests, particularly in view of the fact that Cowpland held the titles of chairman, CEO and president during most of those years, while Matthews served as executive vice-president.

Ultimately, however, Matthews didn't blame Cowpland so much as Ben Webster, the Toronto-based financier who had been a Mitel shareholder and board member since the mid-1970s. Soon after buying into Mitel, Webster and Cowpland began to play tennis and take short holidays together, forging a friendship that would last until Webster's death from cancer in December 1997. "We had a natural affinity because we both love sports," Cowpland recalls. "He's a real fanatical sports guy—irrepressible. Once he came up to the house in Dunrobin to stay over, and we were going to play squash but he'd forgotten his squash shoes. Ben insisted on playing anyway, and since he was playing in bare feet I did the same to make it fair. By the end of the match our feet were covered in blood and there were red streaks all over the court."

Webster was every bit as irrepressible in the game of business. Early in his career, he helped found Velcro Industries, although he bailed out several years before the company's best-known product became a worldwide sensation. His other ventures included Broadway plays, herbal-remedy producers and dozens of high-tech start-ups. By the time Cowpland got to known him, Webster had developed an obsession with psychic phenomena, to the point of sponsoring experiments at Princeton University into psychokinetic power. On one occasion he talked Cowpland into putting up some money for a deep-sea treasure hunt organized by Bob Marx, a famous marine archaeologist. "He was hunting treasure off the coast of Indonesia with a boat, searching for sunken wrecks. The investors got coins from the wrecks and stuff like that."

The problem, as some other Mitel board members saw it, was that Webster's many schemes and adventures were further distracting Cowpland—who wasn't exactly a disciplined manager in the first place—from his work in Kanata. "I really blame Ben for screwing up

Mitel in those early days," the former board member says. "He always had some crazy proposition that he wanted to get Mike involved in, and of course Mike was always looking for more excitement. Eventually, Terry just got fed up with the fact that Mike was always off running with Ben, doing something silly, when Mitel was kind of falling apart."

One deal that provoked more than the usual amount of anguish was the attempted takeover by Mitel of a Long Island, New York, company that manufactured mainframe computer monitors, Applied Digital Data Systems (ADDS). Webster happened to sit on the board of the U.S. company and had somehow managed to convince Cowpland that it would be a good fit with Mitel. Before long, the two corporations were deep into merger negotiations and trading thick piles of confidential technical documents.

Exactly what went wrong is difficult to pin down. One theory is that ADDS became concerned about a possible lawsuit from its shareholders, some of whom feared that the company was about to be sold for far less than it was worth. Whatever the reason, the Long Island company abruptly called off the talks and put out a statement suggesting that Mitel was a hostile suitor. Soon, the entire affair became mired in a legal swamp. Lawyers for ADDS filed a lawsuit against Mitel board member Denzil Doyle, president of the Canadian subsidiary of Digital Equipment Corp. The suit alleged that Digital, which also made computer displays, had taken advantage of the takeover talks to steal proprietary information. Doyle promptly resigned from Mitel's board. In addition, ADDS filed a legal claim against Webster, charging that he had abused his position as a member of both boards. ("That was an interesting experience," says Cowpland, recalling the allegations of conflict of interest. "You find out there's quite a lot of rules about those things.") Matthews, who had not been keen on the ADDS purchase in the first place and only went along to appease his partner, was apparently furious about the trouble it had caused.

Chapter Four

On May 9, 1985, almost a year after Salomon Brothers began the search for an outside equity partner, Mitel accepted a takeover offer. Newly invigorated and flush with cash as a result of its privatization the previous December, British Telecom agreed to acquire 51 percent of the Kanata company for $300 million.

Cowpland stuck around for five more months, then resigned as chairman and cleared out his office. As one who had always chafed at the discipline imposed by large bureaucratic organizations, he knew there was no future for him under Mitel's new owners.

He was also fed up with Bytec and the venture capital business. He didn't mind taking risks, but he hated the fact that as an outside investor he lacked day-to-day management control. "In hindsight, it wasn't a good position for me to be in," he says of his experiences with Bytec. "I found it frustrating because you didn't really have much involvement in the company—you just invested and hoped you'd made the right choice. As an investor you can make suggestions, but whether or not it gets done properly is somewhat out of your hands."

Cowpland's failures as a venture capital lender had also taught him something about his own limitations. "I just sort of got involved in these companies from pure enthusiasm, and probably a bit of naivete, too, because when the only thing you've ever been involved with has been hugely successful you tend to think, 'Boy, I'm good!' like you've got a magic wand. In reality, you just happen to have been in the right place at the right time, doing the right thing, and you've been carried along by this huge surge of momentum. If you try to apply that experience to another business, it's not necessarily going to work as well."

Had he wanted to, of course, Cowpland could have retired after leaving Mitel and never worked another day in his life. Temperamentally, however, he wasn't suited to a life of leisure. He craved the excitement and sense of mission that came from trying to establish a new company. Perhaps more important, he was determined to prove himself again. His critics—and by 1985 there were many—were starting to suggest that Mitel had been a fluke and that Mike Cowpland was just a one-hit wonder. The only way to prove them wrong was to launch a new enterprise and, somehow, build it into a major success.

There was only one question: what sort of company should it be? He really had no idea, beyond a strong conviction that the opportunities were greater in computers rather than in telecommunications. With the Hyperion, he had almost broken through into the front ranks of the world's PC manufacturers—no mean feat for an obscure company based in Nepean, of all places. Even though the initiative had run aground, the short-lived acclaim for the Hyperion demonstrated how much scope there was for a small player with a good idea. The industry was evolving rapidly, creating all kinds of opportunities for new entrants. All that was required was to find the right niche and jump in, the faster the better.

As it turned out, the idea for that new venture came not from Cowpland but from a pair of would-be entrepreneurs who had been trying for some time to launch their own personal computer.

The two men were Peter Wrage, a self-employed economist who worked as a consultant for the federal government, and Lemko Chau, an employee of the federal Department of Communications who had spent years designing computers for broadcast signal processing. Chau had a typical engineer's fascination with new technology, and he also wanted to help his younger brother, a musician with the Canadian Armed Forces Central Band, find a job with a more promising future. He and Wrage, who had done some computer programming at university, kicked around a few ideas and decided to start their own company, which they called Semaphore Corp. Somewhat like the engineers at Dynalogic, they set out to design their own IBM-compatible PC around Intel's 8088 microprocessor. With a crew of six people labouring around the clock in three shifts—Chau worked nights to avoid giving up his government salary—they managed to pull a prototype together in less than a year. Chau and his brother wrote the BIOS, the all-important code without which the machine could not function.

The Sema 1, as they called their dream machine, could do many things, but what it did most of all was deplete its creators' savings. By the fall of 1984, Chau and Wrage had sunk close to $200,000 into the project. Independent tests conducted by a lab in Manitoba had established that the Sema 1 was more powerful than either the IBM PC or the Hyperion, but with no distributor and no immediate prospect of a sale, it was still really more of an engineering exercise than a product on which to build a profitable business. Unless they could find a new source of financing, they were going to have to call it quits.

That's when Chau thought of Mike Cowpland, who at the time was still trying to extricate himself from Mitel. Chau and Cowpland had been students together in the master's program at Carleton University in the 1960s, although they hadn't known each other well. As it turned out, Chau also had a friend, a South African named Mike Anderson, who was a friend of Cowpland's brother, Geoffrey.

It wasn't much of a connection, but Chau didn't exactly have a lot of options.

He picked up the phone one day, called Mitel and asked to speak to Cowpland. Much to his relief, Cowpland listened for a few minutes and then invited him and his partner to drop by with their prototype.

"I guess we knew that Cowpland had a soft spot for innovative technology," Wrage recalls. "A few days later we met him at Mitel and demonstrated our computer. Mike said it wasn't bad and wanted to know how much we had spent to develop it. He was impressed by what we had achieved, but the problem was that, even back then, the field was getting too crowded. A number of other companies were coming on strong."

Chau in particular was disappointed. He had put thousands of hours of work into the Sema 1 and firmly believed that it was better than anything else on the market. Still, he and Wrage seemed to hit it off with Cowpland. As the meeting stretched on past the allotted hour, Cowpland asked his visitors if they had any other ideas that might be suitable for a new company in the personal computer field.

As it happened, Chau had been thinking about one possible opportunity: the still-nascent market for laser printers.

Like several other ground-breaking developments in the history of computing, including the first high-speed computer networks and the first computers with graphical displays (in which icons and menus, rather than words, direct a computer's functions), the laser printer was actually invented back in the early 1970s by a brilliant group of scientists at the Xerox Palo Alto Research Center (PARC) in Palo Alto, California. Fortunately for a lot of other companies, however, the suits at Xerox headquarters in Stamford, Connecticut, did almost nothing to promote those inventions, convinced that the big money would always come from selling photocopiers. That is why, today, Apple is credited with developing the first mass-market computer with a graphical display (the Macintosh), and a company called 3Com Corp., founded by a former PARC researcher, was the first to commercialize a special circuit board (an Ethernet card) that allows PCs to communicate over high-speed networks.

It was a similar story with the laser printer. It wasn't until 1984 that the first popular, affordable commercial laser printer appeared on the market, and when it did it carried Hewlett-Packard's logo rather than that of Xerox. Even then, H-P's LaserJet was of limited practical use since the pages it produced looked as though they had been hammered out by a typewriter. Although it represented a major technical leap beyond the slow and noisy dot-matrix printer, the LaserJet was still something of a work in progress.

The real breakthrough came later that year when Apple's Steve

Jobs heard about the work of two former Xerox PARC scientists named John Warnock and Chuck Geschke, who had started a company called Adobe Systems. Named after a small creek that ran past Warnock's home in Silicon Valley, Adobe was attempting to sell a new computer language that could be used to transmit words and pictures to a printer. Known as PostScript, the language defined letters, numbers and other computer-generated characters as a series of mathematical formulas. The formulas told the printer where to draw a straight line, where to draw a curve, and which parts of the character were to be filled with colour. The result was a document that looked as though it had been designed by a professional typesetter. Better yet, the fact that the characters were based on mathematical descriptions meant that they were "scalable"—they could be made larger and smaller without any loss of detail. Previously, computers had used a much more rudimentary technology that defined characters as "bit maps," which were patterns of tiny white and black squares on a screen or a page. Bit-mapped fonts were available only in specific sizes; if you tried to enlarge or shrink them, the edges of the characters would appeared jagged.

What Steve Jobs recognized in 1984 was that the combination of laser printers and PostScript language would give computer users a powerful new tool for document design and publishing. Defying Apple's senior managers, most of whom considered PostScript a waste of money, he pushed the company into buying 15 percent of Adobe and developing a revolutionary new type of laser printer, the Apple LaserWriter. The LaserWriter used the same laser print mechanism as the H-P LaserJet, but it also contained a powerful circuit board (known as a controller card) that was capable of interpreting Post-Script commands and "rasterizing" them—in effect, translating Post-Script characters into bit maps so that the printer would know where to put black dots on the page.

Priced at $7,000, the LaserWriter was the first computer printer capable of reproducing high-resolution documents and graphical images. As such it became a major success, establishing Apple as a force to be reckoned with in the newly emerging field of desktop publishing.

Even in a good year, however, Apple's share of the microcomputer market was never higher than about 10 percent. To Chau, that suggested that there was a huge market for a similar product that could be used with IBM-compatible machines. The trick would be to develop a machine that possessed the incredible flexibility of the LaserWriter.

It took several weeks and several more meetings to refine the concept. During that period, Cowpland introduced Wrage and Chau to Les Horn, a fellow British expatriate who was running a one-man software company in Ottawa. Horn, who was the same age as Cowpland and had studied electrical engineering in Britain before coming to Canada in 1974, had for several years been the Ottawa sales manager for Hewlett-Packard, a job that brought him in frequent contact with Mitel. In Cowpland's view, Horn's experience at H-P and his background in sales and marketing made him the perfect addition to Chau's small team. He told the three men that if their proposals checked out, he would put up the money to launch a company devoted to manufacturing and selling laser printers.

One Friday morning, however, Cowpland telephoned Wrage to tell him the deal was off. When Wrage asked why, the Mitel co-founder said he had been speaking with a senior executive of Xerox in California about the potential cost of the printing system they were proposing. It turned out to be more expensive than Cowpland had bargained on—so expensive, in fact, that it didn't make sense to go into business.

Wrage couldn't believe it. After he put down the phone, he immediately called the operator, obtained the number for Xerox in California and tracked down the source of Cowpland's information. It turned out that Cowpland was mistaken: the figures he had been given were estimated retail prices, not the wholesale cost. "I got them to give me the wholesale information and drove out to Mitel that same afternoon with a couple of pages of numbers," Wrage says. "Mike looked them over and said, 'Okay—we start Monday.'"

There was one other problem. All along, Cowpland had assumed that Chau—who, after all, had come up with the idea of a business devoted to laser printers—would play an important role in the new company, perhaps as senior engineer. But after talking it over with his wife, Chau decided it wasn't worth quitting his job at the Department of Communications. "To tell you the truth, I was afraid I might not get along with Mike," Chau said. "He was a headstrong engineer and so was I. Besides, I had a young family to support and I already had a government job with a good pension. In terms of the technology it was an exciting time, but nobody knew which way things were going to go. I guess I really wasn't much of a risk-taker."

On a Monday morning in late April, 1985, Peter Wrage and Les Horn reported for work as the first two employees of Corel Systems Corporation, the name Cowpland had given to their new company. At the outset, Corel—short for Cowpland Research Labs—was a three-way limited partnership. Cowpland, who was funding the venture but wanted to keep a low profile because of his involvement with Mitel, took 80 percent of the equity for himself, leaving 10 percent for each of his associates. Wrage, the vice-president of marketing, and Horn, the vice-president of engineering, would each be paid a salary of $50,000 a year, a sum Cowpland later increased to $65,000.

"Our mandate essentially was to put some people in place and get things off the ground," Wrage says. For the first few months of Corel's existence, Cowpland himself was rarely around. "He was sort of the silent partner because the negotiations were still going on between Mitel and British Telecom. He didn't want it widely known that he had started this new company."

One of the first things Wrage and Horn did was to visit the Comdex trade show in Chicago in order to scout out possible suppliers of hardware and software. For three days and evenings they went from booth to booth, soaking up as much information as they could about the latest models of PCs and laser printers. They also gathered a thick file of research on a new type of PC add-on known as a rasterizing image processor (RIP)—a circuit board that, when installed inside a computer, performed much the same function as the controller card in an Apple LaserWriter. Together with some special software that Corel would have to develop on its own, the RIP was the key to developing a flexible, IBM-compatible desktop publishing system.

After a couple of months and several additional exploratory trips, Wrage finally located a small engineering firm in Toronto that was developing its own RIP. The firm agreed to supply Corel with customized circuit boards, as well as some special "handshake" software that would allow the boards to communicate with the computer and the printer. The printer engines themselves were to be purchased from Ricoh Co. Ltd. of Japan, for whose British subsidiary Horn had once worked.

Horn was also in charge of finding a permanent home for Corel. At the beginning, he and Wrage occupied a couple of offices at 99 Bank Street in Ottawa, in a suite leased to Cowpland's friend Rod Bryden. Cowpland, however, believed that the firm needed room to grow. He asked Horn to find a building with at least 900 square metres of available space—enough for about forty employees, a showroom to display the young company's products and a storage area. Finding the space wasn't difficult: one of Horn's friends was vice-president of The Canderel Group, a Montreal-based commercial real estate company that owned a pair of adjoining, octagonal office buildings at 1600 Carling Avenue in Ottawa's west end. Sheathed in reflective gold glass, the development stood right next to the Queensway, the divided highway that bisects the capital from east to west.

The location was ideal, but Horn's friend was initially hesitant to rent to Corel. He'd heard all about Cowpland and his track record at Mitel and with the Hyperion computer. The last thing he wanted to do was sign a lease with yet another Cowpland creation, a company that might not be in business for more than a few months. He needn't have worried.

Horn and Wrage, however, were facing a more uncertain future, although neither man realized it at the time.

"It was an exciting period because we were working with leading-edge technology and everything was evolving very fast," Horn says. "For me, though, the frustrating part was dealing with Mike—his personality, and the way he was always changing his mind. Coming from Hewlett-Packard, I had been used to operating in a very structured organization. Cowpland's style was completely the opposite. Everything was spur-of-the-moment." One time Cowpland decided to charter a plane to check out several possible suppliers in the United States. In a single day, he, Horn and Wrage flew from Ottawa to Toronto, where they picked up a friend of Cowpland's, then on to Chicago and Ann Arbor, Michigan, for meetings, then back to Toronto to attend a party hosted by another of Cowpland's friends on a yacht in the harbour, and finally back to Ottawa.

Despite the culture shock, Horn and Wrage seemed to adapt well to their new environment. Wrage is particularly proud of having organizing Corel's first corporate sales trip. In the late summer of 1985, after they had put the finishing touches on a working prototype of Corel's new PowerPrint laser printer, Wrage hired a small marketing firm to make cold calls to hundreds of big companies in and around Toronto, inviting them to attend a demonstration of the system at the Park Plaza Hotel near Yorkville. On the appointed day, the Corel duo booked themselves into the hotel, booted up their computer and printer and waited. "We were taking a bit of a chance," Wrage says, "but in the end, a hundred and forty companies turned up to see us. We were kept busy for three days solid and we made several sales. I have to admit, I was pretty impressed with myself."

That fall, the publicity machine went into high gear. On October 2, *The Ottawa Citizen* broke the news that Cowpland was a major investor in Corel. Three weeks later, after Mitel announced that he had relinquished the chairmanship to Terry Matthews, Cowpland confirmed that he was also the new company's president and chief executive officer. *Ottawa Business Life*, a local magazine, ran a three-page article about Corel that described its laser printer as "the latest darling of the high-tech world," a fast and efficient product that would allow organizations "to avoid the paper madness" caused by traditional printing technology. "The marketplace is in the process of exploding," Horn told the magazine. "A hundred million dollar market in Canada by 1990 is not an unreasonable estimate. In some circles, the figure of fifty billion dollars worldwide by 1990 is being bandied about."

Behind the hyperbole, not everything at Corel was functioning smoothly. The Toronto company that was supposed to be supplying the RIPs had run into one technical problem after another. Deadlines came and went, and in the end Corel's small band of engineers was forced to perform much of the work itself. There were regular screaming matches over the phone during which Wrage and his counterpart in Toronto would blame each other for the delays. The companies might even have taken each other to court were it not for the fact that Cowpland, contradicting his earlier decision to get out of the venture capital business, had already purchased a minority interest in the Toronto outfit.

Looking back, Wrage remembers his time at Corel as among the most exhilarating periods in his career. "It was one of those seven-day-a-week, twelve-hours-a-day jobs. I literally ate, slept and drank this stuff for more than a year. Often I'd get home at nine, and then around ten o'clock Mike would call with some bright new idea, and we'd discuss it until midnight.

"One of the things I found was that you really had to keep Mike on the straight and narrow. He was like a butterfly, always flitting from one idea to the next. A typical example was when he called me late one night, full of excitement, and said he'd heard about this company in Washington, D.C., that was doing something similar to Corel, and we just had to buy it. That kind of thing happened so often that I gradually developed a system for dealing with him. I used to say, 'Great, Mike, let's talk about it in the morning and see if you still feel that way.' Of course, by the next day he would have forgotten all about it and moved on to something else."

One of Cowpland's bright ideas was to have Corel sponsor a major indoor tennis tournament in Toronto. The event was organized by another of his business ventures, a short-lived sports management company called Greenway Productions that existed primarily to provide employment to two of Cowpland's friends and tennis partners, Chris Troughton and former Canadian Davis Cup player and coach Dale Power. Troughton, an outgoing, muscular man who now runs a limousine service in Ottawa, met Cowpland at a squash round-robin in 1981, when he was twenty-one and Cowpland was thirty-nine. "Back then I was really heavily into barefoot water skiing," Troughton says. "I competed nationally and did a lot of ski shows. The reason I got to know Mike was that we had a mutual friend named Jim Paul, who was a corporate lawyer with Mitel. One day Jim happened to mention what I did to Mike, and Mike thought he was joking. We finally met on a squash court, where [Cowpland] proceeded to kick my butt." A few weeks after that, Mike and Darlene Cowpland drove out to Troughton's cottage in the Gatineau Hills north of Ottawa to watch him perform behind a powerboat skimming across the lake at sixty-five kilometres an hour. "I was just this kid who never went to university, but still he took the time to see what I could do," Troughton said. "That's the thing about Mike. He understands that not everybody is on the same level as he is. Yet he's always able to talk to anybody and he's genuinely interested in what they're doing."

For the next four years, Cowpland and Troughton played squash or tennis once or twice a month. Then Cowpland set up Greenway and hired Troughton and Power to co-ordinate what was billed as the North American indoor tennis championship. The two men shared a room for six months at the Park Plaza Hotel while preparing the groundwork for the ten-day contest. They also organized a separate exhibition match at the Ottawa Civic Centre between John McEnroe and Jimmy Connors, which took place three weeks prior to the Toronto tournament and was intended to raise awareness both of Corel and of the indoor competition. Troughton has vivid memories of a wild post-game party hosted by Cowpland for McEnroe in a private upstairs lounge at the Chez Henri nightclub, across the Ottawa

River in Hull, Quebec. "That was around the time McEnroe was going through his mental crack-up," Troughton says. "For whatever reason, he was just a complete off-the-wall fool. He was doing handstands on the leather couches. It was a night not to be forgotten."

Although he can't help smiling when he thinks back on the experience, Troughton says the two tennis events lost money and probably never should have been organized in the first place. Horn, too, questioned the expenditure. He found out about the tournament only a couple of months before it was due to take place, discovering to his horror that the sponsorship deal was budgeted at almost two hundred thousand dollars—an expenditure that, from his perspective, the fledgling company could ill afford. He was right, but it was Cowpland's money, and the Corel CEO did not appreciate being told how to spend it. Besides, Cowpland was convinced that the publicity would be worth its weight in microchips.

Sure enough, *The Globe and Mail* devoted a quarter page to Corel's January 1986 news conference announcing the sponsorship. Under the headline "Laser printer has Cowpland beaming," the story noted that Corel's founder had been introduced at the news conference by comedian and night-club owner Mark Breslin, who quipped, "The connection between laser jet printing and tennis is obvious." In Cowpland's mind it was. He told reporter Karen Howlett that the tournament was "a quick way to reach a concentrated audience" of lawyers, accountants and bankers, all of whom were potential Corel customers.

Cowpland was now working full-time at the company. The operation that Horn and Wrage had got off the ground a little more than a year earlier had expanded to about twenty employees, including half a dozen sales reps and an equal number of engineers.

As small as it was, however, Corel was not immune to office politics. Horn and many of the other employees especially resented the presence of another Cowpland hanger-on named Gary Cartwright. A former stereo salesman in his mid-twenties with an outrageous sense of humour that, in his less profane moments, reminded some people of Robin Williams, Cartwright never missed an opportunity to remind co-workers that Cowpland and his wife, Darlene, were his personal friends. Officially he was responsible for inventory control and field service, but his influence extended much further than that. Many people were afraid of Cartwright, believing that with a few choice words in Cowpland's ear, he could have them fired or demoted. He spent hours alone with Cowpland in his office, plotting strategy and discussing who among the staff was deserving of a raise or more responsibility, and who was not.

What made it strange was that Cartwright himself had no formal qualifications for the job and no natural talent as a manager of others. "Gary was a good example of the type of person Mike liked to put into management," says Paul Chehowski, an engineer and one of the company's earliest employees. "At any other company, he never would have been in the position he was in. And yet at Corel, he became Mike's right-hand man and helped make a lot of the important decisions."

When Cartwright met Cowpland in 1983, he was working for Wackid Radio, a west-end Ottawa audio store. Cowpland happened to mention that he was looking for someone to install satellite dishes and security systems at his tennis clubs and restaurants, and Cartwright offered to do the work himself. Before long they were playing tennis regularly and had become friends. "I got to know the family quite well," Cartwright recalls. "At least once a month my wife and I would go out with Mike and Darlene for Chinese or Indian food or whatever. We spent a lot of time at the house in Dunrobin and at the condo in Florida."

On the basis of that friendship, Cartwright joined the staff of Corel soon after it was established. Over the next four years he crossed swords with just about everyone at the company, alienating many with his habit of making crude remarks about female employees. He also spoke openly in the office of using cocaine—"I used to go through tons of the stuff," Cartwright acknowledged in a

March 1998 interview—and on several occasions he boasted of having sex with gorgeous young women at the boss's country mansion. His colleagues never knew whether Cartwright was telling the truth or simply trying to shock them.

"Gary really didn't get along well with many people, but he had a kind of strange hold over Mike," Wrage says. Another early Corel employee, Scott Murchison, described Cartwright as "a joker who always says exactly what is on his mind—if he sees a pretty lady walking by he will tell you exactly what he thinks of her, whether you want to know or not." He adds: "Gary's very abrasive, but underneath that rough exterior he's really quite a decent guy. He once told me, 'Mike uses me, so I use him.' . . . Gary was paid around seventy-five grand a year but in all honesty I can't recall what he did at Corel. I certainly never saw any output from him, and he never held any meetings."

Few people disliked Cartwright more than Andy Nellestyn, a retired armed forces colonel and part-time town councillor in Kanata who was brought in by Cowpland early on to instil some discipline. During the company's first year, Wrage had done most of the hiring and had nominally overseen Corel's day-to-day operations, but organization was apparently not one of his strong suits. Nellestyn's job was to impose a more logical structure, a task for which his military training made him ideally suited. He had met Cowpland a few years earlier while serving on Kanata's economic development committee, and then again while serving with the armed forces' directorate of defence sales support, helping to promote Canadian high-tech military exports.

Nellestyn, who joined Corel in December 1985 after taking early retirement from the military, quickly sized up his new workplace and realized that he was in a delicate situation. Cowpland was forever talking about the company as a team effort, yet it was obvious that one member of the team was more equal than others. "Mike had his fingers into everything, never ever letting go," he says. "For me it was a matter of handling expectations and handling the boss. You had to go with the flow and know when to rein things in." He realized that he had to be particularly careful around Gary Cartwright and Chris Troughton, who, at Cartwright's suggestion, had joined the company as a trade show coordinator immediately after the indoor tennis tournament. Neither man had anything like Nellestyn's experience and administrative skills, but both were personal friends of the boss and so had to be treated carefully. "I considered Gary Cartwright to be Mike's puppy dog, his man Friday," Nellestyn says. "Chris was another of Mike's puppies, part of his athletic side. In my experience that is something that's quite characteristic of high-energy, fast-paced people. Mike has a great desire to be liked and to be the centre of things. He needed a certain bevy of people around him to reassure him that he was right, and that's where you get people like Gary and Chris, who know how to pump him up."

As Cartwright and Nellestyn began to play larger roles in the company's operations, it dawned on Wrage that his own days at Corel were numbered. He and Horn gradually found themselves being excluded from key meetings and overruled on decisions that had previously been theirs to make. In one such instance, Wrage hired an award-winning local advertising firm to design some brochures for Corel's desktop publishing systems. According to Wrage, Cowpland took one look at the brochures and pronounced them "fantastic." After Nellestyn complained that the agency was charging Corel too much money, however, Cowpland promptly ordered Wrage to cancel the contract.

"Andy's house was close to mine so he used to give me a lift to work in the morning," Wrage recalls. "Sitting in the car, we'd have these lovely conversations during which he would extract as much information from me as he could about the company's operations. I suppose he thought I didn't realize what was happening, but I did. I still believe it was Andy who was to a great extent responsible for pushing me out the door, because Mike was easily influenced."

What happened next would be repeated many times at Corel in the following years, with only minor differences in setting and execution.

On a Saturday morning in the late summer of 1986, Wrage and Horn were summoned to work to attend what they were told was a breakfast meeting. When they arrived they found Cowpland sitting at his desk, smiling but looking slightly embarrassed. "He said something like, 'Sorry guys, but you're gone and this is the [severance] package,'" Horn says. "I suppose in Mike's view we had contributed all we could to the company and he didn't need us anymore."

Although both men have bitter memories about the way they were let go, Wrage acknowledges that their termination arrangements—which included $30,000 in cash and a desktop publishing system each—were "not ungenerous." They also left with a sizable number of Corel shares and were given the right to purchase more down the road at what turned out to be an extremely favourable price. Wrage, convinced that the company was destined to enjoy a bright future, bought as many shares as he could afford, finally selling them in the early 1990s for a gain of more than $1.5 million. He now decribes himself as a private investment banker in Ottawa.

"I never regretted it for a minute," Wrage says about his time at Corel. "To tell you the truth, I was pretty proud of what I helped to build. It's nice to start something and see it grow."

Chapter Five

There were two reasons why Mike Cowpland was anxious to leave Mitel in the fall of 1985. The first and most obvious was the desire to throw himself behind the task of building his new company. The second—arguably even more important—was that until he severed his ties to the larger company, Corel could not attempt to hire Mitel personnel without exposing Cowpland to a charge of conflict of interest and perhaps the threat of a lawsuit from Mitel shareholders.

That restriction vanished on October 21, 1985, six months after the company's start-up, the day Cowpland relinquished the Mitel chairmanship. Almost precisely two weeks later, Corel welcomed a bearded, thirty-one-year-old ex-Mitel engineer named Patrick R. Beirne as its newest employee.

To describe Pat Beirne as unassuming would be an understatement. Soft-spoken and inward-looking to the point of sometimes seeming aloof, he is every bit as determined to avoid the limelight as his boss is to pursue and bask in it. Yet for all their differences, Cowpland and Beirne share a long history. It is conceivable that Cowpland might never have launched Corel in the first place had he not been confident of his ability to recruit the talented young engineer. Certainly it is no exaggeration to suggest that Corel might never have achieved its eventual success were it not for Pat Beirne.

Probably even he would acknowledge that. For while no one could fairly accuse Beirne of being arrogant or boastful, he has no doubt at all about his own intelligence. Former colleagues believe he is a member of Mensa, the organization for people with extremely high IQs—"although," says one, "he's the last person who would ever tell you that." (Beirne says the story isn't true, which if nothing else, testifies to his modesty.)

Pat Beirne was raised in an upper-middle-class home in Toronto's Rosedale district, the oldest of eight children born to an obstetrician and his homemaker wife. Recognized as gifted from the moment he started school, he skipped grades two and six and invariably scored at the top of his class. In grade eight his parents transferred him from a neighbourhood Catholic school to Neil McNeil, a school that actively sought out the brightest Catholic boys from across the city. "For the first time in my life I was surrounded by a bunch of guys of my calibre," Beirne recalls. "It gave me more incentive." At seventeen he enrolled at the University of Toronto, from which he graduated four years later with an honours degree in applied science.

As a youngster, Beirne loved math the way other boys love hockey or chasing after girls. While other kids were watching "Leave it to Beaver," he sat hunched over the desk in his bedroom, solving algebraic problems or reading voraciously about the new and exciting world of computers, which were just beginning to infiltrate mainstream society. At the age of eleven, having absorbed every book on computers in the local public library, he talked his way into his first computer programming course, part of a continuing education curriculum organized for the benefit of government employees by the Toronto Board of Education. "I was desperate to get on a computer and there were none at my school, so that course was the only way I could find to get access," he says. The students, who met one evening a week at a local public school, weren't actually allowed to see and touch a computer. One of their first assignments was to create a program that could sort a list of names into alphabetical order. The students would hand in written sheets of instructions, which the instructor took downtown to the board's computer centre. A staff member then transferred the commands on to punch cards so they could be fed into an IBM 360 mainframe computer system. A week later the instructor gave the students their results.

There is a popular conception that young men who become hooked on computers tend to be socially inept, that their obsession springs from the fact that a computer, unlike a human being, is an artificial, unfeeling creation that won't talk back and that exists solely to do the bidding of the person who programs it. Surprisingly, Pat Beirne doesn't object to the stereotype. "Yes, it makes sense. I guess it's the same reason I used to take apart clocks and motors and things like that. From very early on I had a fascination with mechanical, man-made objects. Of course, math was always the primary focus. And math and programming are—can be—very tightly coupled."

What he means is that the best programmers are extremely good at distilling complex mathematical puzzles into sequences of simple, precise equations, of the sort that can understood in the binary, yes-or-no language of a computer. The trick is to solve the problem elegantly and efficiently, using as few steps as possible. Beirne, according to those who have worked with him, is an exceptionally gifted programmer, capable of sizing up a problem in his mind, sifting through a jumble of data and spotting the shortcuts that might elude a lesser intellect.

To some people, that makes Beirne a nerd. But that label, at least the way it is normally tossed around, doesn't come close to capturing the other side of Pat Beirne—the emotional and socially progressive side. The vulnerable side. (When was the last time anyone described Bill Gates as vulnerable?)

In the early 1970s, while Mike Cowpland was getting ready to quit Microsystems and start his own company with Terry Matthews so they could both get rich, Pat Beirne was pondering the evils of capitalism. He has the distinction of being perhaps the only engineering students at U of T to take two courses in Communism. "I don't know why, really, except I was always attracted by the NDP and the Left. I came to consciousness in the Sixties, so maybe that has something to do with it." In other ways, too, Beirne belied the image of an introspective math-and-science whiz. In his pocket he carried not only a calculator—he bought his first one for $250 in 1970—but a musicians' union card. Beirne put himself through university by play-ing bass in a rock band called Free Ride, named after a 1973 song by the Edgar Winter Group. The band, which performed most weekends at clubs on the Yonge Street strip, such as the Brown Derby, did cov-ers of tunes by Sam and Dave, the Eagles, the Doobie Brothers and other popular acts of the day.

While at university, Beirne fell in love with a friend of his younger brother, Nora Farrell. They married as soon as he'd graduated. His professors expected him to pursue a graduate degree, but Beirne felt a responsibility to provide for his new bride. He figured he would get a job, work for a few years and then return to university.

His career, however, began inauspiciously. In the spring of 1975, Beirne landed a job with the Department of National Defence in Ottawa, but left less than a year later, after clashing with his superiors. He then went to work for a company called Norpak Ltd. that had just opened its doors in the Ottawa Valley town of Pakenham, west of Ottawa. His boss fired him after three weeks, evidently because he didn't like Beirne's attitude. "In my time there I designed the core of a financial calculator, but really they didn't know what they were doing," Beirne says. Later on, Norpak began to manufacture display terminals and decoders for a pioneering but ultimately unsuccessful on-line system known as Telidon.

On his way to and from work each day, Beirne had driven past the Kanata offices of Mitel Corp. He knew nothing about the company, but the name sounded technical, so he dropped by one day to ask for a job.

Beirne's recollection of his first encounter with Mike Cowpland is hazy, but Cowpland himself remembers it vividly. "In those days, we used to put a lot of effort into recruiting top-quality people," he says. "To speed up the selection process, I came up with a couple of fifteen-minute tests, one of which measured pure IQ—manipulation of geometric objects and things like that—and another that was basi-cally an electronics test. Initially I was a real hands-on designer so I knew the kind of engineer I wanted, which was someone who was extremely bright but was also very practical and had a quick grasp of how things worked. You'd get some PhDs who were so far on the abstract level that they couldn't do the basics. I'd met a few people like that at Northern and at Microsystems, and they weren't the kind of person I wanted to hire because they never got anything done; they'd spin their wheels and soak up a lot of attention without actually producing anything."

One of the questions on the electronics test required the applicant to examine a diagram of an electrical circuit and determine the voltages at various points on the circuit. Some extremely bright engineers would perform pages and pages of detailed calculations to come up with a set of results that were accurate to several decimal places, while others would simply glance at the drawing for a few seconds, work out the approximate voltages in their heads and move on to the next question. Those were the sorts of engineers Mitel was looking for.

One day, Cowpland was working in his office when a secretary poked her head in and reported that a young man had come looking for a job—was he interested in talking to him? "I told her we weren't really hiring at that point, but then she mentioned that this fellow had already taken the tests and scored 25 out of 25 on each, which was incredible considering that a good score was about 15."

Cowpland bounded out of his office and offered Beirne a job on the spot. Before accepting, however, the twenty-one-year-old rookie engineer felt obliged to clear his conscience. He quickly confessed that he had been fired by his previous two employers—for what, he wasn't quite sure. Cowpland figured he knew why, and didn't mind in the least. "Pat's the sort of person who knows a heck of a lot and doesn't mind saying so in front of the chief engineer. I guess his previous employers found him a bit too rich for their liking, and he wasn't good at keeping his head low. But I like that. In my kind of company, I figured we wanted to get it right, and there was no room for sensitivities about people knowing more than they should at their age."

Beirne soon proved to be one of Mitel's most valuable employees. He played a key role in designing the company's first chip-based telephone switching system, the SX-200, and then worked with Cowpland to shrink the size and power requirement of the box so that it became viable for smaller offices with fewer phone lines. The result was the SX-20, the SX-10 and the SX-5. Later, working on his own, he invented a $300 box that could be programmed to intercept and redirect incoming calls, selectively block long-distance and other toll calls, convert tones to pulses and direct calls to any one of several long-distance carriers. Known as a smart-dialler, the gadget ultimately became one of Mitel's most successful products, with sales surpassing one million by 1996.

From day one, Cowpland pampered Beirne the way a gardener pampers a prize hothouse flower. He paid him far more than most Mitel engineers, allowed him to do much of his work at home and saw to it that he received plenty of stock options. By the time he hit his late twenties, Beirne was a multimillionaire. Even so, he might well have left Mitel for another employer—there was no shortage of attractive offers—were it not for the fact that Pat Beirne is and always has been less interested in status and money than in being allowed the freedom to do the kind of raw, leading-edge research he finds most challenging. Cowpland understood that better than most, because, as an engineer, he shared Beirne's giddy, almost childlike sense of wonder at the potential of new technology. As an entrepreneur, Cowpland was clever enough to know that he should treat Beirne the way he had always wished his bosses at Northern and Microsystems would treat him, which meant giving him the scope and the resources to do what he did best.

"At Mitel," Cowpland says, "I'd give him projects and right away he'd come back with designs that you'd look at and say, 'Hey—that's really neat!' So for the first time I started to let someone else do the design. And before long Pat was the chief designer.

"The key thing [at Corel] was, we managed to keep Pat on the technical path. Some people in his position might find themselves being shifted into management, but his forte is actually doing it. So, therefore, Pat could be at a vice-president's pay level when in fact he was maybe managing three or four people, max. And that's good, because you're not forcing someone to do something they're not good at and you never lose the skills they're fantastic at."

Most people in Beirne's situation would have celebrated their financial good fortune, rewarding themselves with a luxurious new car—perhaps two—and a large, expensive house. Beirne, however, felt a growing sense of guilt about the money he was making, as though his success were somehow responsible for depriving somebody else of a decent living. Even now, he, his wife and their three teenaged children live in a modest, two-storey brick house in Kanata. They own two vehicles: an economical four-cylinder Saturn coupe and an aging Ford Aerostar minivan. "I have too much money to really have a clear conscience," he says when asked about his apparent disdain for material possessions. "Anyway, I just don't understand the attraction of cars and things like that. I'd rather read than watch a movie. I get my kicks out of creating things." (Cowpland offers another explanation for Beirne's modest lifestyle. "He and his wife are both from families with eight kids each, so they've got a gigantic extended family, and I wouldn't be surprised if he doesn't have to support quite a few of them.")

In short, and luckily for Cowpland, the last thing Beirne was going to do was to pack up and leave Mitel just because some other employer held out the promise of a higher income. What might tempt him to leave, however, would be the prospect that another company might allow him even greater technological freedom and scope for inventiveness.

When I first asked Beirne why he decided to resign from Mitel and join Corel in 1985, his answer was disarmingly blunt: "Mike asked me to, so I did." (Like a lot of techie types, Beirne doesn't like to talk very much about himself and never offers a lengthy answer when a short one will do. Trying to hold a conversation with him—unless it is about math and engineering, in which case he can be remarkably patient—can be a bit like trying to coax a display of emotions out of Dr. Spock.) Later on, however, he volunteered that the work at Mitel had become less satisfying as the company grew larger, in the sense that his own role—his ability to influence the company's direction—began to shrink. "If I created a new piece of technology or a new product, it went into the pot with all the other products and its impact was therefore diluted. Anything I was doing would contribute at most 1 or 2 percent of the company's revenues in a given year. So you see, along with the security you have this bureaucracy and infrastructure. Whereas with Corel, I was the first technical person in, so I knew that if I did something well I could easily be responsible for a big part of the company."

In point of fact, Beirne was not the first technical person to join Corel—that distinction belonged to Les Horn. But in Cowpland's mind, there was doubt at all that Pat Beirne was the company's ace in the hole, an engineering Mr. Fix-It who could take on just about any technical problem and concoct a solution. Considering that Cowpland himself wasn't exactly sure what kind of business Corel would ultimately find itself in—one of the things he liked about the name was that it wasn't specific to any type of product—Beirne's flexibility was invaluable.

His first assignment at Corel was to design a new controller card for the company's laser printers, a task that took about six months. It was exactly the kind of work he enjoyed: highly technical yet of immense practical utility. "Laser printers were still new at the time," he explains, "and the manufacturers had made sure they could print and feed paper, but there wasn't a lot to help the printer talk to a computer." Beirne, who thrives under pressure, believed that the quality of his work would to a large extent determine the success or failure of the company—laser printers, after all, were its only product.

Soon it became obvious that that exclusivity was also Corel's biggest problem. For while the company had been on the cutting edge when it started to design its printers, the rest of the world was rapidly catching up. By early 1986, computer retailers were carrying a huge assortment of laser printers from all sorts of manufacturers—not just

Hewlett-Packard but IBM, Xerox and a growing list of Japanese companies such as Sharp and Canon. Moreover, each new generation of printer boasted the ability to reproduce an increasing variety of fonts, thereby eroding what Corel had assumed would be its competitive advantage. "We found ourselves right in the middle of a explosion," Horn says. "Suddenly things were changing in all sorts of ways at a very fast rate."

To the outside world, it looked as though Cowpland was merely running with the herd. "He blazed new ground with Mitel," analyst Andrew Toller of Toronto-based Evans Research Corp told *The Globe and Mail.* "With [Corel] he is joining the pack."

That wasn't quite the case. Corel's early work with laser printers and rasterizing image processors had indeed produced a machine that was significantly better than the competition's. But in the computer industry—particularly on the IBM-compatible hardware side, one of the world's most inventive and fiercely competitive markets—few companies manage to maintain a technical advantage for long. Often, dozens or even hundreds of firms are working simultaneously on the same basic idea. Before long, products that once represented a breakthrough are transformed into commodities, as rivals crowd in and profit margins evaporate.

Cowpland's solution was to adopt a new business strategy. Rather than designing and selling laser printers, Corel would become a systems integrator—packaging computers, printers and software for corporate clients, installing networks for multiple users, training staff to use the equipment and providing ongoing customer support. At the time, demand for such services was skyrocketing. Throughout North America, companies were rushing to embrace the information revolution and the advantages of desktop publishing, but because the hardware and software were still in the early stages of development, few enterprises could actually do so without expert assistance.

Moving into systems integration seemed to hold out another attraction, as well: the possibility of higher profit margins. Corel would buy the computers and other hardware devices straight from the manufacturers, slap its own name on the front of the box, add a few pieces of customized software to suit the client's needs and mark up the whole package by as much as 100 percent. The objective was to go after federal government departments and agencies, which tended not to quibble about the price as long as they could be guaranteed that the system would ultimately do what it was intended to do.

Along with its new direction, Corel began to expand its workforce. Although individual managers were encouraged to keep an eye out for potential recruits, Cowpland himself always made the final hiring decisions. He was determined to staff his company with young, high-energy employees, men and women who wouldn't mind working evenings and weekends for the sake of their employer. An enthusiastic personality and a sense of commitment to Corel's cause was essential. Except in the case of engineers, technical knowledge was far less important than a desire to learn and a willingness to work hard.

One of Corel's new employees in the summer of 1986 was a balding thirty-year-old named Paul Bodnoff. Intense, highly ambitious and charming with a wry sense of humour, Bodnoff had worked for several years in the retail industry, eventually becoming the eastern and northern Ontario regional manager for Thrifty's, a chain of blue-jean stores. When he was twenty-seven, he and two other Thrifty's employees, both of whom worked in the information services department, quit their jobs and bought two franchise stores belonging to the Compucentre chain. Bodnoff's role in the partnership was to manage the Compucentre outlet in the Rideau Centre, a large shopping mall two blocks east of Parliament Hill overlooking the Rideau Canal. "I'd never touched a computer before in my life, but on the floor of a computer store in the busiest shopping centre in Ottawa, you either learn or you die. Fortunately, it came very quickly to me."

It was in the Rideau Centre store that Bodnoff first encountered Cowpland, a week or so before Christmas 1985. "He walked in one day and bought a bunch of Macintosh equipment for his daughters," Bodnoff says. "Corel was still in its infancy, but everybody around Ottawa knew who he was because of Mitel." What struck Bodnoff was Cowpland's intensity and drive. Even on a Christmas shopping expedition, he dashed around the store like a madman and made decisions in the blink of a eye. Thin and tightly wound, he looked like someone with a clear sense of where he was going and loads of energy to make sure he got there.

A few months later, Bodnoff was running a Macintosh-based desktop publishing seminar in a downtown Ottawa hotel, one of a series of information sessions intended to drum up business for Compucentre. During the seminar, two Corel staffers dropped in, introducing themselves as Pat Powers, the company's director of research and development, and Mark Charlesworth. Charlesworth, a thirty-year-old former Mitel product manager who had been hired by Powers a few months earlier to help out on the marketing side, explained that Corel was putting together turn-key desktop publishing systems—systems already assembled and ready to use—using IBM-compatible computers to do what up until then had been possible only on a Macintosh. "Mark saw the Mac as the trailblazer in desktop publishing and he wanted us to test their system, to see how it compared," Bodnoff says. "I can remember them delivering one of the Corel systems to us and I can remember testing the system. It was a PC and a huge laser printer, with WordPerfect and a couple of other goodies."

Bodnoff couldn't help but be impressed with what Corel had pulled off. Granted, its publishing system wasn't quite as flexible and simple to use as a Mac, but it was certainly in the right ballpark. And Bodnoff knew from his sales experience that the vast majority of corporate clients would, in any event, much rather buy IBM-compatible computers than anything from Apple. Thanks in part to Apple's own marketing strategy—exemplified by a controversial television ad that depicted IBM as a menacing Big Brother—the Macintosh had been cursed from the time of its introduction in 1984 with the image of an anti-establishment machine, unsuitable for mainstream business applications. A further complication was that the original Mac provided only 128 kilobytes of random-access memory (RAM), which was not enough to run some of the newer, more elaborate programs.

Apple remedied that problem two years later with the introduction of the Macintosh Plus, which had ten times as much RAM, a full megabyte. But by then the Mac had already acquired a reputation as a machine that was really more a toy than a serious computer for the office.

For all those reasons, it looked to Bodnoff as though Corel was on to a good thing. That was more than he could say for himself and his two Compucentre partners. Their franchise business wasn't exactly gushing profits. Landlords, bankers, suppliers—everybody seemed to be making money on their backs. When an opportunity came along in July 1986 to sell the two stores back to the previous owner, they grabbed it without hesitation.

That very day, Bodnoff phoned Mark Charlesworth, told him what had just happened and asked if there were any openings at Corel. Luckily, there were; he started work almost immediately, becoming, by his recollection, the company's twenty-first employee. "I was technically inclined enough to talk to the customers, but I wore a suit so I didn't look like a programmer, which I wasn't, so I became sort of the liaison between the sales people and the customers," Bodnoff says. In later years, Corel would call such people "product specialists": employees who seek out potential clients and meet with them to talk up the company's wares, but do not actually take orders or push anyone to make a purchase. Cowpland refers to them as "evangelists," borrowing a term previously coined by a marketing manager at Apple. The theory is that product specialists are able to gain a better rapport and have more credibility with the prospective customers by virtue of the fact that they do not earn commissions and have no direct responsibility for sales.

With his background in retail management and talent for translating complex technical jargon into simple English, Bodnoff was ideally suited for the role. He also relished the freedom and flexibility he found at Corel. Promotions came fast and furious, and within six months Bodnoff found himself in charge not only of the sales department but of the technical support unit as well. Ultimately, he became one of the most influential people in the company and was responsible for recruiting many of Corel's key marketing and sales staff.

While Bodnoff was putting together his team, Cowpland, Beirne and others were expanding the technical staff. Gradually, word was filtering out in the Ottawa high-tech community that Corel was doing interesting work with PCs and was an inspiring place for a bright young engineer. One person who jumped at the opportunity to work there was Paul Chehowski, a computer science graduate from Waterloo University who, at thirty-three, was already a veteran of five other high-tech firms, including Bell Northern Research and Siltronics Ltd., the custom microchip design company founded by one of Cowpland's former colleagues at Microsystems, David Moore. "The first thing that surprised me was that Mike Cowpland interviewed me directly when I applied at Corel," Chehowski says. "I mean, Mike was an icon to me at that time—I didn't expect someone of his stature to interview me for a regular job. But what I found was that Corel was a lot more unstructured than any other company. The attitude was just, 'Go do it.' As an engineer, you were allowed an incredible amount of latitude, so it wasn't really a defined job. At first I helped Pat Beirne with some of his work on laser printer controllers, then I moved over to some of my own stuff."

Pretty soon, Chehowksi teamed up with another engineer, Roger Bryanton, on a project intended to give Corel's desktop systems the ability to use a revolutionary new type of data storage device known as an optical WORM drive. (WORM is an acronym for "write once, read many times," meaning that information can be stored on the disk and reread as often as desired, but cannot be erased or altered. By the mid-1990s, WORM drives had been largely supplanted by recordable CD-ROMs.) The idea originated with Cowpland, who saw one of the drives at a U.S. computer trade show and was blown away by the fact that it could hold as much as 900 megabytes of data on a removable disk, at a time when most PCs were equipped with a 20-megabyte hard disk and a 1.2-megabyte floppy drive. The new drives made it possible for the first time to save hundreds of large files—for example, graphic images or archived copies of large text documents—on a single portable disk. "A lot of our customers were into desktop publishing and they were running into problems storing their documents because the hard drives weren't big enough," Bryanton says. "Mike figured the write-once drive was the ideal solution, so he brought a couple of them back to Ottawa for us to have a look at."

There was one glaring problem with the optical WORM drive: because it could not be erased, it was incompatible with Microsoft's ubiquitous DOS operating system, which used an obscure file-management system that recognized only rewritable drives. To get around that obstacle, Chehowski and Bryanton set out to create a special piece of software, known as a device driver, that would allow the two otherwise incompatible pieces of hardware to work together, in this case by fooling the operating system into thinking that the WORM drive was erasable. Chehowski relished the challenge. "In my previous job I'd worked on IBM PCs, but at Corel we were actually developing mass-market PC software, which I really enjoyed. Especially in those early days, it was an exciting place to work."

The flip side of all that excitement was the almost complete lack of job security, as Chehowski quickly discovered. The person he had originally approached about a job at Corel was Pat Powers, the director of research and development, with whom Chehowski had previously worked at Bell Northern Research. Powers was on vacation when Chehowski started, but on the day he got back Powers was let go, ostensibly because one of the research projects he had been managing was far behind schedule. "You can imagine how I felt. Here was the only guy I really knew well at Corel, and suddenly he's booted out. Everybody was really upset."

Still, Chehowski and his colleagues gradually came around to the view that Cowpland had made the right decision in removing Powers, if only because the engineering department seemed to be adrift and in need of fresh leadership. "One thing I'll say for Mike: his intuition in most cases is just bang on," says Chehowski, who now does contract work for firms such as Mitel. "His energy is amazing, too. More than once I remember being in the office at three o'clock in the morning, working on some product that had to go out very quickly, and seeing Mike stroll in wearing his track suit. He'd been off playing squash or something but then decided to come to the office and work. It was like the guy never stopped. Obviously he didn't have to take the work as seriously as he did. With his money, he could have sat back and taken it easy. But Mike's a very driven individual, very competitive. And whatever he does, he wants to do well."

Unfortunately for Cowpland, the systems integration field was proving a lot more difficult than he had originally anticipated. One of the big problems was that, almost by definition, it was a local business— you couldn't very well sell workstations to a company in another city unless you positioned a staff of people in that community to provide ongoing service and support. As a consequence, Corel opened sales offices in Toronto in the early summer of 1986 and in Chicago a few months later. It was a step Cowpland himself was extremely reluctant to take, since he knew from his time at Mitel that it was rarely a simple matter to maintain effective managerial control over branch offices. "One thing I really wanted to do with Corel was to keep it simple—everything in one building," Cowpland says. "That way the communication is very natural, and you don't have the problem of different offices taking on different cultures. When you have several locations it's quite a big problem."

Sure enough, the Chicago office became the source of almost constant headaches. Not that it was a terribly large operation. Corel's sales brochures at the time were adorned with a photo of a shimmering, thirty-six-storey glass-and-steel monolith in downtown Chicago, a rather grandiose image given that the U.S. subsidiary, Corel Systems Inc., actually consisted of a half dozen employees who occupied a modest, 140-square-metre suite on the building's seventh floor. Terry Matthews, who had worked so assiduously in Mitel's early days to portray the start-up as a large, well-established enterprise, would have applauded Cowpland's marketing chutzpah.

What bothered Cowpland about the Chicago office was the apparently impossible task of finding a competent U.S. sales manager—someone, in other words, who wouldn't question his direction. "We never could find anyone good to run that place. We'd find that the general manager would turn into a gorilla. Instead of behaving like he was part of the company he'd run his own show, wouldn't take direction. It was almost uncanny. Then we'd interview the next person and they'd seem to be ideal, so we'd give them a go and they'd turn out the same way. I guess it's just not that easy to find people who are clones."

The Toronto sales office encountered problems of a different sort. Initially, Cowpland and Andy Nellestyn recruited a former Xerox sales rep named Howard Bogler to run the operation. Bogler then hired several other sales and service people and a product demonstrator, someone with sufficient skill at the keyboard to show clients all the wonderful things Corel's desktop publishing systems were capable of doing. A Montreal native who had sold every manner of office equipment in his previous job, Bogler swiftly got into the swing of things and loved to lecture clients about the dawning new age of desktop publishing. "It was a brand new product and a whole new concept," says Bogler, who now sells commercial real estate in Toronto. "The market niche Cowpland wanted to burst through was to provide turn-key publishing systems in the IBM environment. He saw a world full of IBM users who had a need, but no one had really gone after it before. We literally were creating something out of nothing."

Bogler actually had two assignments. In addition to cultivating a market for the company's products, Nellestyn told him that he would be helping to lay the groundwork for a planned initial public offering (IPO) by Corel in the spring of 1987, to be underwritten by the blue-chip brokerage firm Midland Doherty (now Midland Walwyn). A strong sales performance by Bogler's group would obviously go a long way toward convincing investors that Corel was a smart bet and that desktop publishing and systems integration were businesses with a rosy future.

Had it gone ahead, the public offering would have generated about $7 million for Corel, enough to repay Cowpland's own investment in the company and provide additional capital for expansion. Bogler, Nellestyn and every other employee would have benefited directly, too, because from the outset anyone who worked for Corel—from secretaries on up—had received generous stock options as an incentive to put in extra effort.

But the IPO never got off the ground. On the very day the shares were scheduled to begin trading, in May 1987, Nellestyn flew to Toronto, gathered up the staff and announced that the offering had been withdrawn. When employees asked why, he responded that he and Cowpland had determined that the timing was not right. One person who was in the room at the time recalls Nellestyn saying something about WORM drives, to the effect that the investment community didn't fully understand some of the technologies Corel was working with. The clear implication was that if the IPO had gone ahead as planned, the shares might have fetched less than their true value.

In the years since then, numerous newspaper and magazine articles about the company have reported that the planned share issue in 1987 was cancelled at the last minute because Corel was unable to attract enough interest from investors, but the truth appears to be more complicated than that. Bogler, for one, says he was assured several times by his superiors during the run-up to the initial public offering that Corel was receiving "an awful lot of interest from investors" and that, based on the volume of advance orders, the shares were likely to be oversubscribed.

Nellestyn, who played a key role in organizing the public offering and participated with Cowpland in a travelling road show to drum up interest among investment analysts and brokers, now paints a slightly less positive picture. In an interview for this book, he explained that there was widespread concern in the investment community both about Corel's singular focus on desktop publishing, a field that was not considered to have sufficient potential for profit, and about Cowpland himself. "Whenever we went into a meeting with these guys, the first half of the session was taken up with questions about what had happened at Mitel and was it going to happen all over again with this new company," said Nellestyn. "By the time you finished with that, half the people would have left the room."

Yet even Nellestyn acknowledges that Cowpland "had an incredible ability, by sheer energy alone, to sell people on his vision for Corel. Once he got started, everybody just got swept up in his excitement."

So what went wrong? As it turns out, there was another explanation for the decision to cancel the share offering at the eleventh hour. According to several former Corel employees, it was widely understood within the company at the time that there were concerns about the accuracy of the revenue numbers supplied by Corel in its preliminary prospectus. "In the early days, the systems integration business was a struggle," says Robert Lendvai, who joined Corel shortly before the planned IPO and stayed with the company for six and a half years in a variety of marketing positions. "But going public was the number-one priority, so whatever it took to get revenues up, the company was willing to do."

According to Lendvai, many of the early orders came from charitable organizations such as the Red Cross, Unicef and the Canadian National Institute for the Blind (CNIB). Within the company, they were referred to as "contra" deals, a term normally used to describe transactions in which two companies exchange products or services but no money actually changes hands. At Corel, it meant something else. "What was happening," Lendvai says, "was that a Corel salesman would take an order from one of those groups for, say, $150,000 worth of desktop publishing equipment. The sale would be recorded on the books as revenue, but then Cowpland would make a donation to the same group for the same amount." In several other cases, the Corel

CEO purchased hardware and software from the company at the going retail price, then turned around and donated the products to an educational or public institution. Either way, the transactions made Corel's revenues look better than they were, while at the same time giving Cowpland a handsome tax deduction.

Nellestyn, for his part, acknowledges that both he and his former boss targeted large charitable organizations as a way of building business for the company. In many cases, the directors of those charities were executives of major corporations that might also be in the market for desktop publishing systems. "It might sound crass and self-serving," says Nellestyn, "but the way we saw it, everybody was a winner. Mike and I would make presentations to the boards of these charities—organizations like the CNIB—and then we would approach the directors individually to see if we could interest them in one of our systems. It was done as a way of getting leads and testimonials so, yes, there were charitable donations made to seed the market. Mike would write the cheques on his own personal account, not from the corporation."

And the amounts were substantial. In the year ending November 30, 1986, when Corel was just getting off the ground, Cowpland gave $122,000 to various charities; the charities then turned around and purchased $209,000 worth of Corel products. In the following three months, as the share offering approached, the donations soared to $865,147, resulting in sales of $988,000—well over half the company's total revenues in that period.

In total, the company's own financial records show, Cowpland donated more than $2.6 million between 1986 and 1989 to organizations that were prospective customers of Corel. Those same organizations purchased $3.1 million in Corel hardware and software.

Nellestyn may be right that the donations made good business sense, but the accounting firm that had been retained to audit Corel's books was none too pleased when it discovered what was going on. Clarkson Gordon insisted that Corel issue amended financial statements for the three months ending February 28, 1987, and then notified the company that it was resigning. "Clarkson Gordon said they didn't want anything to do with Corel any longer," recalls one former Corel executive. As a result, Corel switched to Peat Marwick Thorne, whose accountants have been Corel's auditors ever since. Added the former senior manager, "It was stupid what Mike did, but I don't think he was deliberately trying to deceive the market. He's on the edge sometimes, but in all my years at the company I never saw him cross over that line. I can see him honestly not realizing that what he was doing was wrong."

Be that as it may, the auditors' discovery ultimately forced Corel to cancel its public offering. And that, in turn, sparked upheaval and cutbacks at Corel. With one exception, every employee in the Toronto office—some fifteen in all, according to Bogler—either resigned or was fired by Nellestyn. "When things implode that way, you either wait to be let go or you jump ship looking for gainful employment," Bogler says. "I left the company, and so did just about everybody else."

The one exception was Robert Lendvai, whom Nellestyn had hired only a few weeks earlier to replace the previous product demonstrator, who had quit. For several days in April, he sat bewildered at his desk while other employees cleaned out their offices and disappeared. Bogler, his immediate supervisor, seemed to have vanished into thin air. Lendvai had no idea whether his own job was about to be vaporized. "After the IPO got kiboshed, there was a serious effort to retrench. A lot of people thought the company's doors were going to close for good, both in Toronto and in Ottawa."

Paul Bodnoff, for one, came close to resigning. "I had a chance to go work for Apple, but at the last minute I thought, okay, let's give it one more shot. I think that's probably the power of Cowpland. But I was less than convinced that anything big would ever come out of this company."

Chapter Six

O f all the people who were involved in the planned initial public offering, Andy Nellestyn seemed to take its cancellation the hardest. His colleagues, observing that he no longer arrived at work each morning promptly at seven o'clock, sensed that he was depressed. He'd always been the sort to march around the office giving orders and making sure things were done on schedule. Now he spent hours alone at his desk, mulling over his future.

A short while later he resigned, telling associates he was ready for new challenges. But as was often the case at Corel, the official explanation gave only part of the story. Another part was that Gary Cartwright had never really liked Nellestyn and had been waiting for an opportunity to engineer his departure. Cartwright got his wish one day early in 1987 when he found out that Nellestyn had taken several expensive pieces of computer hardware home from the office. The source of the information was Scott Murchison, a Corel employee, who resented the fact that Nellestyn sometimes asked him to perform personal chores—including, on several occasions, helping to install software on his home computer. "One day I got sick and tired of all these little jobs and I went in to see Gary Cartwright, Mike's right-hand man, and I just said, 'Do you have any idea what Andy has at home now?' I think it was about two weeks later that Andy was gone."

Cowpland flatly rejects that account, adding that the real reason he dismissed Nellestyn was that "we no longer needed his style of leadership." Yet, in typical fashion, Cowpland never questioned Cartwright's own reason for wanting to get rid of Nellestyn. The Corel

CEO had more important personal problems to attend to. Along with a failed IPO, he was trying to cope with a failed marriage. Few people outside his immediate circle of friends realized it at the time, but from as far back as the early 1980s he and Darlene had essentially been living separate lives, spending time together on weekends mainly for the sake of their two daughters, Paula and Christine. They often discussed the possibility of a reconciliation, but Cowpland's heart obviously wasn't in it.

"My wife and I had split but we hadn't totally split, because we still saw each other for the kids," Cowpland recalls. "We took vacations together. It was almost like in-between time where we were both looking for other people and at the same time we spent a lot of time together as a family. But there was dating going on."

Darlene Cowpland doesn't like to talk about that period, preferring to focus on the many good years she and her husband spent together. "Really, we had a great marriage—a lot of fun," she says. "We'd bike together, take little trips, play squash . . . and stay up all night helping the girls with their homework. Mike used to like to take the whole neighbourhood out to the Dairy Queen in our station wagon. He was a great, great father."

Nevertheless, Darlene Cowpland does not hide the pain and anger she felt when she realized her husband had fallen in love with someone else. "I don't feel like a victim today, because some marriages just don't work out. But I would say that when I watched Princess Diana's interview a few years ago and she said there can't be three people in a marrage, I could relate to that."

For a while, there were more than three. Once in the early 1980s, Darlene Cowpland discovered a photograph of her husband in the arms of another, much younger, woman. When she confronted him about the picture, he explained that extramarital affairs, like tennis, helped to keep him mentally young and invigorated. For his part, Mike Cowpland says he was involved in a number of relationships at the time he met the woman who would become his second wife, the former Marlen Therrien. "The thing about Marlen is she's extremely possessive, [so] once we started then the other ones had to stop," he says. "Which was okay, because it made life a little simpler. Initially I thought it was a little bit extreme, but once I got used to it I found it was great—less distractions, you know. No other females to bother about. I kind of broke off all the loose ends. You know, after a while you kind of accumulate all these worldwide connections and then they become a bit of overhead, you could say. Anyway, they disappeared in very short order once Marlen arrived on the scene."

That was in 1986, not long after Corel sponsored the North American indoor tennis tournament in Toronto. When the ten-day event wrapped up, Chris Troughton checked out of his hotel room, flew back to Ottawa and began looking for an apartment to rent. To Troughton's surprise, Cowpland approached him one day and invited him to move into one of the spare bedrooms at Stoke Lacy. By then Cowpland was dividing his time between the mansion and the family home on Parkside Crescent in Nepean. (In addition to working at Corel, Troughton doubled as a part-time bodyguard for his friend. "He's a big guy and around that time there were security problems, threats," Cowpland says. "If Marlen and I ever need security, Chris knows how to get it, because he knows all the cops.")

In all, Troughton spent two years living at Stoke Lacy. "I came back to Ottawa, and Mike was going through a real messy time, yet he would never show it on the outside," Troughton says. "He said, 'I'm going through a little bit of a rough patch [and] the house is too big for me. If you need a place to stay until you get settled, by all means just park yourself there because I would rather have someone [else] around.' So for a time it was Mike and Chris living at the river house and working at Corel."

"We never actually spent a lot of time with each other because we were on different schedules and travelling a lot, but I will attest to the famous midnight squash matches," Troughton adds. "I would be home in bed and the phone would ring at a quarter to twelve and it would be Mike—'I'm coming home tonight. Get out of bed, get your squash gear, because we're going to the squash court.' Honest to

God, I remember one night I had a young lady with me and I had to wake her up because she didn't believe what I was up to. She actually watched us play squash from a quarter after twelve until one-thirty in the morning." The midnight squash games quickly became a regular ritual. "That's Mike just not wanting to go to sleep. He's just—wind him up and watch him go."

The Chez Henri nightclub in Hull was another one of Cowpland's midnight haunts. It was there, in October 1986, that he first met Marlen. She was sitting at the bar in a blue-and-black leopard-print skirt, nursing a glass of white wine. According to Cowpland, it was Troughton who first drew his attention to her. "I was with Chris that night and he said, 'That's the most beautiful girl I've ever seen.' I looked over and said, 'You're absolutely right.' So he's a good spotter."

After that, Cowpland couldn't take his eyes off her. He waved over Walter Grego, the club's owner, and asked him to make the introductions. "At first, Marlen wouldn't pay him any attention, yet he bought her a bottle of champagne, sat down next to her and tried to start a conversation," Troughton says. "He was infatuated, just totally infatuated." Marlen, on the other hand, was cool, almost haughty. "I don't think she had any idea who he was. He pursued her, but it took about a week until there was any response. . . . How quickly it evolved from there God only knows, because that is a very tender area. You know, a lot of guys go through it [marriage break-up] but because of the stature of Mike. . . ."

In an article about the Cowplands in *Elm Street* magazine in March 1998, Ottawa journalist Chris Cobb wrote that Marlen was the owner of a trendy clothing boutique called Rozz at the time she met Cowpland. That is not correct, although the mistake is understandable, since that is the story Cowpland likes to tell. In fact, Marlen opened the store only after meeting Cowpland, while the two were having an affair. What's more, she was married when she met Cowpland, to a Polish-Canadian hairdresser named Roman Kowalski who was part-owner of a salon in the Rideau Centre. Her husband was sitting right beside her in the Chez Henri when the Corel CEO wandered over and began chatting her up.

"My husband had just finished working and he said to me, 'There's a fashion show tonight at the Chez Henri—why don't we go?'" Marlen recalls. At the time, she was selling eyewear at Nelms Opticians on Sparks Street in Ottawa, a job she had held for six years. "I was tired that night and I didn't feel like it, but everyone else was going so I said, 'Okay, but just for one hour.' So we went, and about half an hour after we got there Michael sat down and started talking to me for about three hours, non-stop. The funny thing was, my husband never noticed because he was too busy talking to a very good friend of mine who was an esthetician in his shop. Anyway, now he's married to her."

Just before closing time, Cowpland asked Marlen for her phone number. She refused, insisting that he give her his number. That way, it would be up to her to decide whether to pursue a relationship. Cowpland kept pushing, however, and managed to coax out of her the name of the shop where she worked.

The next day, he sent her six dozen red roses. When she called to thank him, he asked her to come to lunch at his house on the Ottawa River. Once again she tried to put him off. It wasn't that she was happily married—far from it—but she and her husband had been together for ten years and they had an eighteen-month-old boy, Roman. For his sake, she was determined not to get tangled up with someone new. "I went through [my parents'] separation around that age and I wouldn't wish it on anyone," Marlen says. "It always stays with you."

On the other hand, Marlen's childhood had left her hungry for attention. She grew up in Chicoutimi, Quebec, the youngest of five girls raised by a single mother who ran a fitness and bodybuilding club for women. Marlen's father, an RCMP officer, walked out on the family when she was two; except for a brief court appearance twelve years later when her parents were officially divorced, she never set eyes on him again. "In all the years I was living with my mother, a man never set foot in the house," she says.

Another important influence was the fact that three of her four sisters were triplets. "My mother always called them her babies and gave them all the attention, even though I was the last one born. They were one of the only sets of triplets in Quebec, so they were always dressed perfectly and they were always in the newspaper." Once, she said, her mother took the girls on a car trip to the nearby town of Arvida to see a famous aluminum bridge. "My mother told us, 'Go over by the bridge and I'll take a picture of you,' so I went and stood beside the triplets. But then she says, 'Oh, no, Marlen—just the babies. I'll take a picture of you later.' And, you know, I don't think she ever actually pushed the button on the camera, because it seemed like all the time I was growing up the pictures of me never turned out.

"I always was the black sheep," Marlen says. "My mother said I was the hardest to raise—as hard as the other four put together. For a long time I thought I was adopted because I didn't look like my sisters and they were all so beautiful. But when I was eight I asked my mother and she said, 'Marlen, don't worry. I had enough with four—believe me, I would not have wanted a fifth one if it was up to me.' And then I felt good, because at least I knew I was not adopted."

Cowpland's courtship was persistent. Finally, Marlen gave in and agreed to have lunch, but on one condition: they could go anywhere except his house. The next day, he picked her up at work and began driving toward the east end of the city. "I noticed we were heading toward Rockcliffe Airport, so I asked him where were going. He said, 'Oh, we're just going to take a ride in a helicopter.' I said, 'Look, I don't mind airplanes or fast cars, but I don't like helicopters.'" In the end, it didn't matter, because Cowpland's friend Ross Tuddenham, who owned the chopper, couldn't get the machine to start.

Undeterred, Cowpland asked Marlen to get back in the car. Then he began driving toward the west end of the city, still refusing to say where they were going. Forty minutes later, they arrived at Stoke Lacy. "We get there and there's strawberries and champagne—Dom Perignon. And he was very pushy and he tried to French kiss me."

For all of Marlen's protestations, she readily acknowledges that

Cowpland's persistence was what finally won her over. Cowpland, for his part, says he was deliberately employing a pickup style he had learned from Tuddenham. "I knew that Ross was a very good salesman, so I was almost appropriating his style—lines like, 'Oh, wow, you have unbelievable eyes.' I'd seen it work so many times so I thought, well, it seems bogus but it works, so go for it. One example would be when she said she didn't want to go to the house, you just go anyway. You just be very, very assertive and don't take no for an answer."

There was another similarity between Cowpland's and Tuddenham's approach to dating: both men were married. At the beginning, Cowpland told Marlen he and his wife were separated. "I found out maybe a month later that he meant they were mentally separated," Marlen says. "He was still living with her in the house."

A year or so later, he and Darlene began what was effectively a trial separation, during which Darlene moved with the two girls down to the condominium in Florida. "The marriage was in a kind of limbo state, you could say, where I think she was wanting to separate but taking her time, because she wasn't quite ready for it," Cowpland says. "We sort of separated but never really separated, because I was still seeing the kids all the time. That's kind of the way it evolved. I was trying to keep everything as calm as possible."

In an interview for this book, Darlene Cowpland said she had always understood that her ex-husband's relationship with Marlen began only a short while before they divorced in 1991. She sounded surprised to learn that it actually went back to 1986. "I really didn't realize it was that early, because Michael had been seeing me right up until our divorce," she said. "So I guess I was kept in the dark quite a bit. . . . He was still coming back to the house and spending some weekends with us and we were still having Christmases together right up until the end. He was trying to get back together right up until I finally said, 'This is it,' and we divorced."

Regardless of what he told his wife during those years, Mike and Marlen were very much a couple in the late 1980s. According to a family friend who wishes to remain anonymous, Cowpland even rented an apartment for Marlen on Bay Street in downtown Ottawa, just a few blocks from Parliament Hill, so they would have a place to meet.

In 1988, Cowpland sold Stoke Lacy for close to the asking price—$3 million. He'd put it on the market three years earlier, claiming he no longer had the time to enjoy it. (The buyer reportedly purchased the estate intending to develop a golf course and condominiums, but the proposal ran aground after the municipal authorities refused to rezone the land.)

When Chris Troughton found out that the house had been sold, he started looking around again for a place to rent. But Cowpland wouldn't hear of it. He said he had already purchased a luxury condo overlooking the Rideau Canal, and he wanted Troughton to live there. Troughton's first reaction was to politely decline the offer, but then Cowpland explained that he would be doing him a favour. Besides, Cowpland said, he didn't intend to spend much time at the condo himself. The main reason he had purchased it was to reinforce the impression that he was not seeing someone else. Troughton would be acting as a buffer, helping to shield his boss from the prying eyes—and the anger—of a woman who still loved her husband and was determined not to lose him.

"In the transition stage with the marriage I didn't want to make it too public until things were formalized, you could say," Cowpland says. "It was low-key in terms of visibility."

It might have been low-key, but the break-up of the marriage was far from the sort of amicable parting of the ways that Cowpland has in the past sought to portray. "There's a lot of things that went on between Mike and his first wife that would make your head spin," says Gary Cartwright, adding that "his [Cowpland's] regard for other people's feelings leaves a lot to be desired." On the record, Cartwright declines to go into detail, but over the years he has told more than one person that he and Darlene Cowpland were having a relationship in the late 1980s, and that his friend Mike Cowpland knew about it. Darlene Cowpland denies the assertion, but a close friend of the Corel CEO confirms not only that the affair took place, but that it was arranged. "The idea was to give her a companion, give her something to do. I'm glad it was Gary and not me who was asked to do what he did."

According to Chris Troughton, the separation left deep emotional scars. "It's a point in life that everybody may or may not go through, and in some cases it's worse than others," he says. "Unfortunately, this was one of the worse-than-others, and there were a lot of people who were caught in between, protecting or comforting one side or the other. It's not a nice thing to see.... He did everything he possibly could to make it end as easily as possible, but it's tough for some people just to let go."

If the break-up of his marriage left Cowpland's personal life in a state of uncertainty, the feeling would at least be familiar to him from his experiences in business. For whatever else can be said about the Corel CEO, he understands better than most the cardinal rule of high-tech product development and marketing: there are no rules.

There are no sure-fire strategies, no can't-miss products, no guiding principles that, when followed to the letter, will guarantee success and a steady stream of healthy profits. That's why, by some estimates, nineteen out of twenty high-tech start-ups fail. It's why even companies as rich and powerful as Microsoft are forever launching products that turn out to be duds—not just disappointing in terms of their sales, but genuine, certified, Grade A turkeys. Remember "Bob," the dumbed-down, supposedly user-friendly operating system that was going to revolutionize home computing? Bill Gates spent a ton of money to introduce Bob back in 1995, only to see it sink without a trace. Today, Bob is remembered, among those who remember it at all, as the Edsel of computer interfaces, a product that evokes sneers and snickers and bemused comments like, "What on *earth* could they have been thinking?"

Another example, again from the Microsoft archives: in 1995, a Seattle writer named Fred Moody produced a superb book about the company called *I Sing the Body Electronic*. Moody wrote the book after spending more than a year in the company of a team of Microsoft developers who were working on a children's CD-ROM encyclopedia that ultimately became known as *Explorapedia*. Microsoft budgeted $2.5 million (US) for the project. The irony is that while Moody's book became an instant classic, *Explorapedia* has all but disappeared from retail shelves.

Is Microsoft particularly prone to failures? Not at all. In fact, its success rate is the envy of the software business. The point, simply, is that in an industry that is perpetually in a state of flux, in which this year's cutting-edge technology is destined for obsolescence in eighteen months (remember Moore's Law) no one can say where the next big breakthrough will come from or which new products will catch on and which will fail.

"When people ask me for advice about starting their own company," Cowpland says, "I always tell them, 'Well, whatever you do, don't spend all the money on your first idea or even your second, because it's probably going to be the third idea that really makes the money. You've got to make sure you're around to do that.'"

Corel very nearly wasn't around for its third turn at bat. The sudden cancellation of its initial public offering in early 1987 dealt a huge blow to the young company and led to a string of firings, layoffs and resignations, not only in the Toronto office but in Ottawa as well. With no big infusion of investors' cash to look forward to, Cowpland and his crew were forced to depend solely on the revenues from the systems integration business, which, by all accounts, wasn't generating much in the way of profits.

"Frankly, there were no margins to speak of," says Howard Bogler. "We were basically still trying to get a sales and service organization up and running. As far as total sales were concerned, you're not talking about huge dollars here. Maybe in the small millions."

Cowpland himself says that Corel was "more or less" breaking even in 1987. His personal fortune when he left Mitel was something in the order of $20 million—far less than he would have had if he had sold all of his shares several years earlier. Of that, about $8 million went into Corel. "I had to fund the company myself, and it always costs more than you expect, but fortunately I had deep pockets from the Mitel days. That's when you know you're lucky, because if I didn't have deep enough pockets we would have run out of money." Indeed, if Cowpland had known at the start how much money Corel was going to consume before it began to show a profit, it's doubtful he would have started the company in the first place. "Basically, it's like poker. You invest in a situation and if you fold too soon you're going to lose it all, so sometimes you end up putting more in than you want. I mean, I didn't intend to put the $8 million in. It started off with one [million], and then two and then four and then eight. And the more you've got at stake, the more you've got to keep on pushing."

Despite all his efforts, by 1987 the company's future was on the line. Laser printers hadn't proved to be the winning ticket, and from what Cowpland could see, systems integration wasn't likely to be significantly better. The opportunities in hardware sales and distribution were constrained by geography and by the fact that prices for computers, printers and other peripherals were falling rapidly, while quality and ease of use were steadily improving. Over in marketing, people like Paul Bodnoff were finding it harder and harder to talk customers into paying premium prices when someone with a modest amount of technical smarts could buy the components himself, plug them in and immediately go to work.

Corel needed something else, something capable of generating real profits and of extending the company's reach far beyond its immediate environs.

Something, in other words, like software. Something that Cowpland, whose own career had always revolved around hardware—telephone switches, silicon chips, circuit boards and the like—didn't know a whole heck of a lot about. As an engineer, he had always been a machine guy. In the early days of computing, it was always the hardware that was the sexy stuff, with its blinking lights, whirring drives and ever-increasing processing power—not to mention the big profit margins. Software was simply the boring jumble of zeros and ones that made it all run, like gasoline in a sleek Italian sports car. And gasoline is not—never will be—sexy.

Fortunately for Corel and a host of other start-ups that at various times have come out of nowhere to achieve fame and fortune, the computer business is not like the car industry. If it were, Bill Gates would probably still be a tiny parts supplier in suburban Seattle, trying his darnedest to avoid being stomped on by unassailable giants like IBM and Digital Equipment.

Roger Bryanton (who, along with Pat Beirne and Cowpland himself, is one of only three senior people to have spent more than ten years at Corel), thinks he knows the exact moment at which Cowpland woke up to the enormous opportunities that lay waiting in software.

It was early in 1987, not long after Bryanton had created that little device driver that made it possible for an IBM-compatible PC running MS-DOS to store and retrieve information from an optical WORM drive. All along, the thinking had been that Corel would use the software as a kind of marketing tool for its high-end desktop publishing systems. That way, the company might be able to talk computer purchasers into buying a 900-megabyte optical drive to go along with the rest of their systems. The software, in other words, wasn't really a product itself, merely some lines of computer code that allowed the hardware to do what the engineers wanted it to do, like the software in the PBX telephone switches Cowpland had previously designed for Mitel.

But then a funny thing happened. The software turned out to be a great deal more lucrative, at least from Corel's standpoint, than the optical drives themselves.

The reason is that Maxtor, the U.S. distributor from which Corel was buying the Japanese-made optical drives, got wind of what Bryanton had come up with and decided that it wouldn't mind having some copies of the software for itself. Up to that point, Maxtor had been selling the drives primarily to owners of mainframe computer systems—libraries and corporate accounting departments, for example—who used them to archive large amounts of data. Now that Corel had devised a way to connect a WORM drive to a standard-configuration desktop computer, Maxtor saw the potential for a whole new market, one that was growing far more rapidly than the mainframe market.

Exactly who got the ball rolling is difficult to pin down, but at some point an executive from Maxtor called somebody at Corel and asked how much the Ottawa company would charge for copies of its optical-drive device driver. One hundred dollars, U.S., the answer came back. Fine, Maxtor said, we'll take a hundred.

"I can remember almost seeing a light go on over Mike's head," says Bryanton, who was with his boss when the order came in. "He made some comment about it being very easy to make a lot of money selling software. Not that ten thousand dollars was an enormous sum, but we'd already written the software, so there was not a lot of cost for us to ship it out." Hardly any cost at all, in fact, since all that was required was to copy the software on to one hundred standard five-and-a-quarter-inch floppy-disks, each of which was worth about seventy cents. Add in the cost of shipping and you were still looking at less than a hundred bucks in expenses—1 percent of revenue from that transaction—not counting the cost of research and development, which Corel had already absorbed.

And that was just the beginning. After the initial sale to Maxtor, Cowpland decided that Corel should approach other makers of optical disk drives and offer to produce device drivers for them as well. In the language of business, those companies—Pioneer, Mitsubishi, Toshiba, Sony and several others—were known as OEMs, or original equipment manufacturers. The idea was that Corel would go after the OEM market, supplying hardware companies with interface kits that consisted of a floppy-disk with some software, an installation manual and an interface card that the final purchaser would install in his or her PC. The complete package would be included, or "bundled," with every optical drive that was sold.

Eventually the company became so successful at targeting OEMs with its device drivers that Corel software became the de facto industry standard for optical disk interfaces, not only for PCs but for Macintoshes as well. The biggest single customer was Matsushita, better known in North America as Panasonic.

According to Paul Chehowski, most of the credit for landing the Matsushita account belongs to Cowpland. "Very early on, we were trying to win some contracts from Matsushita and we had put together a kit that included a plain, laser-printed manual. Mike looked at it and said, 'No, we've got to do a really good job on this manual,' so even though we had already committed to a schedule we delayed everything by two weeks and did a really special job on this manual—a nice, coil-bound book with a fancy graphic cover and stuff like that.

"I really disagreed with him at the time because I felt our commitment to the schedule was more important than something silly like doing a fancy cover. Well, in the end we got some significant contracts because of that fancy cover—because the quality of our product looked a lot more professional than the competition. And because of that, we developed a very close working relationship with Matsushita and Ricoh and a number of other Japanese companies."

Around the same time that Roger Bryanton and Paul Chehowski were developing their first optical disk drive interfaces, Pat Beirne and another Corel engineer, Michel Bouillon, were looking for ways to extend the word-processing capability of the company's PC-based workstations. In so doing, they unwittingly laid the foundation for Corel's metamorphosis from a small Ottawa systems integration firm into a leading producer of retail software, and the world's number-one maker of graphics applications for the PC.

To understand how it happened, it's useful first to look back over the brief history of desktop publishing.

Back when Cowpland, Peter Wrage and Les Horn initially decided that Corel should be in the business of putting together computers and laser printers, the phrase "desktop publishing" did not even exist.

The most popular brand of word-processing software at the time happened to be WordPerfect, owned by the Utah-based company of the same name, so Corel generally installed that application on its computer systems. In addition to the standard tools for writing and editing on the screen, WordPerfect offered a number of useful formatting options, including the ability to turn a document into multiple columns of text.

One thing it could not do, however, was combine text with photographs, illustrations or other graphics. Nor could it display characters on the screen in a form that would look exactly like the printed page, a feature known as what-you-see-is-what-you-get, or WYSI-WYG (pronounced "wizeewig"). The fundamental problem was that the operating system for which WordPerfect had been designed, MS-DOS, offered only rudimentary support for handling fonts and graphics. (The first true WYSIWYG version of WordPerfect did not become available until 1992, with the introduction of WordPerfect 6 for Windows.) For all those reasons, WordPerfect could not be used to lay out pages, design brochures or produce newsletters.

The first software that could do that was PageMaker, introduced in 1985 for Apple's Macintosh computer. PageMaker was the brainchild of a brilliant former journalist named Paul Brainerd who, in the early 1980s, was working in Redmond, Washington, as a vice-president of Atex Systems Inc., a Boston-based producer of mainframe publishing systems for newspapers and magazines. When Atex decided to close its Redmond operation, Brainerd quit, recruited a handful of Atex engineers and gambled his life's savings by founding Aldus Corporation to create page-composition software for desktop computers. It was Brainerd who coined the term desktop publishing. PageMaker quickly became a cash cow, and it, more than any other application, was responsible for driving early sales of Macintosh computers and LaserWriter printers.

When PageMaker hit the market, there was nothing even remotely like it in the world of IBM-compatible computing, in part because the PC market had been slower than Apple to embrace the graphical display. In 1984, however, Digital Research introduced a DOS-based graphical environment it called GEM. A year later, Microsoft followed with Windows, which in many ways was inferior to GEM but had the advantage of Bill Gates's win-at-all-costs marketing approach.

At one point in 1985, three Digital Research engineers proposed that the company create a dedicated desktop publishing package for GEM similar to PageMaker. The company rejected the idea, so they resigned and formed their own company, Ventura Software Inc., which was soon taken over by Xerox. Their first product, Ventura Publisher, introduced in 1986, was a huge success, shipping 200,000 copies in its first three years to become the best-selling desktop publishing software for MS-DOS systems. In the opinion of many users, Ventura Publisher 1 was even better than PageMaker, since it automated many of the functions that had to be performed by hand on PageMaker—drawing vertical lines between columns of text, for example, or anchoring illustrations to blocks of text so that the two elements stayed together whenever the layout changed.

Ventura Publisher's page-composition software was exactly what Cowpland figured he needed to create demand for his computer workstations—"real breakthrough technology," he called it after returning from a trade show in San Francisco at which he had seen a pre-release version. Corel eventually put together a line of workstations based on Ventura Publisher. At the top of the range was the Corel Publisher Station, which for $30,000 included a 20-megabyte hard disk, 640 kilobytes of random-access memory, a 1.2-megabyte floppy drive, a forty-eight-centimetre colour monitor, a PostScript-capable laser printer and a mouse. For $7,000 less, customers could choose a similar system with a thirty-eight-centimetre monochrome monitor and a laser printer that used Hewlett-Packard's HPL font language rather than Adobe's PostScript. To launch the new products, the company printed up glossy brochures declaring itself "the leader in desktop publishing." Inside, there were photographs of two attractive blondes sitting in front of Corel workstations. To avoid having to hire models, both were Corel employees—Patti Hall, a former secretary whom Cowpland had recently promoted to director of sales, and Kathy Bryden, the daughter of Cowpland's close friend Rod Bryden.

Luckily for Corel, Ventura was an extremely good product. Even more luckily for Corel, it wasn't perfect. If it had been, Corel would never have gone on to make so much money.

To someone outside the high-tech industry, that might sound illogical. But in the software business, it is a fact of life. Generally speaking, when a company releases a popular new application, myriad smaller companies look for ways to cash in on its success by dreaming up additional features—variously called third-party add-ons, utilities or extensions—which can then be sold independently of the original product. (So-called value-added resellers do much the same thing, except they package their add-ons together with the original software to produce what is sometimes referred to as an enhanced version.) Far from objecting, the company that produced the application in the first place typically encourages this kind of piggybacking, for the simple reason that the availability of those add-ons makes the software even more attractive and useful to potential customers. Everybody wins—at least until the first company gets around to designing the next version of its software, at which point it tries to build in as many of those additional features as possible, and any others it can think of. Then the cycle begins all over again.

Corel didn't deliberately set out to become a producer of third-party add-ons for Ventura Publisher, but that's what happened. It started when Patti Hall's sales department complained that the company was losing sales to the federal government and other large clients that needed to create documents in both official languages, because there was no easy way for users of Ventura Publisher to create French accents. Cowpland assigned Roger Bryanton to come up with a solution and he designed a handy little software utility that eventually became known as VP Help. Once it was installed, a mouse-click in the appropriate spot on the screen was all it took to open a small window containing not only all of the accents necessary for

French and Spanish, but also Greek, mathematical and typesetting characters. When the user clicked on one of the characters, it was immediately inserted into the text. "This was all part of our added-value, doing a little bit of extra software customization for our customers," Bryanton says.

Meanwhile, Paul Bodnoff and Mark Charlesworth were racking their brains trying to think of other ways to improve upon Ventura Publisher, aware that if they didn't, there was nothing to stop other companies from putting together similar desktop publishing stations and selling them for less money. Either that, or customers might just go and buy the hardware themselves, along with a copy of Ventura Publisher, saving thousands of dollars in the process. The trick was to dream up extensions that people were sure to want, and then make them available only to customers who purchased entire systems from Corel. "Mark and I spent a lot of time trying to figure out what we should be doing that would help drive this stuff," Bodnoff says. "Those [Ventura] utilities were created for one reason and one reason alone, which was to create sole-source justification for the government so that the pricing could be maintained."

In time, Corel produced three other significant Ventura add-ons. Tabin was a relatively simple utility that made it possible to import a table of numbers from Lotus 1-2-3, the most popular spreadsheet application of the day, without messing up the tab alignments. Newfont, which Pat Beirne created, expanded the range of typefaces available to owners of PostScript-compatible printers by allowing them to slant, stretch or shade individual letters or alter the proportion and density of fonts. After experimenting with various effects on the printer, the user could install the modified font in Ventura Publisher to create a matching screen font.

The last and technically most sophisticated of Corel's Ventura utilities was Headline, so named because that is what its programmer, Michel Bouillon, intended it to be used for. Bouillon was twenty-three and had just finished a computer science program at Sherbrooke University in Quebec's Eastern Townships when he applied for a job at Corel in the summer of 1986. Pat Beirne interviewed him for the position and came away highly impressed. He didn't care that Bouillon had no experience. "When I evaluate somebody," Beirne said, "I'm looking for their ability to think on their feet, to innovate— any evidence that the person enjoys learning."

It took Bouillon about ten months to design Headline, a period he looks back on fondly. "It was enjoyable work because I was really making use of a lot of things I learned in my computer graphics course." At the same time, he can't remember who first came up with the idea. "It might have been partly my own idea, or it might have come from one of our regular brainstorming sessions on what we could do to enhance the capabilities of our system. All I know is, I was a very junior engineer in those days. So I guess internally the project didn't really have the highest priority."

Perhaps not, but the software Bouillon created represented a break-through for PC owners in terms of its ability to manipulate text. Using a series of menus into which the user entered co-ordinates, sizes, angles and so on, it could produce an almost limitless variety of PostScript special effects—for example, making lines of type appear to cast a shadow, adding patterns, or turning text into spirals. "Head-line's menus are clear but complex, and you'll spend hours generating text printouts," PC Magazine said after testing the software in 1988. "But the results can be spectacular." Both Headline and Newfont, the publication added, "let you produce extravagant variations on PostScript fonts without spending months learning how to be a PostScript pro-grammer."

Headline and Newfont were so good, in fact, that they soon became the targets of a software custody battle. Patti Hall and the rest of the sales reps were in one corner, insisting—demanding, in fact— that the company stick to its original plan to make the Ventura add-ons available only to purchasers of Corel desktop publishing systems. The sales reps earned a hefty commission on each desktop system and were convinced that the improvements Corel's engineers had come up with would mean a flood of new orders. Not wanting to sound overly greedy, Hall also argued that a decision to flog software on the open market would destroy the company's competitive advantage in systems integration and allow Corel's competitors to close the gap.

In the other corner were Paul Bodnoff, Mark Charlesworth and several other managers, who were being bombarded with calls from users of Ventura Publisher across North America, all of whom were desperate to get their hands on the utilities. It was a bit like the shampoo commercial that was running on television at the time, the one in which a satisfied customer told two friends, and they told two friends, and so on and so on. In this case, word was spreading fast among members of Ventura Publisher user groups, organizations of computer owners and software buffs who met regularly in person or through online discussion groups to exchange tips and useful information.

Hall put up a determined fight, but the outcome of the struggle was never really in doubt. Even if Corel had refused to sell its software to customers who were not owners of Corel systems, it would have been a simple matter for someone to pirate the code and distribute the utilities for free. In general, most people were quite willing to pay for software as long as it performed some function that they deemed valuable or necessary, but if the software was for some reason unavailable through conventional retail channels, they were equally willing to beg, borrow or steal a copy of it.

Besides, Cowpland's mind was already made up. Software, he had concluded, was where the real money was. For a few thousand dollars, he placed several small mail-order ads in the back pages of American computer magazines, offering to make copies of Tabin available for $99 (US) and Headline and Newfont for $185 (US) each. Soon the company was pulling in $40,000 a month from the utilities, almost all of which was pure profit.

"That was when we found out that we'd become quite good at writing software," Cowpland recalls. "And the Ventura utilities sold like hot cakes. I remember one of the turning points was when we thought, well, we can't sell systems beyond Ottawa and Toronto, but we could in theory sell the utilities independently—debundle them.

So we decided it was worth putting up with the flak from the sales-people. And when we started doing that, we were amazed at how great it was, because the profit margin was huge. I mean, software is great! Never mind buying expensive components and putting them in a warehouse and then waiting to sell them and waiting to get paid. Suddenly you could put this stuff together for virtually nothing and you'd get orders from all over the U.S."

Chapter Seven

Outside the high-tech universe, people often assume that computer programming and software design are one and the same thing. They aren't. Without the contributions of both skilled programmers and talented product managers who are concerned with the big picture, you could divide all of the world's software into two categories: the kind that looks really cool but has so many bugs it is impossible to use; and the kind that is technically perfect down to the last binary digit, yet so deeply flawed in concept that it is of no practical value.

Pat Beirne is a brilliant engineer, but even he acknowledges that he is the last person you'd want to put in charge of deciding what kinds of software Corel should produce. His strength is the nuts and bolts of programming, not the broader issues of product development. "Down in the trenches, writing code, those kinds of things just don't come into it," he says. "You simply look at a problem and go for it."

Says Cowpland: "Pat Beirne's got some blind spots. His main blind spot is really understanding the market, and I think he'd be the first to admit he calls a lot of wrong shots. You've got to work around it. You've got to keep pointing Pat in the right direction because his technical abilities are second to none."

Sounding a lot like the exasperated parent of an exceedingly bright but confused adolescent, Cowpland tells of a conversation he had with Beirne in the summer of 1997. At the time, Corel's chief engineer was waist-deep in technical problems arising from the development of a new type of machine known as a network computer (NC), which Cowpland is betting will soon replace the personal computer in many business settings. "Pat tends to get discouraged—he needs a bit of a steadying influence," Cowpland says. "Like I'd challenge him by saying, 'Well, what's the good of having an NC versus a PC?' and he'd say, 'Nothing, really.' It's almost discouraging. So finally I said, 'Well Pat, you're designing the damn thing. What are we wasting our time for?' But as he gets closer to the reality he starts to find out, hey, this thing actually does fly. He's got the ability to put it all together, but in between times he tends to go through these ups and downs."

Beirne's counterpart at Corel in the late 1980s was Mark Charlesworth. Although Charlesworth has never written a line of code in his life, he knows an enormous amount about computer graphics, which is vastly more complicated than many other types of computing. No matter how powerful it is, a computer is essentially a machine for storing and retrieving large numbers of binary digits or bits—ones and zeros. Those numbers then act like switches in the microprocessor chip, opening and closing thousands or millions of electronic pathways. The flow of signals can be made to represent numbers, letters, pictures or sounds, depending on how detailed the information is and how rapidly the computer can process it. A typical page of text might require 3 kilobytes (or 3,072 bytes) of storage, with each byte (a byte equals eight bits) representing one character of ordinary language. In comparison, a simple two-dimensional colour image might require 256 kilobytes of storage. If the image is of an object, and you want to be able to rotate that object in three dimensions, the complexity increases by several orders of magnitude.

The reason Mark Charlesworth became an expert in computer graphics is that it married the two things—outside of his own family—about which he cares most: math and drawing. Growing up in Deep River, Ontario, the son of a research scientist at the nearby Atomic Energy of Canada facility in Chalk River, he was an inveterate doodler, constantly scribbling in the margins of his notebooks and dashing off cartoons of his best friends. He was also the top math student in his graduating class at Mackenzie High School, consistently scoring in the mid- to high-90s, and he won the Ottawa Valley championship in a 1977 mathematics competition sponsored by Waterloo University. On the theory that his talent for calculus and geometry was more likely to yield a steady income than his ability as an illustrator, he enrolled in electrical engineering at Queen's University, winning the Annie Bentley Lillie Prize for mathematics in first-year engineering, the Major James H. Rattray M.C. Memorial Scholarship in Applied Science in his second and third years, and the Peter R. White Memorial Award in his final year: "awarded annually to the graduating student from the Faculty of Applied Science who has made the most outstanding contribution to the creative arts and the development of interpersonal relationships both on and off the University campus."

Ironically, by the time he completed his degree, Charlesworth had decided against a career in engineering. What changed his mind were the three summers he spent as an engineering intern at General Motors of Canada Ltd. in Oshawa, Ontario. "GM Canada doesn't do much design work, so maybe that influenced my opinion," Charlesworth says. "But from what I could see, engineering didn't look like a lot of fun. The result was that when I came out of Queen's in 1981, I decided I didn't want to work as an engineer. There'd always been this creative side of me, so I started looking for a job in advertising or marketing. For me, that was always as interesting as the engineering itself. I mean, you can have a great product, but if you don't know how to market it, it won't become a success."

As luck would have it, Mitel was looking for an engineer that summer to join its marketing department. Charlesworth spent the next three years there, handling corporate advertising and marketing for the SX-20 phone system and digital telephone sets. As a product manager, he had little direct contact with Mike Cowpland, but worked closely with Terry Matthews, a man he describes as a "true master" of marketing.

All the while, Charlesworth continued to draw in his spare time. One of his cartoons from that period is a sympathetic caricature of

Matthews and Cowpland, the latter posing with a champagne glass in his hand. Another sketch, which appeared in the in-house newsletter, depicts Mitel as frenetic and disorderly, with managers shouting instructions at one another over the tops of cubicles and employees scurrying madly in all directions. "This was around the time the SX-2000 was taking over the company. It was pretty hard times for a while."

Charlesworth might have stayed at Mitel had his younger brother not landed a summer job in 1984 with Imapro Corp., an Ottawa company that was a world leader in the design of high-end film recorders for business presentations. When the owner mentioned that he was looking for someone to sell a new product—an integrated system with a PC, a film recorder and some DOS-based graphics software—Charlesworth jumped at the chance. "Being into all this cartooning and drawing, computer graphics looked really interesting compared to telephone systems. And in that job I got to meet a lot of graphic artists who were doing business presentations, so I got a sense of what was important to them in terms of layout, use of type and that kind of thing. It was great experience."

Because of its work in the area of computer graphics and integrated systems, Imapro later became an important breeding ground for Corel employees. Three of Corel's early software developers came from Imapro—Roger Bryanton, Ian Rae and Ken Shimizu, who played a key role in the design of CorelDRAW 2—as did Ian Gibson, the first sales manager for CorelDRAW, and Trevor McGuire, who joined Corel as a junior technician and eventually rose to become the second most powerful person in the company, after Cowpland himself.

Imapro's founder and president is Fred Andreone, whom Cowpland holds in high regard. "Fred's a brilliant guy who started off in PEI of all places making copying cameras—very specialized technology. Later on he moved the company up to Ottawa. The thing is, he's a pretty tough guy to work for, very demanding. But for us that means good training, because if you've worked in that environment you're going to find everything else easy. Apparently he fired Mark in a fit of fury one day, and that's how Mark came over to work with us."

Charlesworth, who was hired by Pat Powers in January 1986, was the first Imapro employee to join the new company. He took the job partly because Corel was getting involved in publishing systems, a hot growth area, and partly to work with Cowpland. "To me, Mike was like a rock star. He was legendary. So here was a start-up that was into desktop publishing, with Mike Cowpland, who was already phenomenally successful. I was really excited—totally excited. And I wasn't let down."

Indeed, the next year and a half was a whirlwind of activity and new opportunity. When Charlesworth started at Corel, the company was just getting ready to introduce its first integrated desktop system using WordPerfect 4, the Corel PowerStation, and a more advanced version of its laser printer with full H-P LaserJet compatibility. By that fall WordPerfect had given way to Ventura Publisher 1, while over on the Macintosh platform Adobe was preparing to introduce a ground-breaking application called Illustrator, a PostScript program that allowed graphic artists to create freehand illustrations and technical drawings of great complexity on the screen. Previously, most computer graphics applications had been paint programs in which the illustration was composed of a matrix of dots, or pixels, called a bit map. Although easy to edit, bit-mapped graphics had an unfortunate tendency to degrade when enlarged. Adobe Illustrator, on the other hand, was a vector-based application whose drawings could be blown up or stretched without any loss of resolution.

Charlesworth attended a demonstration of Adobe Illustrator at a publishing trade show in Chicago in March 1987, and was bowled over by what he saw. Here was an incredibly flexible new tool that took full advantage of the Mac's graphical interface; there was nothing even remotely like it available for the PC. The best-selling IBM-compatible graphics programs at the time were GEM Draw Plus and Lotus Freelance, both of which were underpowered and amateurish compared to Adobe Illustrator.

By that point, Corel's engineers were well into the development of Headline, Newfont and the other stand-alone Ventura utilities. Charlesworth spent part of the summer writing manuals for the software, while Cowpland engaged Aili Kurtis, then a freelance graphic artist, to design the covers. The final results were shown publicly for the first time that fall at a trade show in Boston attended by Cowpland and Charlesworth together with Pat Beirne, Michel Bouillon and Paul Bodnoff. It was a heady time for Cowpland and his staff. Orders were beginning to pour in, trade journals were applauding the company for its utilities, and customers were phoning or writing in with suggestions for future enhancements.

Among all those suggestions, one in particular popped up repeatedly. A huge proportion of buyers wanted a what-you-see-is-what-you-get version of Headline—the market was practically crying out for it. As written, Headline had only a single DOS screen into which the user entered parameters, specifying the size of the text, the angle and so on. You couldn't actually see what you had created until it was printed out or imported into Ventura, which meant that achieving a desired effect was generally a process of trial and error, taking some users as much as an hour. Given that no other program offered anything like as much flexibility, it was still a great utility. But now that PC users had sampled the graphical capabilities of their machines, an experience previously available only to Mac users, they wanted more. They wanted to be able to pick up a mouse, draw an object and immediately see it on the screen. "With every copy of the utilities, there was a little blue registration card that people could fill in and send to us with comments, and those cards turned out to be really important," Charlesworth says. "With Headline especially, people told us over and over again that they loved it. But they also kept telling us, 'Make it WYSIWYG, make it WYSIWYG.'"

It was Cowpland who finally decided to seize the opportunity. In October 1987, as work on the remaining Ventura utilities wound down, he convened a meeting with Mark Charlesworth, Pat Beirne, Michel Bouillon and Ian Rae to kick around ideas for a follow-up project. Everyone knew what he was thinking. With Headline and the other utilities, Corel had proven that it could create popular, leading-edge PC software. In addition, the chorus of requests for a WYSIWYG version of Headline demonstrated that there was a huge, as yet untapped market among PC users for something roughly comparable to Adobe Illustrator on the Mac. Recalls Charlesworth: "Mike came in that day and he decided, 'Yep, let's go for it. We know people are dying for this, so let's take a run at doing a graphics package for the PC.' "

If you took a poll among the several hundred people who worked at Corel in the late 1980s and early 1990s, most would probably agree on the names of the six or eight most influential men and women who, for better or worse, shaped the company in those formative years.

Other than Cowpland himself, none inspires such widely differing reactions as Mark Charlesworth. A slight man with curly brown hair and a broad, toothy smile, Charlesworth was for many employees the heart and soul of the company, a passionate believer in the power of the computer as a tool for graphic artists. It was Charlesworth, they would argue, who gave life to the company's core product, Corel-DRAW, only to be abused and cast aside by ruthless megalomaniacs who couldn't stomach the thought that someone else might deserve a share of the glory.

"This has to be said carefully, because Mike's not going to like it," says John McFetridge, a senior engineer who worked at Corel from 1988 to 1992. "But when they fired Mark, that was the day the music died."

There were others, however, Cowpland among them, who saw Charlesworth as stubborn and arrogant, a man with obsessive tendencies and an inflated sense of his own importance. "Mark thought that CorelDRAW and Corel were largely dependent upon him, and it wasn't true at all," says former creative director Aili Kurtis, who quit the company in 1995. Although Kurtis doesn't hesitate to criticize Cowpland's management style, she maintains that the Corel founder was ultimately left with no choice but to dismiss Charlesworth. "Mark would take stands and be very dogmatic, and Mike would listen to him. But after a period of time he just became so inflexible that Mike had to get rid of him."

Two things about Mark Charlesworth are beyond dispute. Number one, he was the first person at Corel with a clear vision of what CorelDRAW could and should be—how it should look and feel from the vantage point of the user, the way it would function, what it could be used to create. His contribution to the product's eventual success is impossible to overstate.

Number two, Charlesworth was a disaster when it came to office politics. At many companies, that shortcoming would qualify as a serious career impediment, the kind of thing that might cost you a promotion or a raise. At Corel, it was a guarantee that, sooner or later, someone was going to put a gun to your head, metaphorically speaking, and pull the trigger.

And because Corel was Corel, they'd probably be smiling when they did it.

For Charlesworth, the creation of a graphics software package was a dream project, one that would combine his engineering background with his love of drawing. "I was so excited I said I'd do anything to work on this. I'd sweep floors, I'd digitize fonts. I would do whatever it takes to be part of this thing." Beirne, Bouillon and Rae had their own reasons for wanting to sign on. Up to then, their work at Corel had mainly involved the creation of add-on products—software utilities, drivers and circuit boards that were intended to supplement and extend the capabilities of Corel's desktop systems. Here, at last, was a chance to create a full-featured software product in one of the fastest-growing and most challenging segments of the PC industry. None of the three men was given to effusive displays of emotion, but each knew instinctively that this was a glamour assignment, the engineering equivalent of moving from a supporting role to star billing.

Of course, there was no assurance that other companies—companies much larger and with far more experience and resources than Corel—weren't thinking of launching similar products. Adobe itself was almost certainly planning a PC version of Illustrator, in the same way that it had recently produced a PC version of PageMaker. The assumption made by Cowpland and his engineers was that Adobe would unveil a PC illustration package around the same time as Corel, if not before, and that it would immediately grab as much as 95 percent of the market. Even if Corel managed to get only 5 percent, however, that would still generate a significant stream of revenue, particularly since Cowpland was sure the market would grow rapidly.

If Adobe happened to stumble—if, for some reason, John Warnock's company were late in introducing a PC graphics package or failed to produce a product that was as easy to use and as powerful as its Macintosh counterpart—so much the better. But Cowpland and Charlesworth knew they couldn't count on that. Adobe was one of the world's most successful software companies. The idea that it might be beaten by a small outfit up in Canada, a company that had only just entered the retail software market, was far-fetched, to say the least.

The first decision facing the Corel team, made within hours of Cowpland's go-ahead for the project, was the selection of a graphical interface as a platform for the software. It was a crucial step in the development process, since the choice of a platform would influence almost every subsequent decision, from the look of the product on the screen to the way the software would interact with printers and other peripherals. Once you started to write code for a specific operating system and platform, there was no going back—at least not without creating a huge volume of additional work.

There were two possibilities, each with its own set of advantages and drawbacks. The first and in some ways most obvious was GEM, the platform on which Ventura operated. On the plus side, GEM was already well established in the desktop publishing market, and it was slicker and faster than its main competitor, Microsoft Windows. Corel also had plenty of experience with GEM as a result of its work on the

Ventura utilities. Less encouraging was the fact that GEM had been developed by Digital Research, a company with a poor track record for supporting and marketing its own products. To Cowpland, it spoke volumes that Digital Research had turned thumbs down on desktop publishing in the first place, prompting three of its best engineers to quit and form Ventura.

As for Windows, it seemed clunky and almost toy-like compared to GEM. The first version of Windows had shipped in 1985 and was so widely criticized that one trade publication declared all the excitement over graphical interfaces was a flash in the pan. The second version, which appeared two years later, wasn't much better. On the other hand, the Microsoft product included a wide variety of printer drivers and screen drivers, which would save Corel several months of work. (In GEM, developers had to write their own drivers for each application.) In addition, Microsoft was famous for its persistence. If at first it didn't succeed, it kept trying until it got it right. It was all part of Bill Gates's master plan for software supremacy: get it out fast to stake a claim in the market, and worry later about correcting the flaws. And Microsoft already had DOS, the operating system that formed the underpinnings of both Windows and GEM. Microsoft's near-monopoly in operating systems had to count as a huge advantage over competing platforms.

For all those reasons, the Corel team opted for Windows. "It wasn't necessarily a straightforward decision," Charlesworth says. "But we just believed, hey, in the long term there's no question Microsoft is going to win. They're DOS. No way GEM is going to win."

Another critical early step in the development effort was the decision to include high-quality text display and type manipulation as core features in Corel's illustration software. The success of Headline, combined with Charlesworth's previous contact with professional graphic artists, had taught him that type was an integral element in almost all commercial illustrations, and that the greater the product's ability to deal with text, the more useful it would be for designers. At lunchtime, he often went for long walks along Carling Avenue, gazing at all the storefront signs and business logos and marvelling at how every one of them used type in a different way.

During one of the preliminary brainstorming sessions, Charlesworth stood at an electronic whiteboard and listed seventeen potential product attributes in order of priority. The top three were that it be WYSIWYG, that it be capable of converting freehand illustrations into mathematically defined curves—allowing users to alter the scale of their graphics without any loss of resolution or detail—and that it provide a high degree of control over type styles, sizes and the spacing between letters, known as kerning. Also listed as priorities were the ability to rotate, flip and skew characters, the availability of various screen effects and patterns, the ability to import and export files in a variety of formats, and the inclusion of what the software industry calls macros, which allow users to combine several program commands and implement them with a single keystroke, thus saving time when repeating specific actions.

Over on the far right of the whiteboard, next to some notes about text styles and editing capabilities, Charlesworth scribbled four other words that summed up the team's objective: "Ventura of draw packages." By that, he meant that Corel's product should be the first of its kind on the market, easy to use, packed with features and relatively inexpensive. It was a tall order, but there were plenty of examples of software products that had failed—he knew of four in the desktop publishing field alone—either because they had been introduced too late or because they lacked one or more features that users considered important.

While Charlesworth concerned himself with the overall design of the product, Pat Beirne grappled with several pressing technical problems. Right off the top, he and the other developers had to learn how to program in Windows—a comparatively simple task now, but extremely complicated back then, given that Windows was still in its infancy. "Back in '87, there was virtually no engineering documentation for Windows, and much of what did exist was wrong," Beirne says. "Of course, we didn't know that at the time. So we took everything at face value and several times we went down the garden path. We'd have to turn around and start over. The other big problem was the way things were explained. The author at Microsoft, a real technocrat, had probably been working on this stuff for three years, so when he wrote the documentation, in all probability it made sense to him. But as outsiders, never having seen the stuff before, we faced a big learning curve."

A further complication was Microsoft's unwillingness to offer any direct assistance over and above the documentation. Though Microsoft often lends a hand when it wants companies to develop software that is likely to increase demand for its products, Corel, a virtual unknown in the software industry, simply didn't rate that level of attention. (Much later, Beirne discovered that Microsoft had provided help to two of Corel's competitors, Adobe and Micrografx, both of which were already well established. "I talked to the guy who was the chief engineer at Micrografx—he and I are on good terms—and they got all kinds of advice and assistance. Microsoft people were right there in their offices, lending support.")

By November, the project was in full swing. Ian Rae, a short, quiet man with youthful features and wavy brown hair who had known Charlesworth since they were both kids in Deep River, decided that the product needed a code-name. His proposal, Waldo, a name he liked because it sounded fun and offbeat, was promptly endorsed by the rest of the team. Charlesworth picked up on the idea and drew a character to go along with the name, a whimsical little cartoon man with a bowler hat and a handlebar moustache. The more he thought about it, the more he liked the idea of a mascot to give the product a bit of personality, an image customers might relate to.

For all the hurdles they knew they would encounter, it was shaping up as an enjoyable project. Seated at a row of four workstations in one corner of a large room, surrounded by packing boxes and inventory from the systems integration group, the four men divided up their responsibilities and set to work. Largely as a result of his experience with Headline, Michel Bouillon agreed to look after most of

Waldo's printing capabilities and the software's main architectural points—deciding how files should be structured and what would happen behind the screen when the user pushed a button. Ian Rae would handle file input and output, text storage and dialogue boxes—the windows that would appear on screen to ask the user a question or offer a list of alternative actions. Finally, Pat Beirne would address most of the key graphical issues: how illustrations would be displayed on the screen, the use of colour, the thickness of lines and how objects would behave when they were moved around on screen. Devising solutions to each of those problems would require prodigious feats of mathematics and complex algorithms, sequences of code that tell a computer how to perform a certain task. "I couldn't tell you who actually wrote the most code," Paul Bodnoff said years later, "but if there was a wacky algorithm that needed to be written, Pat was the man for the job."

None of those technical hurdles was as difficult, nor as critical to Waldo's eventual success, as the application of the Bezier curve. Named after Pierre Bezier, an engineer at the French car company Renault who, in 1972, developed a series of mathematical formulas for modelling the surface of a automobile, a Bezier is a curve defined by several "control points," most of which it does not actually pass through. Because they are based on mathematical equations, Bezier curves can be calculated accurately and stored digitally on a computer. Adobe used the Bezier curve as a basic component of Post-Script, and Michel Bouillon had done some work on Beziers for Headline, which was a PostScript program. But that still left a huge amount of original engineering work for the developers of Waldo, particularly since Headline, a DOS application, did not require that curves actually be displayed on the screen.

In Waldo, everything depended on Bezier curves—even straight lines, which were defined as curves with only two control points, at the beginning and at the end. Suppose, for example, that a person took a mouse, clicked on the screen and traced a long, squiggly line. The software's job was to convert that squiggly line into a mathematical equation, so that it could be reproduced accurately, printed out or simply recorded in digital format on the computer's hard drive. It did that not by drawing a squiggly line but by analysing the mouse points and replacing them with a series of precisely defined Bezier curves that merely looked like a squiggly line to the person using the computer. All of this had to happen instantaneously, which meant that the software had to be constantly reviewing the input from the user, figuring how out what kinds of Bezier curves were required and making sure that when it replaced the user's scribbled line with Bezier curves, it wasn't introducing an unacceptable degree of variation from what the user had originally intended. In places where there was too much error, the program would have to go back and break that section of the curve into two pieces, attempt to match Beziers against each of those pieces, and continue that process until the difference between the user's drawing and the image rendered by the computer was so small as to be, in practical terms, undetectable.

It took Beirne a solid month of research, poring over academic material at the National Research Council and in the library at Carleton University, before he felt he knew enough about Bezier curves to compose an algorithm that would tell the computer how to perform that analysis. "What we do," he explained, "is we fit curves to within a certain error, but naturally the acceptability of the error changes depending on whether you are zoomed in on the illustration or zoomed out. If you're zoomed in, working on the details, there's a different error limit than when you're just drawing just a slash across the page. And, you see, this math didn't exist anywhere—there's no reason for academics to be tackling this kind of thing. So I can safely say that the only other people in the world who have done this math are the other people who are doing [computer] drawing packages. You probably won't even find it at Adobe and PostScript because for what they're doing they don't have to do this kind of analysis—they do a kind of synthesis."

Waldo presented a similar problem when it came to dealing with circles. In mathematical terms, a circle is a line on which the curvature (or turning radius) is constant all the way around, as opposed to the curve on a Bezier, which is always changing. A Bezier, therefore, can never accurately match any portion of a circle. Nevertheless, Charlesworth's specifications called for Waldo to include a circle tool—a small button that, once activated, allowed the user to click anywhere on the screen and create a circle, then stretch it out to the desired size. To achieve that effect, Beirne had to determine the minimum number of Beziers that were required to approximate a circle given that the resulting illustration would eventually have to be converted to a bit map—a pattern of dots or pixels—so that it could be printed out. His calculations showed that the maximum degree of variation from a true circle was 2 percent with three Beziers, .0033 percent with four Beziers and .001 percent with six Beziers. "Four was the number I decided was acceptable, bearing in mind that when you print it on a laser printer at three hundred or six hundred dots per inch, you're actually going to be off by less than one pixel. So even though it's mathematically impure, by the time you put the dots on the page the curve is practically in the same place it would have been anyway."

In addition to curves, Beirne had to figure out all of the mathematics of colour and pattern manipulation, so that users of the software would have as much flexibility as possible when filling in arbitrary shapes and objects. For example, what if an artist wanted to create a rectangle covered with woodgrain, and the word "wood" etched on top? After months of work, Beirne came up with a way to do that, employing a technique that software engineers call "exclusive or," an operation in Boolean logic that yields a desired output (generally defined as "yes," or the number one) only if one or the other of two inputs, but not both, is also "yes." Using "exclusive or," he would first instruct the computer to fill the object with a pattern that was the opposite colour of woodgrain, somewhat like the effect created by colour negative film. Once that was completed, the computer would superimpose on the rectangle the word "wood" in black. Finally, the entire shape would be gone over again with opposite colour, thereby converting the rectangle to the desired colour but leaving the text in the opposite colour, so that it was still visible. (In effect, painting the object twice with opposite colour produced the original colour, just as two "yes" inputs produce a "no" using the "exclusive or" operation.) "That was a big deal, that took a while to figure out," Beirne recalls.

In some cases, Beirne admits, his contributions to Waldo duplicated work that had already been done by developers at other companies, although he only realized it years later. In other instances, he, Bouillon and Rae were aware that the problems they faced had previously been solved by other engineers, but thought they could do better. Looking back, Beirne is convinced they did. "There's a lot of math in our product that I haven't seen anywhere else, that lends it speed and agility," he says. "One of the things about a computer tool is that if you can make it faster and closer to the brain, it feels more natural, more like part of the mechanics of actually doing something. If you move the mouse and you have to wait one and a half seconds for a reaction, it becomes less of a tool and more of an impediment. Whereas if you move the mouse and the screen reaction occurs instantly, it's almost part of the thought process. You just think and do, think and do, and everything happens much more smoothly. That's what we were aiming for, and that's what we got."

Inevitably, the team underestimated the amount and complexity of the work that lay ahead of them. In a planning document drawn up in January 1988, Mark Charlesworth calculated that it would take another thirty man-months of production to complete Waldo. He appears to have based that figure on the assumption that the entire team of four would spend six more months on the project, assisted in the final three months by two other employees, who would check for bugs and carry out a variety of supporting tasks. The completed software would then go on sale in July at a recommended retail price of $295 (US), of which $140 would be Corel's wholesale price. Sales were forecast to be one hundred units in the first month, ramping up over the following year to twelve hundred units a month. With a marketing budget of $25,000 a month and a staff of four engineers, at $5,000 a month each, to plan upgrades and correct any flaws that had not previously been detected, Waldo was projected to earn a profit of several hundred thousand dollars in its first year on the market.

As it turned out, every one of those numbers was off by a wide margin.

One reason Waldo's development took much longer than expected is that Cowpland and Charlesworth kept raising the bar, adding new features to the wish list of specifications. At the beginning, there was talk that Waldo should be a monochrome product, capable of printing in colour but using black and white to display graphics on the screen. Only much later was it decided to incorporate screen colours.

In a similar vein, the original plan called for Waldo to be designed for use with PostScript printers only. After much internal debate, however, Cowpland and Charlesworth decided that the software should be reconfigured so that it was capable of downloading to H-P LaserJet-compatible printers as well as the more expensive and sophisticated PostScript machines. The rationale was simple: by 1988, there were 700,000 LaserJet-compatible printers in use across North America, compared to an estimated 50,000 PostScript printers. "Waldo will be a great product, but it is focused at a very narrow niche," Charlesworth said in a memo to his boss in the spring of that year. "By adding an LJ [LaserJet] driver, we multiply the size of our potential market by a factor of ten. We can go head to head with GEM Draw Plus and Freelance [two non–PostScript illustration packages] for owners of a laser printer."

The logic may have been inescapable, but that didn't make it any easier from an engineering standpoint. The result of that decision, Beirne said, was that "in some areas there was twice as much to do, a real manpower hurdle. For instance, if you're drawing and you create an arbitrary shape, fair enough. It's fairly straightforward to print that in either PostScript or LaserJet. But if you take that same arbitrary shape and fill it with a pattern—bricks, say, or bubbles—it's relatively trivial to do in PostScript but it's a real brain-bender to try to figure out how to do it in LaserJet, at least back in 1987."

In November 1987, Corel's president returned from Comdex in Las Vegas full of excitement about a new Macintosh graphics package called Digital Darkroom, from a small California company called Silicon Beach. One of the first products of its kind, Digital Darkroom had the ability to trace automatically a bit-mapped image, which meant you could scan in a photograph or other graphic and transform it into an object that could be manipulated by an illustration program. In the Macintosh version of Adobe Illustrator, by contrast, the user had to do the tracing manually. Since it was likely that other software vendors would be scrambling to keep up with Silicon Beach, Cowpland decided that auto-tracing should also be included in Corel's product. That kept Pat Beirne busy for several more weeks, working out the math so that Waldo would be able to locate the edge of an object in a bit-mapped image and convert it into Beziers.

According to Paul Bodnoff, it was Charlesworth who carried out most of the detailed analysis of competing products, while he, Cowpland and others contributed ideas and took part in brainstorming sessions at which potential features and marketing strategies were kicked around. "Between us we did a really good job of what is described as marketing, which is figuring out what the customer might be interested in and then communicating that to the engineers. It was like, 'It would be very cool if we could do this,' and sure enough the engineers would go away and do it—things like being able to put text on a curve, being able to trace stuff and so on. All of those things were complex technically and still they were able to pull it off. It was a great team effort."

Another labour-intensive addition to the product specs was the decision to equip Waldo with a wide selection of fonts. The simplest solution would have been to license several dozen of the most popular fonts from Adobe, but Cowpland rejected that idea because Corel would have been required to pay royalties to the California company. To save money, he asked the team to find a way of pirating Adobe's fonts.

Once again, Beirne came up with a solution. Using the technology he had developed for converting hand-drawn lines to Bezier curves, he created a stripped-down prototype of Waldo designed specifically for copying and reproducing—in other words, pirating—fonts. Charlesworth then hired three students, friends of Cowpland's daughter Paula, to work evenings, weekends and full-time during the summer in what became known around Corel as "the font factory." The procedure was time-consuming but effective. One by one, the students would call up Adobe fonts on their computers using Ventura Publisher, enlarge them, print them out and scan them into another computer that was equipped with Beirne's special pirating software. The students—Peter Kenny, Craig Dunphy and Brad McDonald— would then manually trace the characters with a series of mouse clicks. Finally, the outline would be stored and converted into a vector-based image. For every font, the process had to be repeated as many as two hundred and fifty times: once for each letter of the alphabet in both upper and lower cases in normal, bold, italic and bold-italic typefaces, plus all the punctuation marks and a standard assortment of symbols.

With the font factory going flat out, Corel was eventually able to accumulate a library of fifty-seven fonts for Waldo, of which thirty-five were shameless knockoffs of Adobe products. Adobe, not surprisingly, was furious when it found out what had happened, but was powerless to do anything because its copyright extended only to the programming code used to create the font, not to the actual shape of the letters. Thanks to Pat Beirne's font-copying software, Corel had created its own code, which just happened to achieve the same effect. It had also assigned new names to the fonts, names that in some cases bore a striking resemblance to the ones used by Adobe. Bodoni became Bodnoff, Optima became Ottawa, Charlemagne became Charlesworth, and so on. To make sure there was no confusion, the software came with a handy chart that identified all of Corel's fonts by their original names. Another helpful addition was an editing feature that gave Waldo users the ability to rename any font—if, for example, they deemed it desirable to revert to the names used by Adobe.

Scott Murchison, a former Mitel employee who joined Corel in 1986 and became its first quality assurance specialist, recalls sitting around with several other employees trying to dream up new names for Waldo fonts. He was disappointed when the company chose to go with "Mystical" rather than his own last name to replace Adobe's "Mistral."

"The thing was, our tracing program didn't actually give us that fine a resolution," Murchison says. "To tell the truth, a lot of the times the characters were kind of coarse. I used to laugh about the percent signs more than anything—they looked like two bagels with a slash. I was never really satisfied with the quality of our fonts, but nobody else around there seemed to mind. Even Pat would say, 'Who cares? They're free.'"

Just as important as the number of fonts was the way they were displayed on the screen. In the late 1980s, Adobe Systems boasted the highest profit margins of any major software company in the world. Most of that money came from selling fonts, so Adobe had understandably gone to a great deal of trouble to discourage people from copying them. A key part of that strategy was the fact that PostScript fonts were stored not as part of the computer's software but inside the printer. As a result, when Adobe Illustrator for Macintosh was released it used only low-resolution bit-mapped screen fonts, which appeared rough and jagged when enlarged. Only when an illustration was printed out was the text converted to smooth, high-resolution outline fonts. "They may have thought that was sufficient for their customers, but when you're doing a graphic design that heavily depends on the precise look of those characters, it's just not good enough," Charlesworth says. "For us, the outline font technology was really critical. We felt it was going to be one of our unique differentiators."

For all that, he and the rest of the Waldo team knew they could not afford to be complacent. There were bound to be a number of rival products on the market by the time Waldo was finally ready to ship, and it was impossible to know in advance how Corel's entry would stack up against the competition.

The first of those competing products, Micrografx Designer, went on sale in April 1988, a full nine months before Corel's product finally hit the market. Charlesworth, Beirne and the others were relieved to discover that it had been developed primarily for sophisticated users who specialized in technical and mechanical illustration. Because text was very much a secondary element in those sorts of drawings, Micrografx Designer used generic stick fonts that were useful for judging size and position but nowhere near as convenient as true WYSIWYG type. Even so, Micrografx Designer was good enough to win a 1988 award for technical excellence from PC *Magazine*, a highly respected industry publication.

Meanwhile, the main competition was still presumed to be Adobe. As summer progressed and the Waldo team began putting in longer hours in a desperate effort to meet a deadline that kept slipping farther away, rumours of a soon-to-be-released PC version of Illustrator abounded. Charlesworth was convinced it would be the one to beat.

"Adobe was like this ghost, this spectre hovering over us the whole time," he says. "We didn't know anything about it, but we knew it was coming. I remember many times thinking that it would just be so great if we could beat them by a few months and get a bit of a spotlight, because otherwise people would probably ignore us. You know: 'Adobe is here and, oh, there's this other product too, but it's not Adobe, so who really cares?' That's what we were up against."

Chapter Eight

For the first nine or ten months of Waldo's gestation, Cowpland left the development team more or less alone to run its own show, intervening only occasionally to ask that some new feature be added to the growing list of specifications. But as the product began to take shape and the launch date approached, he assumed a much more active role. Software development might not have been one of his strengths—he was more than happy to leave that in Pat Beirne's capable hands—but marketing most assuredly was. There was no way on earth he was going to let Corel's biggest and most important product to date go out the door without putting his stamp all over it.

That approach—giving managers free rein in the early stages of a project, but then stepping in at the end and making all of the key decisions—is typical of Cowpland's management style. On one level, he genuinely believes that the best way to foster an intense competitive spirit at Corel is to delegate authority and give project supervisors a wide degree of latitude in tackling assignments. It's just that, when all is said and done, he trusts no one's judgment but his own.

"I know from experience that I have that ability to create a world-beating product," Cowpland says over a late lunch one afternoon in his Rockcliffe mansion. "A lot of other people think they can but they haven't proven it. So there's no way I'm going to, if you like, sub-contract all that decision-making and say, 'See you next year—hope you make the budget.'"

Characteristically, Cowpland shifts into a tennis metaphor to drive home his point. "It comes back to this competitive tennis thing. You know: Rod Laver can win, but how many would-be Rod Lavers are there out? How many would-be Pete Samprases are there? A lot of people have picked up a tennis racket and said, 'I can play tennis as well as the next guy,' but have they actually won anything? It's a subtle thing. You have to give people a fair amount of slack and you don't want to prejudge, because otherwise you stop innovating. But at the same time, if you give too much rope you're going to waste a lot of money with people who don't really have the capability."

Back in the summer of 1988, Cowpland was beginning to feel that way about Mark Charlesworth. There was no question in his mind that Charlesworth had done a superb job of managing the Waldo project and of making sure that Corel's graphics package would be both powerful and easy to use. Still, Cowpland was becoming increasingly convinced that Charlesworth's ambitions for Waldo were too modest. In part, the difference was one of perspective. To Cowpland, it hardly mattered whether Waldo was a vector-based illustration package or the world's greatest software for cataloguing recipes, so long as there was an opportunity to break out of Corel's small, unprofitable niche and establish the company as a major producer of software. Charlesworth, in contrast, had been drawn to the project precisely because of his interest in, and knowledge of, computer graphics. That made him the ideal person to oversee Waldo's creation, but it did not necessarily qualify him—in Cowpland's mind at least—to decide how it should be sold.

The main issue now was how to position Waldo in the market. In a twenty-five-page document titled "Waldo plan," dated August 19, 1988, Charlesworth endorsed Cowpland's view that the objective was to establish Corel's software as "the drawing program of choice for owners of PostScript or LaserJet printers hooked to PCs." To achieve that, it was important that the software be more powerful than Adobe's Illustrator for PC, at a comparable price, and easier to use. "We don't want to be perceived," wrote Charlesworth, " as a 'professional artist-only' niche market product."

All of that was fine and good, yet later on in the same document

Charlesworth seemed to imply that it would be difficult, if not futile, to sell Corel's software to novice users. He predicted that 50 percent of Waldo's customers would be professional graphic artists "who for some reason . . . have a PC rather than a Mac," while the remainder would be "business communicators who [are] not trained graphic artists."

"Because drawing and graphic design is accepted as a talent or skill," he wrote, "non-artists will shy away from the package except for the gray segment which will buy the package to spruce up their publications. . . . Most PC users will not buy Waldo, because they believe you need artistic abilities to draw and/or they feel creating good-looking graphics is a waste of their time."

From Charlesworth's point of view, he was only stating the obvious. After all, why would anyone go to the expense of purchasing a sophisticated, state-of-the-art graphics package if he or she wasn't already convinced of the need for such a product? To Cowpland, however, that sort of thinking bordered on defeatism. He had his eye on a far larger and more lucrative market, one that would encompass professional users as well as those people whose previous graphics experience might have been limited to the crayons and finger-paints they used in kindergarten. The key to winning over that crowd was to pitch Corel's software not as a high-end graphics illustration product but as a tool that anybody could use, regardless of how much or how little they knew about art.

In truth, the difference between the two positions was really more a matter of degree. It was Charlesworth, after all, who had pushed hard to ensure that the software would be as user-friendly as possible, and it was Charlesworth who, in that same strategy document, proposed that every copy of Waldo be accompanied not just by a user manual, tutorial guide and other standard reference materials, but also by a step-by-step beginners' introduction to computer graphics. "This is in recognition that eighty percent of the market are people who put together publications who aren't professional graphic artists," he wrote.

Nevertheless, it was becoming increasingly obvious to those

around them that Cowpland and Charlesworth were pulling in different directions when it came to some of the key marketing questions surrounding Waldo. One of the first concrete expressions of that divergence concerned the design of the product's packaging—a crucial element, since the packaging would in many cases represent the company's one and only shot at communicating a positive message to potential customers. Even if a buyer had already heard good things about the product, a poorly executed package could easily cost Corel a sale.

Charlesworth wanted the packaging to convey an impression of sophistication and high quality: it would be similar to the box used by Adobe for PageMaker. "There should be a heavy stock sleeve with full colour photograph and text showing traditional tools (rich colours, parchment detail)," he wrote in his August 18 marketing plan. "This would slide over a graphics-only colour box (two pieces, sleeve design) which contains the miscellaneous items which make up the Waldo product."

That left unsettled the question of who exactly should be given the responsibility for package design. Charlesworth's mind was not made up, but one possible candidate was an Ottawa-based graphic artist named Stanley Berneche. Charlesworth was a big admirer of Berneche's work and had already pencilled in his name on a tentative work schedule as the person who would be hired to design and lay out the promotional poster for Corel's new software. He had also frequently sought Berneche's advice on the design and usability of the software itself. Having functioned for several months as a kind of one-man beta test site, Berneche already knew the product better than anyone else outside Corel.

Cowpland, however, had other ideas.

Ever since the Mitel days, when his newfound wealth had given him the means to sample some of the finer things in life, Cowpland had fancied himself something of a patron of the arts. At one point in the early 1980s he had donated $50,000 to the Ottawa School of Art, a publicly subsidized institution that was perennially in need of additional financial assistance. By way of thanks, the school had then invited him to join its voluntary board of directors.

One of the school's other directors at that time was Aili Kurtis. A former head of design for CJOH-TV, the local CTV affiliate, Kurtis had spent ten years as a self-employed graphic artist, doing courtroom sketches for a variety of local television stations, teaching at the art school and, whenever possible, selling her own paintings. Life as a freelancer wasn't always easy or artistically gratifying, but she was a single mother and couldn't afford the luxury of picking and choosing her clients. She lived, she was proud to say, by her wits and her talent.

One year, in the midst of one of the art school's frequent financial crises, several of the outside directors launched a campaign to oust the executive director, alleging mismanagement. To Kurtis, it seemed as though the executive director was being made a scapegoat, so she sprang to her defence in the midst of a particularly raucous board meeting. Cowpland evidently didn't feel strongly one way or the other, but he was intrigued enough by Kurtis's intervention to suggest that they get together afterward for coffee.

"It was one of those instances where it wasn't easy in light of the public mood to stand up and defend someone, but I always tend to act without thinking about the future," Kurtis says. "Anyway, I guess he noticed me, because over the following few weeks we had lunch a couple of times and I showed him my portfolio. Pretty soon he asked me to do some freelance work for this new company he had set up, which turned out to be Corel."

What most interested Cowpland about Kurtis was her chameleon-like versatility as a graphic artist—the way she could juggle a variety of assignments and give each client exactly what he or she wanted. He passed on her name to Debbie Boucher, Corel's advertising director at the time, suggesting that Kurtis be given the job of designing covers for the user manuals that accompanied Headline and Newfont. His instructions were to come up with something "bold and simple."

A day later, Kurtis returned with a proposal that fit the bill perfectly: a plain grey background across which was painted a sort of

Japanese brushstroke, magenta for Headline and aqua for Newfont. Nothing subtle, but then Cowpland didn't go in for subtlety. He took one look and approved both of them.

"I'd had some experiences with artists where you ask them to do something and they give you what they want," Cowpland says. "This time, what I got back was exactly what I'd asked for. I thought, wow, that's an unusual artist—talented but not obsessive about her style. Some people are so narrow and they just do one type of thing. Whereas Aili and I had a natural affinity, I would say. Her style was colourful and very flexible. She added a graphics flair to our organization, which we needed because we were doing graphics software but none of us were artists."

Roughly a year after that, in early September 1988, Cowpland talked Kurtis into accepting a full-time position at Corel in the newly created role of creative director. Instead of receiving freelance assignments from Boucher, Kurtis was suddenly her boss. The move was vintage Cowpland: he considered the arrangement to be advantageous for Corel, so he didn't spend five seconds thinking about how Boucher might feel.

Kurtis's appointment came just as decisions were being made about the packaging design for Waldo, but Cowpland did not concern himself with how Mark Charlesworth might react. Although he never spoke to Charlesworth directly about his intentions, it was clear to several other senior managers that Cowpland had brought in Kurtis in order to help him personally exercise control over the way Waldo would be positioned and marketed. Henceforth, Charlesworth would be responsible only for what went inside the box. Kurtis and Cowpland would work together in deciding what face it would present to the world.

Before an image could be chosen for the product, it would need a catchy name. For months, Charlesworth had been promoting the name Textures, in part because it played on what he considered to be Waldo's single most valuable feature: its ability to customize and manipulate the appearance of text. He had even produced several hand-drawn sketches of a box bearing that name, with the first four letters in roman typeface and the rest in italics. The use of two difference typefaces was deliberate and, to Charlesworth, rather clever, given that one of the defining features of the software was its ability to alter the attributes of characters within a text string.

Cowpland, however, detested the name. He was looking for a name that was as generic as possible, much like Mitel or Corel—a name that would allow the product to evolve in whatever direction seemed most likely to generate sales. Textures was stylish, to be sure, but who cared about style when the goal was to flog as many boxes as possible? Besides, it made it sound as though the software were really useful only for printing textures and patterns. It was, he complained to Kurtis, "way too narrow."

His solution was to throw open the naming process to suggestions from the rest of the staff, of which there were about fifty at that point. Someone proposed Corellustrator, and several others wanted to stick with Waldo. Two or three people, however, put forward Corel Draw. It wasn't exactly original—GEM Draw, a low-end illustration product from Digital Research, had been on the market for some time—but it expressed clearly and unmistakably the software's purpose, without in any way imposing limitations.

"The thing I would say about Mike is that he would make the stupidest decisions you've ever heard and then make it work," says Merri Lemmex, who was working as a product demonstrator in the systems group at the time. "It was amazing. At one point we took a vote and a number of us thought Waldo was a great name. Mike said, 'No, no, no—it's got to be Corel Draw.' And we thought, How stupid, how boring can you be? It's graphics, so the name has got to be fun. But Mike said, 'Look, I want it sold all around the world and I want it easy to remember.' And you know what? He was right. I guess that's why I'm sitting here in my little house and he lives in that big, fancy mansion."

There were two other things about the name that Cowpland liked. First, the word "draw" was so generic that Corel would not have to commission an exhaustive and potentially expensive search of product names to avoid duplication. And second, it was so stark that users would likely feel compelled to use the full name when speaking about the software, thereby emphasizing Corel as the brand identity. For the same reason hockey arenas and other large public facilities have for some time been given names that end in "centre." In the old days, a Montrealer might have told his friends that he had just been to the Forum, and everybody would know precisely what he meant, but now, to avoid confusion, hockey fans have to say they have been to the Molson Centre. Similarly, by the late 1990s, theatregoers in Toronto, Vancouver and New York were attending musicals at the Ford Centre for the Performing Arts (Ford Centre for short, naturally). The name might not have had the same romance or sense of history as the Royal Alexandra or Broadway's Music Box Theatre, but you sure weren't going to forget the name of the megacorporation that had so generously put up the sponsorship money.

For good measure, Kurtis decided to make Corel Draw all one word, incorporate Charlesworth's notion of two different fonts and cap it all off with an exclamation mark. Presto: CorelDRAW! No, it wasn't subtle.

"Some people didn't like it, but that's one of those times when somebody has to make a decision," Cowpland recalls. "Most things I like to be by consensus and collegial because it should be obvious, but you can never get buy-in on things like names or colours. In my case I look at the person I'm disagreeing with and decide whether I've got a bigger mandate than him, in terms of experience or track record. That's where the CEO calls the shots."

Next on the agenda was the question of package design. Here again, Charlesworth was in one camp, Cowpland in another. Kurtis had not one iota of doubt about where her loyalties belonged. She considered her boss a marketing genius and was prepared to let his opinions take precedence over anything she might have come up with on her own.

"Mark had this idea that we should give it the appearance of a very sophisticated product, a quality product, which was completely against how Mike wanted to position it," Kurtis recalls. "Mark came to me and said, 'Look, we've got to design this advertising to make it look very exquisite,' and I asked him to show me some examples of the kind of advertising he meant. He brought them to me and I took them to Mike. He laughed and said, 'No, no, no—we gotta do the *opposite* of this.' The important point was that Mike wanted something colourful and flashy and exciting, something that wouldn't alienate the average person."

"I believed in Mike—that was the main thing," Kurtis adds, conscious of sounding like the follower of some charismatic sage. "He was the kingpin and I was wide open to his suggestions. I felt that way from the moment I met him."

One day, about a month and a half before Corel was planning to announce the product at Comdex in Las Vegas, Cowpland picked up the phone and asked Kurtis to join him in his office for a brainstorming session. Seated at the small round table beside his desk, he explained that he wanted an image that would be simple and fun. In no way should the product appear technical or intimidating to those whose knowledge of computers or graphic design was on the skimpy side: the idea was to attract buyers who might not otherwise purchase a PC graphics package and who, in all likelihood, wouldn't know or care about the difference between a Bezier curve and a bit map. Nor should the design employ muted colours. The purpose was to attract people's attention—to grab their interest before their eyes moved on to some other product. In retail, there are no marks for tastefulness or pretty designs if customers wind up giving their money to someone else.

"We started talking about things the average person would like, because we knew we were going to market this not just to graphic designers but to secretaries and managers and people who couldn't really draw but who wanted to put something out quickly and easily," Kurtis says. "So we started brainstorming about things that people love and aren't controversial. We thought of things like ice cream and sailboats and balloons, and suddenly Mike said, 'Well, what about hot-air balloons? Everyone likes hot-air balloons, and you can put lots of colours on them.' It was a friendly image and very accessible. So I said, 'Great—sounds great,' and off I went."

That afternoon and evening, Kurtis airbrushed a large canvas and then painted over it with acrylics. The completed picture showed eight colourful hot-air balloons floating over a silhouetted Ottawa skyline, from which jutted the neo-Gothic Peace Tower of Parliament Hill. It was sunset, and a radiant, orange-pink glow illuminated the office towers in the background, while overhead the moon and the stars glittered in a deep blue sky. In the foreground was a large, rainbow-coloured balloon with the name "CorelDRAW!" painted in black across a brilliant yellow stripe. The whole thing had a playful, old-fashioned feel that was completely at odds with the designs on most software boxes.

It was also, not to put too fine a point on it, garish and more than a little cheesy. You couldn't miss it if your eyes were closed. Charles-worth's heart sank when he saw what Kurtis had come up with as the principal image for his labour of love, but Cowpland's reaction left no room for debate. "Love it," he declared, flashing Kurtis the thumbs-up sign. "Let's go with it."

Soon Kurtis had designed an entire marketing campaign around the CorelDRAW balloon, with posters, four-page brochures and mock-ups of magazine ads. "CorelDRAW! does it all," one of the brochures proclaimed. "Great architecture! Amazing type selection! Versatile input & output! Superb drawing power! Incredible type control! Dazzling low cost colour!" If the schlockmeisters at K-Tel had been in the business of hawking computer software, they could scarcely have come up with anything more tacky and blatant.

"The main thing with Mike was that he wanted everything to be colourful," Kurtis says. "He knew that when people flipped through magazines you just had a fraction of a second to grab their attention, so he wanted it to look really bright and full of information and exciting. He didn't want a soft, sophisticated look, he wanted it to be loud and flashy. He's like that himself and he wants to be noticed. Personally, I wasn't used to that kind of garish advertising, but that was his vision, so I adapted to it."

Ironically, the only thing Cowpland didn't seem concerned about was Kurtis's decision to create the image the old-fashioned way, with paint and brushes, rather than on a computer. Her choice was dictated by her lack of computer skills at the time, and the fact that early versions of CorelDRAW were incapable of creating customized colour palettes or colour blends. To Cowpland, however, the choice of medium was irrelevant. "Mike liked it so much that, even when the product was at the level where it could be used to illustrate something like that, he still hung on to the painting," Kurtis says. "Eventually I insisted, because I thought it was important to use our own product."

Down the road, Cowpland's hit-them-between-the-eyes marketing instinct would rebound on Corel by offending some of the more discriminating members of the professional graphic arts community, who couldn't bring themselves to buy an illustration program—even an extremely refined and powerful one—whose packaging looked as though it had been dreamed up by Ronald McDonald. But at the time of its introduction, aesthetic concerns took a back seat to Corel's primary challenge, which was to catch the attention of software buyers. Kurtis's colourful balloon seemed tailor-made for that task.

Partly for that reason, the mood at 1600 Carling Avenue in the fall of 1988 was overwhelmingly upbeat. Cowpland himself was practically giddy with enthusiasm about the upcoming launch, as was Paul Bodnoff. He knew the Macintosh better than almost anyone else at Corel, and he believed that CorelDRAW was more than just a great PC program—it was a great program, period, every bit as good as Adobe Illustrator, and significantly easier to use, thanks to the user-friendly interface that Charlesworth had dreamed up. The only question was whether Adobe's PC version of Illustrator would prove to be even better. Fortunately, Adobe still had not announced a launch date for its long-awaited product, which meant there was a reasonable chance of upstaging its introduction. Even if Adobe ultimately came out with a superior package, Corel might at least have the field to itself long enough to capture a modest share of the market.

The key would be the reception at that fall's Comdex in Las Vegas, the biggest and flashiest trade show on the computer industry calendar. In addition to all the hardware and software executives who attended each November, Comdex attracted writers and editors from every significant computer magazine and newsletter in North America, not to mention a sizable number from Europe and Asia. It was at Comdex that the world got its first peek at many high-tech innovations. Any product or service that managed to generate a favourable buzz among the digital elite who gathered there could look forward to months of positive media coverage, publicity that had the power to transform otherwise unknown companies into veritable gushers of revenue.

Given what was at stake, it might have seemed surprising that Cowpland opted for a low-key approach to Comdex. Rather than setting up its own booth, Corel arranged to do what it had done a year earlier when its main software products were Headline and Newfont—sublet a few square metres of space from Xerox, the company that distributed Ventura Publisher. Of course, doing Comdex that way was a heck of a lot cheaper than renting space for a stand-alone booth, but Cowpland also had another reason for wanting to ride on Xerox's coattails. As one of the giants of the office-machine industry, Xerox always drew large numbers of visitors to its display. The way Cowpland saw it, it made a lot more sense to have a dinky refreshment stand smack dab in the middle of a crowded beach than a fancy ice-cream parlour on the other side of town.

The decision to appear at Comdex as a Xerox partner also meant that Corel could send only a handful of people to Las Vegas. Paul Bodnoff, the head of marketing, would lead the contingent. He would be accompanied by engineer John McFetridge, who had joined the company earlier that year to work on an IBM mainframe version of CorelDRAW, Debbie Boucher, who had shifted over to media relations, and Ian Gibson, who would oversee sales of the product. Because the software was still at a pre-release stage—the final version wouldn't be ready to ship until some time in January—the engineers who had actually created CorelDRAW were forced to stay behind in Ottawa, working day and night to find and correct bugs.

Meanwhile, Mark Charlesworth was spending most of his time at home, hunched over a keyboard on his kitchen table in a mad scramble to finish putting together the user manual—or rather, two manuals, since Cowpland had decided that a preliminary, or beta, version of the guide should be ready in time for distribution at Comdex, with a more complete version to follow at the time of the official release. For Charlesworth, the manual was his one remaining opportunity to put a personal stamp on CorelDRAW, and he was determined to make the most of it. Not only did he write the entire 237-page book himself, he also drew several cartoons which he inserted in the text as illustrations. One of them, captioned "The CorelDRAW team," showed Pat Beirne, Michel Bouillon, Ian Rae and himself standing behind a table on which was scattered an assortment of empty pizza boxes, discarded soda cans, burger wrappers and other reminders of the many late nights they had spent developing the product. "I put in those cartoons just to give us a more approachable, friendly face, so we wouldn't seem staid and corporate," Charlesworth says. "My feeling was, this is the only way you touch your customer."

Once again, however, Cowpland questioned Charlesworth's judgment. As soon as he saw the beta version of the manual, he complained that the cartoon, with its collection of fast-food detritus, made the company seem disorganized and unprofessional—never mind that all those eighteen-hour days and all that greasy food were as much a part of the culture of software development as computers themselves.

"I was so disappointed," Charlesworth says. "I mean, I thought this was a great image. I really wanted it to stay in, so I said to Mike, 'How about if I clean up all the junk—would that be okay?'" Cowpland didn't object, so Charlesworth scanned the drawing into an image-editing program and erased most of the trash, leaving only a single pizza carton and a half-eaten pizza. The amended version made it into the official manual, along with a smaller sketch of four other men who played a part in Waldo's creation: Scott Murchison, John McFetridge, Christian Gingras and Adam Nelling.

Almost a decade later, Charlesworth still savours the memory of one of the few times he felt he had slipped one past the Corel president. "See?" he says, pointing out the relatively minor differences between the original and sanitized versions of his CorelDRAW team cartoon. "It's really the same picture!"

John McFetridge has always worn his emotions on his sleeve. His life, he admits, has been one unending roller coaster of spectacular highs and wretched lows. The four years he spent at Corel encompassed both extremes.

"I have mixed feelings about the place," he says one afternoon, gazing out the window of his Florida townhouse at his sailboard, his hot-tub and his six-metre Searay powerboat docked in the Inter-coastal waterway near Clearwater. "I loved the early days. In fact, in many respects it saved me. I had just come off a real bad divorce and I was real negative. Corel gave me reason to get excited again, to live again and dream again."

A native of Halifax, McFetridge graduated from university with a degree in math, started in med school at Dalhousie and then dropped out, having decided that computers were a lot more fun to be around than sick people. His father and his friends thought he was nuts to walk away from the prospect of a doctor's income, but McFetridge stubbornly refused to reconsider. At the age of twenty, he boarded a plane for the first time in his life and flew to Ottawa in pursuit of a Statistics Canada programming job he had seen advertised. The truth was that he knew only a smattering of FORTRAN, but he was a fast learner—faster, at any rate, than his boss, which in the end was what mattered.

That was in 1974. In 1982, after a couple of years at StatsCan and six more at the University of Ottawa's computer centre, McFetridge started his own company, Simware Inc., which today is a thriving developer of networking software. "I've heard that as many as 90 percent of the people who start companies are no longer there after four years, and that's exactly what happened to me," he says. "There was a dispute over the direction of the company and I was forced out in 1986 by all the people I'd given shares to. It was a bitter dispute and it cost me a lot, including my marriage, because she was one of the problems. The thing is, I'm not a businessman, I'm a techie. She was pushing me to run the company and I didn't want to. Anyway, the whole messy situation was not a highlight in my life."

Angry and embittered, McFetridge licked his wounds for while and then landed a consulting job with the Department of National Defence (DND), which had a clunky old mainframe system and wanted it rejigged to run some of the newer PC publishing applications, such as WordPerfect and Ventura. While he was working on that, a friend introduced McFetridge to Cowpland, who proudly showed him an early version CorelDRAW.

McFetridge was stunned by the demonstration. "I'd been looking for a drawing product for my DND customers and, believe me, there was nothing on the PC that could touch this. In 1988, the PC platform was essentially restricted to drawing boxes and lines and maybe applying a couple of colours. The idea that you could stretch and manipulate characters, wrap text around irregular paths and all that great stuff was revolutionary. . . . The font technology was way, way ahead of its time."

No less impressive than Corel's new software was its dynamic, high-spirited founder. To McFetridge, Cowpland seemed like the boss he had always wished for—brilliant, overflowing with creativity and willing to throw his energies and his financial support behind any new idea, no matter how unconventional. Here, McFetridge thought to himself, was a CEO who wasn't afraid of taking risks and who understood that business and pleasure were not mutually exclusive. Cowpland was letting his engineers run wild—and the results spoke for themselves.

Evidently, Cowpland thought highly of McFetridge, too, because in September 1988 he announced to the Waldo team that he was thinking of hiring the engineer to develop a means by which Corel's software could work on IBM mainframes—a huge market, and potentially very lucrative. Ironically, Pat Beirne and Mark Charlesworth initially objected and tried to keep McFetridge away from their project. They had heard all about the internal feuding at Simware and figured McFetridge for a troublemaker. Cowpland, however, brought him in as a consultant, gambling correctly that familiarity would erode any mistrust. After a couple of months, McFetridge joined the company full-time.

In a roundabout way, McFetridge's knowledge of IBM mainframes was the reason Cowpland sent him to Comdex later that fall. McFetridge was a friend of IBM's top man in Ottawa, Paul Koch, who was sharp enough to realize that Corel's software could give Big Blue a powerful boost in the field of desktop publishing, the only significant market in which the Macintosh was solidly trouncing the IBM PC. Koch decided to tip off his superiors at IBM's Canadian headquarters in Toronto, who in turn passed the message on to the corporation's main publishing group in Boulder, Colorado. Several phone calls later, it was agreed that McFetridge and Paul Bodnoff would stop over in the Rocky Mountain city on their way to Las Vegas.

The biggest computer trade show of the year, an audience with a bunch of IBM honchos and a software product that was already creating waves two months before its official introduction—McFetridge and Bodnoff could scarcely contain their excitement. "I'll never forget when we left on that trip," McFetridge says. "We jumped in the car to drive to the airport and Paul was all giggly, saying, 'Isn't this an insanely great place to work?' And he was right, because we had such a blast."

Bodnoff doesn't recall that part of the trip, but he does remember the reception they received when they arrived in Boulder and were escorted up to a conference room to conduct a demonstration of CorelDRAW on an IBM PS/2. McFetridge gave a short introductory speech, after which his partner fired up the software and performed some simple yet impressive tricks—typing a few words on the screen, varying the fonts, rotating and skewing the text and, finally, fitting the words to a curved path. "They could not believe it," Bodnoff said. "We were manipulating type, and that was supposed to be the unique domain of the Mac—it had never been done before on a PC. And as staid and as conservative as IBM people were at the time, I watched as seven or eight guys just came unglued."

Though the session in Boulder went like a dream, the two Corel representatives arrived in Vegas still haunted by the fear that Adobe was about to pull the wraps off a PC version of Illustrator that would put their product to shame. Big bad Adobe, Bodnoff called the California company. Nobody knew fonts and graphics like Adobe. Its founder, John Warnock, was a legend, one of the greatest programmers alive, and one of the only men in the world that Apple co-founder Steve Jobs looked up to—in part because, if it hadn't been for Adobe's software, the Macintosh might never have found a market.

It's been fun up to now, John McFetridge told himself during the cab ride from the airport to the hotel, but let's get real. We're about to get creamed by some of the smartest guys in the business.

They were so nervous, in fact, that immediately after meeting up with Debbie Boucher, who had arrived in Vegas a day in advance to help co-ordinate Corel's tiny display, McFetridge and Bodnoff made a beeline for Adobe's booth. To their relief, the company was showing only the two Macintosh versions of its software, Illustrator and Illustrator 88. "That's their old stuff," Bodnoff said, smiling. Corel, they realized then, had beaten its chief competitor in the race to introduce a PC product.

As a Xerox partner, Corel was supposed to be showing Headline, Newfont and the other Ventura utilities that it had been selling since late 1987. But those applications never made it out of the box. Instead, Bodnoff loaded CorelDRAW onto a computer, and within minutes the crowds started to flow in.

One of the first visitors was Daniel Will-Harris, a well-known desktop publishing guru from San Francisco and the author of several guides to Ventura Publisher. A longtime critic of the Macintosh, which he complained was overpriced and underpowered, Will-Harris was perpetually on the hunt for new products that could extend the capability of his preferred machine, the humble PC. Each year at Comdex, he made it a point to check out the Xerox booth before anything else, just in case there was some new Ventura add-on that might provide fodder for one of his regular magazine columns.

Will-Harris knew Corel as the company behind Headline, a product he had reviewed favourably several times in print, but he was in no way prepared for what Corel was touting as Headline's successor. Watching Paul Bodnoff perform a brief demo of CorelDRAW, he felt a bit like a Hollywood producer who had just wandered into a drug store and stumbled across the next Lana Turner. CorelDRAW wasn't just good, Will-Harris thought, it actually out-Mac-ed the Mac. He was so astonished and overjoyed that he promptly headed off to tell his friends and acquaintances in the industry about this amazing new software from Canada. A chubby, gregarious man with an unruly black beard and eyes that seem to sparkle when he is excited, Will-Harris knows practically everyone there is to know in PC desktop publishing. Thanks to him, the word, if not on the street, was most certainly on the convention floor.

Recalls Bodnoff: "Dan Will-Harris wandered by and I did a demo for him, not really knowing who he was, and within an hour we had a hundred people deep and it was like that for the next five days, the entire show. It was wild.

"The next thing we knew, Paul Grayson, the CEO of Micrografx, and John Warnock from Adobe were being hustled over to take a look at what we had. Their attitude was, 'Who the hell are you guys and where did you come from?' I recall Grayson looking straight at me and saying those exact words in a very unfriendly way, with about a hundred people looking on. We had arrived and peed in their cornflakes."

Not long after that, Bodnoff and McFetridge found themselves shaking hands with Paul Brainerd, the father of desktop publishing and the hugely successful CEO of Aldus, maker of PageMaker. They learned later that Will-Harris, after leaving the Xerox booth, had marched across several football fields of exhibition space, located the Aldus display and buttonholed Brainerd. Bubbling with excitement, he'd proceeded to lecture Brainerd to the effect that if he was smart, he would look at acquiring CorelDRAW as a companion application for the Windows version of PageMaker, in the same way that Aldus had earlier licensed a graphics program called FreeHand for the Mac.

To Will-Harris, it seemed like an ideal marriage: Corel had a great product but virtually no experience in the retail software business. Aldus, on the other hand, was the biggest distributor of page-layout software in the world. And CorelDRAW was exactly the sort of illustration software that Aldus needed to fill out its PC product line.

That night, Brainerd took Bodnoff, McFetridge and Boucher to dinner in an attempt to learn more about the hotshot little company from Ottawa. "If I remember correctly, we went to this Italian restaurant across the street from the convention centre," Brainerd recalls. "As part of our business plan we were definitely looking at either developing internally or working out a joint marketing deal or acquisition of a drawing product. We reasoned—correctly, in retrospect—that we would need additional revenue streams to justify the marketing and other expenses associated with where the industry was going." (Six years later, besieged by cutthroat marketing competition and unrelenting pressure from Microsoft, Brainerd sold Aldus to Adobe in a stock deal worth $525 million. He is now retired from the software business and runs his own charitable foundation, doling out grants to organizations that dedicate themselves to saving the Pacific Northwest rainforest.)

By way of breaking the ice, Brainerd talked about a trip he had made to Ottawa in the early 1980s on behalf of Atex, to check out Norpak's then-revolutionary technology for transmitting words and graphics via telephone lines or television broadcast signals. He also described fond memories of an early morning spent jogging along the Ottawa River below Parliament Hill. Canada's capital and Aldus's home base of Seattle had a lot in common, Brainerd said, which was one of the reasons he felt sure that his company and Corel would be a good fit.

As he spoke, it dawned on McFetridge that Brainerd must have assumed that he and Bodnoff were the owners of the company. "I was just so honoured to be in this man's presence that I wasn't sure what to say," McFetridge says. "I knew Paul and I were there under false pretenses, and I was terrified that as soon as Brainerd discovered who he was talking to, he would get up from the table and leave."

That didn't happen, however. After Bodnoff explained the situation, the Aldus CEO promised that he and one of his senior executives, Mike Solomon, would get in touch with Cowpland personally to work out a deal.

The next morning, after a follow-up conversation with Brainerd and Solomon, Ian Gibson phoned Mark Charlesworth to pass on the good news. "This is exciting!" Charlesworth scribbled in his logbook as the two men conversed. "Key points: They are interested in buying the product. They have two hundred and fifty people in sales out of six hundred and fifty people worldwide, plus marketing. Seventy-five people in R and D. . . . Six thousand hotline calls a week, two hundred thousand users, one call per year per user on average. No PC version of Freehand under development. Draw is a hole in their product line they want to fill." The bottom line: Aldus had the means, the money and the experience to market CorelDRAW to the world.

That same morning—day two of Comdex—Cowpland arrived in Las Vegas, anxious to find out how his troops were faring. Bodnoff's first words to him were, "Mike, we're going to be rich." It was no exaggeration.

Chapter Nine

In his 1995 book *Inside the Tornado*, author and marketing consultant Geoffrey Moore describes the fate of a company that finally hits on a hugely successful product: "Billions of dollars in company revenue appear from nowhere. They're yours, and all you have to do is ship. Congratulations. You've managed to get your product across the chasm of market acceptance and into the tornado of market demand. It's all you can do to keep up with orders and keep track of all that money."

As the reception at Comdex demonstrated, Mike Cowpland and Corel were indeed standing smack in the path of an oncoming tornado—or was it an Ottawa blizzard? Either way, there was an awful lot of money blowing around out there, just waiting to be scooped up. Cowpland's never-say-die business instincts, combined with Mark Charlesworth's meticulous product management, Pat Beirne's ingenious algorithms and the contributions of more than half a dozen other employees had miraculously produced a graphics program that was not only better than the competition's, but exceeded most people's expectations of what was possible on a PC.

It would have been nice to sit back and savour the moment, but in many ways the work had just begun. There were a thousand decisions, both large and small, to be made before CorelDRAW's official introduction. The first was whether to accept Brainerd's offer of an exclusive marketing agreement with Aldus. Under the terms of the proposed deal, Aldus would assume full responsibility for manufacturing, distribution, advertising and customer support, in return for which Corel would collect a 15 percent royalty on sales. Henceforth,

Corel could concentrate all of its efforts on software upgrades and new product development. Patterned on the traditional arrangement between author and publisher in the book trade, similar marketing deals had been commonplace in the software industry since the 1979 introduction of VisiCalc by a Boston company called Software Arts, which subsequently became part of Lotus.

On December 8, a team of four Aldus representatives, including two third-party liaison managers, flew in to Ottawa to present a detailed offer. Among other things, they pointed out that Aldus had struck an identical deal a year earlier with Altsys, the Texas company that had developed FreeHand. Now, thanks to Aldus's unmatched marketing and distribution skills, the guys at Altsys were raking in the bucks.

"I kept thinking about the power of Aldus, their size and their ability to make our product successful," Bodnoff recalls. "Compared to them, we barely even had a sales force. Given our limited resources and the strength of Brainerd's company, there were all sorts of good reasons to do a deal. Seems stupid in retrospect but, you know, it wasn't illogical."

Mark Charlesworth was even more persuaded that Corel should embrace Aldus's offer. On a personal level, he clearly felt a closer affinity with Paul Brainerd—an idealistic, thoughtful man who respected his senior managers and carefully nurtured his company's reputation for quality—than with the hard-charging, high-living and notoriously impulsive Mike Cowpland. Brainerd, he felt sure, would understand and attend to the needs of the Waldo team, whose members were, after all, Corel's most valuable assets. "My ideas on the Aldus deal: our team has been crucial to the success," Charlesworth wrote in his logbook on November 17, the day Ian Gibson informed him of Brainerd's interest. "No one individual makes the team, it is only as a group which enjoys working together with each individual's strengths. For our long-term success, we must keep the core team together: Pat, Ian, Mark, Michel."

Below that entry, Charlesworth mapped out two scenarios which, for his money, demonstrated convincingly that a marketing agreement with Aldus, if not essential, was certainly in Corel's best interests.

"Alternative 1: Keep group small, R and D focused. Licence software. Let Aldus handle packaging, documentation, promotion, distribution." Under that sort of an arrangement, Charlesworth predicted, Aldus would sell between 10,000 and 20,000 copies of the software per year, at a retail price of $695 (US). Assuming a dealer cost of $350 per box, total revenues could be anywhere from $3.5 million to $7 million. Based on a 15 percent royalty and annual development costs of $500,000 for a team of twelve engineers, Corel could count on about $500,000 a year in profit.

The second alternative was for Corel to go it alone. In that event, Charlesworth predicted, sales would probably max out at between 3,000 and 5,000 copies a year at a list price of $495 (US). "We will sell less because we don't have the manufacturing, distribution, marketing support of Adobe, but Aldus does." Assuming a dealer cost of $300, the annual revenues from the software would be $1.5 million a year at best. And on top of its R and D costs, Corel would have to shoulder a long list of additional expenses for manufacturing ("$3.50 US per package"), technical support ("will be a load on the development team"), sales ("20-50,000 inquiries per year!"), advertising and travel. Always a stickler for detail, Charlesworth included in his calculations everything from postage to the cost of printing flyers and the 2 percent commission charged by Visa on credit-card sales.

He also made a point of jotting down the names of Corel employees who would be responsible for particular areas of the business. Cowpland, interestingly enough, was listed under "marketing," alongside Aili Kurtis, Debbie Boucher, Paul Bodnoff and several others.

Adding it all up, Charlesworth arrived at a ballpark estimate for sales and marketing of $1 million a year. Factor in the cost of engineering and ongoing product development, and there it was in black and white: if Corel forged ahead and tried to sell CorelDRAW on its own, it would be lucky to make any money at all.

To Cowpland, the idea of climbing into bed with a larger, well-established software company was so far removed from his way of doing things as to be laughable. His philosophy could be summed up in four short words—no guts, no glory. He was frustrated and annoyed that nobody else seemed to recognize the tremendous opportunities ahead.

"I could tell everybody was really flattered, particularly Mark Charlesworth, because Aldus were like kings—this was almost like getting their seal of approval," Cowpland recalls. "But from my point of view it wasn't very attractive because I could see we would never get any recognition or value out of it. We'd become an invisible development team, just a bunch of engineers who code all day and leave the marketing and management to someone else. My view was that we had a really good shot at being a major player, so let's go for it."

Those around Cowpland were left in no doubt of where he stood. As soon as the Aldus advance team left Corel's offices on December 8, Ian Gibson telephoned Charlesworth at home—he was still two weeks away from completing the official user manual—to report what had happened. The deal wasn't going to fly, regardless of how good it was, Gibson said, because Cowpland was insistent that Corel operate as a fully integrated company. If CorelDRAW proved to be as successful as he expected, it would erase all memory of the abortive 1987 public offering. A stock sale would be sure to follow, bringing many millions of dollars into the business.

Despite his strong convictions, Cowpland hesitated to impose his decision without allowing others an opportunity to air their views. If Corel was going to enter the retail software business in a big way, it was going to require the commitment of every employee. At this stage, at least, he couldn't afford any defections, particularly on the part of disgruntled senior managers who felt their opinions didn't count.

A few days after Aldus made its pitch, Cowpland called together the entire staff—about fifty people in total—to discuss Corel's next move. Mark Charlesworth, who phoned in to say he was too busy working on the manual, was the only senior person who did not attend.

"It tells you a lot about the way Corel worked in those days," McFetridge says of the meeting. "Mike was sitting at the head of the table and Pat [Beirne] was next to him, and one by one we went around the table. Everybody in the room said 'sell' until it got to me. You had to express your confidence level, so I said 'don't sell,' and I think I put it at an 80 percent confidence level. And then Pat said the same thing and so did Mike. We all knew it was Mike's decision, but he still listened to everybody in that room. Afterward, the whole company was mad at me and Pat because, you know, it was a start-up and anything could have happened."

Referring to the same incident, Paul Chehowski says that Cowpland's handling of the Aldus offer was very much in keeping with his approach to management. "I think Mike's attitude was that he didn't mind people disagreeing with him, but in the end he's steering the ship and he's making the decisions. You're either following your leader or you're not. And if you don't want to follow your leader, you're working for the wrong place."

Like many current and former Corel employees, Chehowski has spent a lot of time thinking about how Cowpland makes decisions, a process which to outsiders—not to mention the vast majority of his own staff—frequently seems haphazard and arbitrary. "I've talked to people who used to work with him at Microsystems," Chehowski said, "and my theory is that Mike's an intuitive thinker—he uses inductive logic as opposed to deductive logic. What that means is, you can't always see how he arrives at his decisions. He does have a logical approach, a real process he goes through when he evaluates things, but most people can't see it so they're afraid of it. And sometimes what looks to be the risky course actually turns out to be the opposite."

That certainly proved to the case with the Aldus offer. For what it's worth, Cowpland spurned two more offers for CorelDRAW that winter, one from Adobe and the other from Software Publishing Corp. of Fairfield, New Jersey, distributors of a DOS-based business presentations package called Harvard Graphics. In neither case was there so much as a murmur of dissent from the staff. By then, even

Cowpland's most intractable doubters had been forced to admit that his instincts were bang on.

Shortly after the meeting to discuss Aldus's offer, there was another staff get-together that has become part of Corel lore. This time, however, Cowpland wasn't invited. A few days before Christmas of 1988, about twenty of the company's senior managers and staff gathered at John McFetridge's house in Ottawa South to discuss what to do about Cowpland's crony Gary Cartwright, nominally in charge of the optical division, who was driving many of the women at Corel crazy with his crude sexual jokes and crass behaviour. There were also complaints about his irregular hours. Some days he never even bothered to come into the office, telling subordinates that he had worked late the previous night when, in fact, he'd been out partying. Says Paul Bodnoff: "It had been obvious for a long time that Gary was going to be detrimental to the company. He thought he was a bigshot. Certainly bigger than he should have been."

After talking it over for a couple of hours, all but one of those in attendance—in addition to McFetridge, the group of dissidents included Bodnoff, Merri Lemmex, Mike Slaunwhite, Michel Bouillon, Patti Hall and others—agreed to present Cowpland with an ultimatum. He could either get rid of Cartwright or everyone else would quit, leaving Corel bereft of experienced managers on the eve of the launch of its most important product.

The only holdout was Pat Beirne, who couldn't bring himself to threaten to walk out on his mentor. Nevertheless, Beirne did agree to act as go-between, communicating the group's position to Cowpland.

Cowpland didn't put up any resistance. After talking it over with Beirne and Slaunwhite, he took Cartwright out to lunch and gently broke the news that it was "time for a change." Recalls Cowpland: "When I heard there was a mutiny, that made me understand the group dynamics. Personally I got along well with Gary, and he was useful in a certain way, but in terms of the company, he didn't belong. And the CEO's job is to facilitate that."

Cowpland did make sure that Cartwright was well compensated. Using his own money, he set his friend up in business a few blocks away as the owner of a company called ArtRight Inc., which produced ready-made illustrations known as clip-art. ArtRight's only significant customer was Corel, but the arrangement proved extremely lucrative for Cartwright because, less than two years later, Cowpland bought him out for a million dollars. On top of that Cartwright made—by his own account—about four million dollars selling Corel stock in the wake of the company's successful 1989 initial public offering. "He took major advantage of Michael," says Marlen, who doesn't hide her dislike of her husband's former friend. "He's a yes man. Michael used to be surrounded with a lot of yes men."

Cartwright now lives with his wife, Joanne, and their two children in a lavish home near Stittsville, Ontario, half an hour west of Ottawa. But in spite of his wealth, he is far from comfortable. Less than a year before his ouster from Corel, he was diagnosed with a brain tumour and spent two months in Ottawa's Civic Hospital, undergoing tests. Later, after Cowpland set him up with his company, medical specialists realized that he was also suffering from cancer of the bladder and lesions on his spinal column, conditions that eventually forced him to stop working. His doctors say it is impossible to know how much longer he will live, but in the meantime he receives regular doses of morphine to dull the pain. He's proud that during a prolonged stay in hospital in 1990, Mike Cowpland visited him every second day or so, and Darlene Cowpland visited him every day, bringing freshly prepared Italian food from Cartwright's favourite restaurant. These days, however, he has no contact with either Cowpland or his ex-wife. "Things have changed, and Mike has gone on with his life," Cartwright says, evidently bitter that his old friend wants nothing to do with him.

The final few weeks before the release of CorelDRAW were a mad scramble of activity. Pat Beirne spent one weekend in December writing his own script for a tutorial video that was to be included with the software. "The quality/effectiveness may not be top notch, but it's better than nothing," Charlesworth wrote in his notebook. Beirne, John McFetridge, Ian Rae and several others flew down to Bethesda, Maryland, for a show-and-tell with an IBM engineering design group that was gearing up to launch an illustration package called DisplayGraphic. "IBM wanted to see what we had," McFetridge recalls. "As soon as we demoed DRAW they packed in their project." Both WordPerfect and Hewlett-Packard called and volunteered to do joint marketing, a clear indication that some of the most powerful players in the business were expecting big things from Corel's software and wanted to capitalize on the momentum. In a similar vein, IBM contacted Cowpland to request that a group of Corel representatives appear in its booth at a computer graphics trade show in New York City in mid-January.

On December 19, *PC Week* ran the first significant article on CorelDRAW in a major computer trade publication. The article quoted Dan Will-Harris calling the application "the first [PC-based] program to rival what you can do on the Macintosh." Soon after, *Personal Publishing* magazine lauded the program as "an impressive product that comes as close as anything we've seen to bringing the power of the Mac's FreeHand to the PC. . . . We got a real idea of just how hot a product it is at Fall COMDEX. During a demonstration of the product, we looked over to see a programmer from Micrografx's Designer team. He stood through most of the presentation with his jaw hanging open."

The first boxes of CorelDRAW finally left 1600 Carling Avenue on Monday, January 16, 1989. By that point, there was a backlog of several thousand orders from Comdex attendees, software distributors and journalists impatient to get their hands on a review copy. "When the product was ready and the boxes were ready, we actually stripped out the reception area, put in folding tables and on our first day we packed and shipped fourteen hundred boxes," says Merri Lemmex, who had joined the systems integration group a year earlier. "It was phenomenal. We had most of the people in the company getting these boxes ready."

Meanwhile, the phones were ringing off the hook, with calls from as far away as Europe. "Fellas, you've got another [Lotus] 1-2-3," said a software distributor in Britain who had managed to secure a pre-release copy. "We could sell four or five hundred copies a month over here." Somebody else called Corel's toll-free customer support hotline and reported that the product was "so much fun that I don't even want to stop to eat."

Those and other laudatory quotes were gathered up by Mark Charlesworth and printed in a five-page newsletter he circulated to the staff at the end of CorelDRAW's first week in the market. All of a sudden, the man who more than anyone else had doubted his employer's ability to make it in the retail software business was doing his best to sound like its most impassioned believer:

This week CorelDRAW rocketed out of the development labs and into the real world. The product is well on its way to becoming a major success in the PC software industry. But our work has only begun.

There are three main steps to success in the PC software business:

1. Develop an innovative product that fills a significant customer need.
2. Promote and Sell it like crazy.
3. Keep your customers happy.

Step #1 has been completed, and we did an A+ job of it. The development team is to be commended. We have a world-class product that we can all be proud of. In 16 months, we have blown by competitors who have been developing graphic software for years.

Our challenge is now to accomplish steps #2 and #3 with equal proficiency. I KNOW WE CAN DO IT! WE HAVE THE TEAM AND THE OPPORTUNITY!

Although Charlesworth didn't know it, his newsletter became the source of some amusement around Corel's offices. There was hardly a person at the company who didn't consider him a brilliant product manager and talented graphic artist. But after the product's release, many of those same people had a hard time taking him seriously on matters related to business strategy. Let Mark design the products, the consensus went, but let Mike market them.

"Mark was a real perfectionist, but he could also be a bit of a strange guy from time to time," Merri Lemmex says. "Later on, he didn't even want to buy shares because he wanted to pay down his mortgage—he wanted something stable. When he was asked to estimate the sales in the first year he said it would be three thousand copies. And after the first week or so, when the orders were piling up, they went back to him and said, 'Well Mark. . . . ' So he said, 'Okay, I'll have to change that. . . .' Mark raised the estimate to five thousand, and then he had to raise it to ten thousand, and after that I think he refused to put his name to a number. He wouldn't do it. It was really quite funny."

A few days after the launch, Cowpland flew to New York City with Debbie Boucher and another recent addition to the marketing staff, Arlen Bartsch, for a news conference at the Marriott Marquis Hotel. Cowpland had thrown it together on the spur of the moment, realizing that he'd have to make a trip to the Big Apple to attend a computer graphics trade show to which IBM had invited him. Bartsch, twenty-nine, was a slim, fair-haired University of Ottawa communications grad whose penchant for management-speak—his sentences were sprinkled with terms such as "mentoring," "paradigm" and "synergy"—belied his fundamentalist Mennonite upbringing on a dairy farm in rural Saskatchewan. Determined to, in his own words, "see the world and make a name for myself," he had left home at twenty-three, married outside the faith and nursed ambitions of a career on the stage or in television. In his final year at university, however, one of his courses focused on the impact of desktop publishing, a subject he found engrossing. "I had a very good mentoring relationship with a professor who really encouraged me," Bartsch says, "so I spent a lot of time trying to understand the paradigm of computers and what this new technology was doing."

Armed with his degree, Bartsch landed a contract position at the Canadian Museum of Civilization, across the river from Parliament Hill in Hull. He was supposed to help transfer some of the institution's archeological research on to desktop computers running Ventura Publisher, but Bartsch spent just as much time thinking about the company that had installed the hardware and software: Corel Systems Corp. "I began to wonder about Corel and who was behind it, and then I heard it was Mike Cowpland. I knew his name from Mitel days and thought, wow, if ever there was someone I'd like to be mentored by—would like to get close to—it was Mike Cowpland, because of his entrepreneurial winning ways."

At first Bartsch applied for a sales job, but Patti Hall turned him down because of his lack of experience. On his second try, he was shocked to hear Cowpland himself invite him to have lunch down the street at a restaurant called the Rose Bowl. A day later, Paul Bodnoff phoned to offer him a junior position in marketing. "I was completely enamoured of Mike," says Bartsch, reflecting on the eight years he spent at Corel, during which he rose to become director of sales and marketing. "I was a little intimidated, too, but I found that we had a lot of similar personality characteristics. I felt that he and I gelled in the idea space. We both loved to think about things from the thirty-thousand-foot perspective. I thought it would be very valuable from a career perspective if I could begin to think like him, strategically as opposed to just tactically."

The trip to New York City in January 1989 beautifully illustrates Cowpland's strategic thinking. Thrown together with only a few days' notice, the press conference could easily have exploded in his face. Corel's media relations department was all but nonexistent at that time, so Bartsch found himself having to make cold calls to scores of journalists, practically begging them to attend an announcement by the head of a company most had never heard about.

To Bartsch's immense relief, about fifteen reporters responded to his solicitation, including representatives of PC *Magazine,* PC *Week, Byte* and *Computer Graphics World,* publications whose influence more than compensated for the relatively small turnout. After a quick demo of CorelDRAW, Cowpland announced plans to award a $10,000 grand prize to the person who, in the opinion of a panel of judges to be chosen by Corel, submitted the best graphic design or illustration created entirely with the software. The contest winner would be chosen in March 1990. "Mike and Aili dreamed this up as a way to showcase what people could do with the application," Bartsch says. "The original thinking was that it was a wonderful way to leverage the graphics community, because we didn't have a lot of in-house graphic designers."

Over the years, the annual CorelDRAW design contest has grown far beyond even Cowpland's original expectations. In the first year, Corel received 300 submissions from graphic artists in a dozen countries. By 1996, there were 4,800 entries from sixty countries. The total value of the prizes that year was $3 million—$200,000 in cash and the rest in computers, printers, scanners and assorted equipment donated by other companies in return for the publicity.

In addition to generating millions of dollars' worth of media coverage, the event guarantees a turnout of several thousand people each year for a black-tie awards gala conveniently timed to coincide with the launch of the latest version of Corel's software. Another benefit for Corel is that, under the contest rules, every entry automatically becomes the property of Corel and can be published, used or sold by the company for any purpose, without payment of fee or royalty. With few exceptions, every significant example of computer-generated art used by Corel in its ads and publicity material since 1990—including the black-and-white photo-realistic image of Hedy Lamarr used on boxes of CorelDRAW since the fall of 1997—has been acquired through the design contests, saving the company many hundreds of thousands of dollars in licensing fees. On top of that, Corel publishes a book and companion CD-ROM after each awards ceremony that features more than a thousand images from the contest. In the early 1990s, when demand for CorelDRAW was at its peak, those books alone were pulling in some $2 million in revenue a year.

Among everything that happened in those first few weeks after CorelDRAW's launch, few events provoked more elation around the company's offices than the release, early in February, of Adobe Illustrator for Windows. It turned out that Adobe—the one company that everyone, Cowpland included, had feared could blow Corel out of the water—had flubbed it. It wasn't a total surprise. John Warnock's sour face at Comdex back in November had suggested to Paul Bodnoff that he and his companions would have little to fear from their much more powerful rival. A month after that, some of the trade publications ran stories implying that Adobe's product would disappoint graphic artists who were familiar with the existing Macintosh versions of Illustrator.

But nothing prepared Corel's engineers for their first real hands-on experience with Illustrator for Windows. It wasn't just bad, it was awful—so slow and lacking in important features that the folks at Adobe eventually came to refer to it as the "landfill version." Clearly the California company had underestimated the enormous technical challenges inherent in translating, or "porting," an existing Macintosh application so that it could run on a PC. In point of fact, the two platforms were so different that it would have been faster and easier for Adobe to have rewritten the software from the ground up. That way, it could have developed a whole new version of Illustrator that took into account the unique features and limitations of a PC running DOS and Windows.

The fundamental problem concerned memory. At the time, the standard configuration for a PC called for 640 kilobytes of random access memory (RAM), of which the operating system and Windows itself consumed 340 kilobytes. That left 300 kilobytes for a program that on the Mac required many times that much RAM. To get around the problem, Adobe's engineers used something called "extended memory" to swap programming code between the main system memory and the computer's hard disk storage space. They also had to make, in the words of one Adobe executive, "some hard choices about features," omitting such things as the ability to display graphics on the screen in colour, the ability to blend colours in an illustration and the ability to add patterns. Even then, Adobe Illustrator for Windows ran well only on a high-end machine equipped with an Intel 386-series microprocessor and at least 256 kilobytes of expanded memory, which required the installation of an optional card in the PC. For optimal performance, the company recommended 1 to 2 megabytes of expanded memory, which at the time could set users back as much as $600.

In contrast, CorelDRAW performed well on an older 286-based machine with the usual 640 kilobytes of memory. CorelDRAW was cheaper, too: $495 (US) compared to $695 for Illustrator.

Michel Bouillon remembers the day that Corel obtained its first copy of Adobe's software. "We all crowded into Mike's office to look at it on his computer, because we'd been really anxious to see it. And people were pointing at the screen and saying, 'Wow, it's great, it's great! It's slow as hell!' I remember colour was a big deal—whether or not we would put it in our version 1.0. In the last few months we decided to put it in and that turned out to be a big advantage for our side, because Illustrator didn't have it. Plus the Adobe product was a real memory pig. It would take something like thirty seconds just to do a simple rotation. It was so slow you had time to go out and have a cigarette. The whole thing was certainly not what you would have expected from a company like that. . . . I mean, we thought they were going to own the market. Instead, the product was such a flop we sat there and had a good laugh."

After that, it seemed Corel could do no wrong. Long the exclusive preserve of the Macintosh, graphics were suddenly the fastest-growing segment of the PC software industry. And CorelDRAW was the hottest product in that niche. Not only was it one of the one of the cheapest vector-based illustration packages—Cowpland's strategy from the beginning was to grab market share with aggressive pricing—it was also acknowledged by almost everyone to be the best.

A key factor behind CorelDRAW's early success was the enthusiastic coverage it received from the major computer magazines, whose reviews can often make or break a new software title. In part, this is because of the nature of the product itself. With most types of consumer goods, shoppers have a wide range of sources of buying information. Someone interested in a new car, for example, might be influenced by a magazine or newspaper article, but he or she might just as easily drop by the nearest dealer and take it for a test drive. That opportunity to try out a product before you buy is simply not available with most software purchases, except in special circumstances. Moreover, until relatively recently a large proportion of computer users outside of the office were dedicated hobbyists or high-tech professionals, who naturally looked to trade publications for advice on choosing a new product.

In the case of CorelDRAW, the critical tone was established by a head-to-head comparison with Adobe Illustrator for Windows that appeared in *PC Week* on March 13, 1989. The writer, Dale Lewallen, had spent a total of fourteen hours on the phone with Mark Charlesworth gathering background information and discussing technical details, leaving the CorelDRAW manager in suspense as to his conclusions. When the story finally appeared, Charlesworth was ecstatic. Among his many criticisms of the Adobe product, the reviewer took aim at Illustrator's black-and-white screen display, its excessive memory requirement, the lack of support for industry-standard Pantone colours and the fact that it could only print high-quality colour graphics on an expensive PostScript printer, forcing LaserJet owners to settle for low-resolution, monochrome images. As for speed, Lewallen found that it took Illustrator one minute and twenty-six seconds to load one of its own 36-kilobyte files. CorelDRAW could import the same file and load it in one minute and twenty-one seconds. After converting it to its own file format, CorelDRAW could load it in a mere thirty-nine seconds.

"In the end Corel Draw provides, feature for feature, significantly more value than the Windows-based PC version of Adobe Illustrator and does so at a far lower total cost," Lewallen wrote. "Corel Draw offers professionals as well as novices the chance to use existing PC systems without requiring relatively expensive printer technology or memory upgrades."

Still, even that conclusion was understated in comparison with some of the subsequent reviews. "This new vector-based drawing package truly deserves the exclamation point that rounds out its name," raved PC Magazine in its April 11, 1989, issue. Writer Luisa Simone was particularly impressed with the friendly, intuitive user interface—which, as it happened, was one of the aspects of Corel-DRAW of which Charlesworth was most proud. He had spent countless days refining and simplifying the on-screen "toolbox," a series of buttons running down the left side of the display. Where Illustrator's toolbox had fifteen tools and Micrografx Designer's had twenty-one, CorelDRAW's product had nine, of which only three were drawing tools. In his determination to make the program easy to use, Charlesworth had hit upon the idea of making each tool perform a variety of functions, depending on how it was used. Instead of one tool to draw straight lines and another to draw curves, CorelDRAW gave you what amounted to an electronic pencil. Straight lines were produced by clicking and releasing the mouse, then moving the mouse and clicking again. If you moved the mouse while holding the button down, the program assumed you wanted a curve. Then, if you imported a bit-mapped image, the pencil tool automatically changed into an auto-trace tool. Another could be used to draw rectangles or, by hitting the Control key, squares. Double-clicking on any of the lines opened a pop-up menu with a variety of additional editing tools.

"Apparently they didn't ask programmers how they thought artists should work; they asked artists how they do work, and they listened to the answers," PC Magazine said in a major comparison of five PC-based graphics packages on June 27.

Actually, that wasn't quite true. Apart from his friend Stanley Berneche, Charlesworth hadn't really consulted anyone outside Corel during the sixteen months of development that went into Corel-DRAW 1. The reason the software was so good was that Mark Charlesworth, the math whiz from Deep River whose love of drawing was equalled by his compulsive attention to detail, had set out to create a program that fit *his* needs. And if CorelDRAW was good enough to satisfy Charlesworth's demanding expectations, it was a pretty safe bet that a lot of other people were going to like it, too.

"Mark was not a graphics-elite person," Arlen Bartsch says. "He was a cartoonist, an Everyman kind of user, so he was really creating the kind of product that he would like to use. The calligraphic pen [a feature that allowed users to automatically vary the width and end style of the electronic pen instead of simply drawing lines of uniform thickness] was something he wanted to create in the computer so you could use it the same way he used a pen for cartooning.

"At the time a lot of us were naive, just out of school, but Mark knew what had to be done and made sure that all of the elements in the product plan were successfully executed. And Mike gave him a lot of latitude. I think Mark was almost educating Mike in terms of his sense of what the product needed and what kind of features needed to be built into it. The two of them spent hours together in Mike's office. As I would go home at night I'd see the two of them in there just talking over strategy."

On top of the favorable press, CorelDRAW received a big boost in those early days from established players such as IBM, Aldus, Hewlett-Packard, Canon and Microsoft, each of which had its own reasons for wanting to assist Cowpland and his company.

IBM's motivation, made clear during the visit to Boulder in November 1988, was to strengthen its competitive position in the rapidly growing desktop publishing market. At the time, Big Blue's publishing workstations consisted of a PS/2, a PostScript printer and PageMaker. Without a full-featured illustration application to show clients, the company was losing sales left and right to Apple. Similarly,

Aldus figured it could sell more copies of PageMaker if customers knew that they could also buy a high-quality graphics package to go with it. Despite being rebuffed in its attempt to license CorelDRAW, Aldus recognized that it was in its own interest to lend Corel a helping hand. H-P and Canon, meanwhile, were always on the hunt for new software that might fuel demand for their high-end colour laser printers. And Microsoft liked CorelDRAW because it reinforced Bill Gates's efforts to position Windows, which was still fighting to attain broad acceptance, as the leading graphical environment for IBM-compatible PCs.

One of Paul Bodnoff's jobs during that first year was to translate those good intentions into a more formal series of agreements—strategic alliances—that would help drive sales of Corel's software. Happily for him, it was not an arduous task. The positive reviews and sudden explosion of interest in CorelDRAW meant that many of the most powerful companies in the industry were falling over themselves to have Corel as a partner.

The extent to which CorelDRAW had become an industry darling hit home with Bodnoff during a visit to Houston two months after the product's introduction. Once again, the host was IBM, which had assembled several hundred of its desktop publishing specialists for a series of pep talks and seminars about new software and hardware products. "There were three or four hundred people from all over the world, and John and I got to sit in a huge party room and demo CorelDRAW for them," Bodnoff says. "As impressed as those guys in Boulder had been, this time we had guys standing on chairs and whistling and cheering. It was hysterical—people were yelling out, 'Put text on the curve!' If there was ever anything that could make your head swell, that was it." When the demo ended, Bodnoff stood up and announced that Corel had shipped in four hundred copies of the software, enough to give everyone in attendance a free sample. Says Bodnoff: "I'd never seen anything like it. We had four hundred people lined up down the hall, down the stairs, to get their free copy of CorelDRAW."

Cowpland and his first wife, Darlene. The marriage began to disintegrate in the early 1980s, when Darlene discovered her husband's weakness for younger women.

Corel co-founders Peter Wrage (left) and Les Horn with a prototype of the company's first product, a laser printer. Cowpland, says Wrage, "was like a butterfly, always flitting from one idea to the next." (Photo by Richard Desmarais.)

The original
CorelDRAW team:
(clockwise from left)
Ian Rae, Pat Beirne,
Michel Bouillon,
Mark Charlesworth.
(Photo by Lynn Ball,
The Ottawa Citizen.)

Mark Charlesworth' sketch of the CorelDRAW team. Cowpland
vetoed an earlier version of the drawing because, he said, it made the
company seem disorganized and unprofessional.

As sales of
CorelDRAW
took off, the
company's pay-
roll exploded.
This photo was
taken in the
Corel lobby for
the 1989 annual
report. Creative
director Aili
Kurtis, who
coordinated the
shoot, is in the
lower left-had
corner.

Cowpland in 1998. Out on the tennis court, he can wage daily battle against the aging process.
(Photo by Phill Snel, *Maclean's*.)

Marlen Cowpland earned her pilot's licence in 13 days at a flying school in Florida. Here, glass of champagne in hand, she takes the controls of a chartered Lear jet en route to Comdex in Las Vegas.

Marlen Cowpland at the 1997 Corel
gala in Ottawa, with dress designer
Richard Robinson (top). "Michael
said if the stock goes up, next year
he'll buy me the other half of the
dress," she told reporters.
(Photos by John Major, *The Ottawa Citizen.*)

Trevor McGuire, who became Cowpland's hatchet man, was a 22-year-old service technician when he started at Corel in 1987. By the time he left the company in 1994 he had made $10 million from stock options.
(Photo by Wayne Hiebert, *The Ottawa Citizen*.)

Susan Wimmer, who oversaw the development of CorelDRAW 4. "Mike's philosophy from day one was that a certain percentage of bugginess is acceptable."

After he was fired in 1992, John McFetridge went public with his complaints about Cowpland's harsh management style. "This isn't the Golden Tower," he told *The Ottawa Citizen*. "This is the Dark Tower."
(Photo by Wayne Cuddington, *The Ottawa Citizen*.)

Michel Bouillon gets a backrub from his wife, Danielle Morasse, in 1994. The long hours and punishing pace of work at Corel took a severe toll on many employees.
(Photo by John Major, *The Ottawa Citizen*.)

Paul Skillen joked that his unofficial job title was Demolition Man—the person Corel called on whenever it licenced some clapped-out piece of software that was in desperate need of renewal.

Eid Eid with a prototype of the NetWinder, Corel's Linux-based network computer. Along with Skillen, he was fired in 1998 in a company-wide reorganization.
(Photo by Phill Snel, *Maclean's*.)

Not long after that, Corel negotiated an agreement whereby IBM's customers could purchase CorelDRAW directly from any one of Big Blue's thousands of PC sales reps. A similar deal allowed Aldus's field reps to sell PageMaker and CorelDRAW together at a discounted price. Whatever the benefits for IBM and Aldus, the significance for Corel was obvious: with each such arrangement, the company acquired the services of a huge, unpaid sales force.

By the summer of 1989, Corel was selling a thousand copies a week of CorelDRAW, ten times Charlesworth's most optimistic forecasts before the product launch. Demand for the software was continuing to increase, as was the chorus of critical acclaim. In its July issue, *Publish!* magazine ranked CorelDRAW the "clear standout" among five PC-based illustration programs; the others were Adobe Illustrator for Windows, Micrografx Designer, Digital Research's GEM Artline and Computer Support Corp.'s Arts and Letters. CorelDRAW, the review summarized, "has it all: precision drawing tools, strong text handling, lots of choices for color, and quick response. All add up to a product that you'll find equally appropriate for fine art illustrations, text-heavy fliers, and complex logos."

Around the same time, Corel signed its first major distribution deal, with a U.S. company called Softsel, soon to be renamed Merisel. Now, instead of filling customer orders directly or sending a small number of boxes by courier to each retailer who expressed an interest, Corel could ship hundreds of copies of CorelDRAW at a time to a distributor's warehouse. The distributor then assumed responsibility for supplying stores and independent vendors, known as resellers, throughout North America.

Initially, Softsel tried to force Corel to sign an exclusive agreement, but Cowpland was adamant that his company would not allow itself to become dependent on one distributor. He was gambling that Softsel wanted CorelDRAW so badly that it would agree to a non-exclusive deal, and he was right. Later on, Corel negotiated similar arrangements with Ingram, Techdata and more than half a dozen other big distributors, each of which gave Cowpland's company access to thousands of additional retailers.

The Softsel deal in particular proved to be a boon to the Ottawa company in terms of increasing dealer awareness of CorelDRAW. Several times a year, the distributor would invite Corel representatives to take part in a promotional roadshow that was intended to introduce software dealers to new products. Typically, the production would cover six cities in the span of six weekends. Merisel and its suppliers, including Corel, would arrive in town, set up their displays in a big hotel and invite every computer reseller in the area to drop by. As an additional incentive for dealers to place an order, Cowpland dreamed up a gimmick he called "One to show, one to go"— basically a two-for-the-price-of-one deal by which retailers who contacted the company after the roadshow would be sent one copy of CorelDRAW for display purposes and another to sell. The offer was such a success that Corel's people found themselves having to rush back to Ottawa every Sunday evening after the Softsel events so they would be ready when the orders started to flood in the next morning. "On Mondays the phones would just light up," Bodnoff says, "and all of a sudden we'd have hundreds and hundreds of new dealers."

Best of all, from Cowpland's perspective, was that Corel was acquiring all of this new business without having to open a single new sales office outside Ottawa. "I'd rather sell less software and *not* have any remote offices to manage," the Corel president had told his senior managers during a meeting shortly before CorelDRAW's launch. By then, the company had closed both its Toronto and Chicago offices and laid off most of the staff, moving only a handful of the more hard-working employees to Ottawa. The problems encountered in both those cities had reinforced Cowpland's belief, dating back to his experiences at Mitel, that branch offices were nothing but a pain in the neck. Even though Corel was beginning to expand rapidly to meet the rising demand for its software, he was determined to see the company remain as compact and as tightly focused as possible. Henceforth, he vowed, all Corel employees would be based in Ottawa, where he could keep an eye on them.

According to Paul Bodnoff, one of Cowpland's other guiding principles was his refusal, outside of the engineering ranks, to hire people who had previous experience in the software industry. This was partly because he didn't want to bring in people who might challenge his way of doing things, and partly because he believed that the most important quality in an employee was his or her sense of devotion to the company. Given a choice between a twenty-one-year-old job applicant, fresh out of school and unencumbered by spouse or children, and a thirty-six-year-old with fifteen years of marketing experience, a wife and two kids, Cowpland would take the former almost every time. Not only did younger people command lower salaries, they also tended to display more energy and were much more likely to want to put in longer hours for the sake of their employer.

"One quote I really like is, 'Find a job you love and you'll never work a day in your life,'" Cowpland says. "The culture [of Corel] is there for high performance, and those are the kind of people who are attracted to the company, not people who want a semi-retirement existence. If they want that, they can go somewhere else."

Merri Lemmex was one Corel employee whose drive and initiative fit Cowpland's needs perfectly. She was working as a real-estate agent in the fall of 1987 when she came across a help-wanted ad for Corel. The company was looking for people to teach WordPerfect to its systems integration clients. Lemmex, then twenty-eight, had never used WordPerfect before, but she knew Corel was Mike Cowpland's company and figured that any firm associated with the Mitel co-founder was bound to be an exciting place. She also had some experience as a computer instructor, so she applied for the job and went for an interview with Bodnoff. She was sure the job was hers.

When the phone rang a few days later with bad news, Lemmex couldn't believe it. Straightaway, she jumped in her car, drove over to Corel and demanded to speak to Bodnoff. "I've got two questions," she blurted out. "Why didn't I get the job, and what does it take to get one here?" Bodnoff was momentarily speechless. Then he stammered out something to the effect that perhaps Corel could find something for her.

A short while after that, Cowpland himself invited her to an interview. "I walked in thinking, Mike Cowpland, wow, he's a rich guy— I'd love to work for him. This nice-looking, white-haired gentleman came out to the reception area and asked me to follow him, so I assumed he was Cowpland. But when I went to sit down in his office he said, 'Oh, no, you go this way.' And I turned around and there was this little tiny office and this younger guy standing there beside a whiteboard that looked like someone had been typing on it—it was absolutely covered with all these facts and figures, sales numbers and technical information. And I thought, oh my, he's obviously very detail-oriented. The first thing he asked was, what did I know about Corel? I said, 'Well, obviously not enough to be sitting in here with you,' and he looked at me and said, 'Good answer.' I hadn't done my homework and it was the first thing he picked up on. Then he glanced at my résumé and started firing all these questions: 'What did you do in '74? And in 1976 you were doing what? And what did you do between summer of '76 and . . .?' Honestly, I couldn't even follow it, but you could see how fast his brain worked. In retrospect I think he hired me because I was straight with him. In those days, he had no respect for people trying to suck up with him."

About a year later, after a stint in training and several months as a product demonstrator in the systems group, Lemmex walked into Cowpland's office and asked to join the CorelDRAW marketing team, which was just getting ready for the product launch. Cowpland agreed, and before long Lemmex became one of the very first Corel-DRAW product specialists, people whose responsibility it was to whip up excitement about the product at trade shows, in meetings with user groups and anywhere else prospective customers might be found. Cowpland and Bodnoff had hit upon the idea of product specialists after reading about a team of Apple employees known as evangelists because their only job was to spread the good word about the company's products. As with Apple's evangelists, CorelDRAW's product specialists were, without exception, attractive, vivacious and energetic. As much as anything, they helped to make Corel's software a major success.

"It was amazing when CorelDRAW first came out—none of us had every been involved in anything like it," Lemmex says. "We started off working for this little company, and pretty soon it got to the stage where we would go to trade shows and people would stop and say, 'Wow! You work for Corel!' And I was getting job offers everywhere I went."

The first time it happened to Lemmex was at the spring Comdex in Atlanta in 1989.

"We had this little booth about the size of a computer and my job was to stand there and do demos all day long. At one point I wandered over to another booth where they were giving watches away and on my way back somebody came up and asked for my business card. Then when I got back to our booth there were two men in dark suits waiting for me in this little glassed-in meeting room—they were from Micrografx and they wanted to know what it would take to hire me. I was making peanuts at the time, but they said they were opening an office in Toronto and I could name my salary—whatever it took. I turned them down so they left, asking me to keep them in mind. Next thing I know, Mike Cowpland bounces in—'Hi, Hi! How's it going?' I said I'd just been offered a job by Micrografx and he said, 'Hope you didn't take it.' I said no. 'Good girl' was all he said and then, boom—off he goes.

"After that I got offered jobs all the time. Of course, I found out many other people did, too, which kind of hurt my ego. But it was one of those things. You worked for Corel, anyone would want you."

Another one of the early product specialists was Susan Wimmer. Wimmer and her husband Frank were both high-tech devotees. He was working on his thesis for a PhD in experimental psychology, the subject of which was computer/human interaction. Unusually for Corel, Wimmer was thirty-six when she joined the company in 1989.

She was hired because she loved computers and because, at the time she applied, it was all Corel could do to keep up with the growing demand. She also had a enthusiastic personality and a proven ability to take on new challenges, as evidenced by a résumé that included jobs as an advertising director and a local TV news anchor.

"Susan Wimmer was probably our most brilliant demonstrator ever, and we've had some great ones," Cowpland recalls. "Of course, being a former talk show host she's great with crowds, but at the same time she's a wizard with a mouse—she just lives and breathes computers with her husband. We had the best product, too, but then you need someone to get those ooohs and aaahs from the audience. It's all in the timing."

Just as Cowpland admired Wimmer, she in turn relished working for Corel during the frenzied few years after CorelDRAW's introduction. In her previous jobs, she had often become frustrated by the slow pace of corporate decision-making. Corel was nothing like that. In most cases, Cowpland made up his mind right on the spot, without so much as a moment's hesitation. His idea of careful deliberation was to think about a problem over the weekend and announce his decision first thing Monday morning. If, as often happened, he had a subsequent change of heart, the entire strategy might be scrapped and replaced with some other plan by noon on Tuesday.

"At least for the years I was at Corel, there was something about the company that attracted people who went the extra mile," says Wimmer, who now lives in Raleigh, North Carolina, and designs computer games with her husband. "Are you familiar with the concept of buccaneer versus farmer in business theory? The buccaneers are entrepreneurs who go out there and get things started, while the farmers take fewer risks and tend to want to do things the way they've always been done. Well, Mike is the ultimate buccaneer. He just kind of says, 'Yeah, go out there and make it happen.' If you really wanted to make your name and be recognized, he was right there with you. And that's all the encouragement most of us needed."

That was the positive side of Cowpland's brash, head-first approach to business. But the metaphor cuts both ways: when buccaneers start waving their swords around, people nearby are apt to get hurt. At Corel, Wimmer said, the culture of individual empowerment was so strong, and the organizational structure so weak, that loyal, hardworking employees were constantly being harassed or shoved aside by nakedly ambitious co-workers. Cowpland himself encouraged that kind of rivalry and on numerous occasions intervened to shake things up by promoting junior employees to positions of authority over their former supervisors. The result, as Corel grew in size, was a kind of corporate free-for-all in which the power and the spoils went to those who fought hardest to get ahead.

"Part of it," Wimmer says, "was that so many of the employees were just out of school, not accustomed to business life. There was an immaturity that ran through the company. I tried to figure it out a couple of times, and what I decided was that with that open doorway came the temptation for people to rush right at it. And not everybody is capable of handling that kind of freedom and opportunity. You'd have people at the lowest levels really duking it out to get up the ladder."

That, too, was part of Cowpland's way of doing things. He didn't want his managers—or anyone else, for that matter—to get too comfortable, for fear they would slack off. He'd seen that happen many times at Northern and Microsystems, he said on several occasions, and he was determined not to let a similar mentality take hold at Corel.

Chapter Ten

B y the fall of 1989, Cowpland's relentless drive to establish Corel as a leader in the PC graphics market was generating both recognition and reward. *PC Magazine* had given CorelDRAW an Editor's Choice designation, while *InfoWorld* had honoured it as "graphics product of the year" and *PC World* had praised it as a "best buy." Similar trade publication accolades were arriving at the rate of about one a month from as far afield as Britain, France, Spain and New Zealand. With 40,000 copies distributed in only its first ten months on the market, Mark Charlesworth's progeny was well on its way to becoming the world's best-selling PC illustration software.

The money was pouring in, too. On November 9, the company went public on the Toronto Stock Exchange, issuing 2,666,667 common shares at $7.50 each. After deducting the underwriter's fee and other expenses, Corel's net proceeds were $18,446,036. Cowpland, his wife, Darlene, and his two daughters, Christine and Paula, held an additional 5,794,895 shares, worth $43.5 million at the issue price.

Back in 1987, Cowpland had tried to take Corel public in order to recoup his investment and raise capital for future expansion. Now, the company was growing so rapidly that the money from the initial public offering was hardly even necessary—except, of course, as a way of enriching Cowpland and all of those current and past employees whose compensation had come partly in the form of stock. As of November 30, the end of its fiscal year, the company had almost $19 million sitting in the bank. Sales for the previous twelve months totalled $21.7 million, compared to $6.6 million in 1988. Profits were $2.9 million, up sharply from $169,401 in 1988 and a loss of $1.3 million in 1987.

There was only one problem. Having hit the jackpot, Corel was under enormous pressure to keep doing it—to make sure that revenues and profits continued to increase at a rapid clip. If the growth so much as slowed, shareholders would pummel the stock without mercy, reckoning that the initial success of its software had merely been a fluke.

For that reason, Cowpland knew that Corel would have to change. During its first five years, the company had pursued one potential business opportunity after another. Now, instead of trying to pioneer new products—a risky bet at the best of times—it would have to concentrate as much of its resources as possible on CorelDRAW, the company's one cash cow. The challenge was to come up with upgrades to the core product that would expand CorelDRAW's market share while enticing existing users to shell out more money for the newest version.

Right from the start, Cowpland's company proved adept at the upgrade game. In July 1989, the engineering team delivered Version 1.1 of CorelDRAW, which added forty-five—count 'em—more fonts, some additional file import/export capabilities and a special add-on utility developed by Pat Beirne that could decode Adobe's heavily encrypted PostScript fonts and convert them to Corel's own proprietary font format. Known as the WFNBoss (in a nod to Corel-DRAW's history, the first three letters were short for Waldo font), the utility marked a major breakthrough for Corel and helped to precipitate Adobe's decision later that year to lower its font prices.

For months afterward, Corel employees swapped theories about how Beirne had managed to decipher Adobe's secret font specifications. "They had something like four levels of encryption in there and Pat broke the encryption," says Scott Murchison, who was manager of testing and quality assurance for CorelDRAW between 1988 and 1992. "He was probably one of only two or three people in the world who had done that. I'm pretty sure he had some help from a phone call, but I don't know who it was from. I just know that suddenly we had this amazing program that could read and convert Adobe fonts."

The next major step forward for Corel was the worldwide intro-duction of Microsoft Windows 3.0 on May 22, 1990. At the time, it was the most hyped media event ever in the personal computer indus-try. Backed by a $10-million advertising campaign, Windows 3.0 quickly became the best-selling computer software product in history, shipping an estimated six million copies in its first year (the previous two versions had sold half that many in five years). Up until then, Microsoft's graphical operating environment had been merely a rough-around-the-edges experiment. The third generation, however, was slicker, better designed and much easier to use. Eventually it would find its way onto 80 percent of the world's personal computers.

The phenomenal popularity of Microsoft's new platform fuelled a huge surge in demand for programs that were designed to run on top of it, including CorelDRAW—which, in fact, was one of the applica-tions selected by Microsoft during the Windows 3.0 launch to show off its versatility. Cowpland wanted to take full advantage of Micro-soft's success, so he ordered the development team to accelerate its work on CorelDRAW 2. The goal was to introduce the new version at Comdex in Las Vegas that fall.

Launched on November 12, CorelDRAW 2 was three times bigger than the original version, with 900,000 lines of code on 10 floppy-disks, more than 150 scalable fonts, a wide assortment of additional special effects and a sophisticated new colour auto-tracing program called CorelTRACE, developed by Eid Eid, a Lebanese-born engineer. The brother of a hairdresser, Eid had joined Corel after a disastrous attempt to market a $20,000 computer-imaging system that could be used to show salon clients how they would look in a range of popu-lar hairstyles. The system was a flop, far too expensive and technically advanced for the average hairdresser, but Eid's knowledge of colour science and tracing technology made him an important addition to Corel's engineering department. His partner in the hair salon venture, Paul Skillen, joined the company two years later. Both men eventu-ally rose to the rank of vice-president before leaving the company as part of a corporate reorganization in June 1998.

One of CorelDRAW 2's other features was a library of 3,500 clip-art images and symbols, simple, off-the-shelf illustrations that were designed to make the program even more attractive for inexperienced users. As with fonts, Cowpland instructed Charlesworth's team to throw in as many clip-art images as possible, on the theory that too much was never enough. And once again, the most efficient way to satisfy Cowpland's expectations was to pirate somebody else's work. Many of the first clip-art images included with CorelDRAW were lifted without attribution from catalogues and digital collections issued by commercial clip-art suppliers. When those companies discovered what was going on and threatened to sue for copyright infringement, Corel coolly responded with a letter offering to credit the supplier in subsequent versions of the software. It would also promise to include one of the clip-art company's ads in a listing of "Corel partners" that accompanied the software, just in case the user wanted to order more.

Not wanting to miss out on a potentially lucrative marketing opportunity, the clip-art vendors invariably dropped their complaints against Corel, allowing Cowpland free use of their intellectual property. "Mike would say, 'Listen, I'll let you put twenty or thirty images in the next version of Draw and I'll promote you,'" says Gary Cartwright. "That was his way of getting away from being sued."

Cowpland's business tactics might at times have seemed questionable, but the bottom-line results were undeniably impressive. Corel-DRAW 2 was an even bigger hit than its predecessor, driving the installed base of users up to 300,000 by the end of 1991, at which point the company had grown to almost two hundred full-time employees. *Publish!* magazine, in a poll of its readers that year, found CorelDRAW to be ten times more popular than its nearest rival, Micrografx Designer. "I was as excited and as proud of that second version as I was of the first," Charlesworth says. Referring to the Texas company, he adds: "Draw 2 was like dropping a bomb on those guys—they didn't stand a chance."

Neither, however, did Charlesworth. Only a year after the success of CorelDRAW 2, he was pushed out the door, seething with anger about the way Cowpland had treated him. His dismissal, and the internal clashes that led up to and followed it, signified an important turning point in the company's history. The energetic start-up was rapidly maturing into a major corporation, one that would become known as much for its revolving-door employment practices as for its industry-leading software. In the eyes of most Corel veterans, it was very much a transition for the worse.

"Like a lot of public companies, it became a very quarter-to-quarter driven business," Paul Bodnoff says. "In the first few years I remember my friends being very jealous of me, of that feeling [Corel employees had] that you'd get up in the morning and couldn't wait to go to work. But then the company exploded and it changed, just like anything when it grows. I didn't like some of the things I was seeing. I didn't like the way some people were being treated. And after a while, it just stopped being fun."

Mike Cowpland wants to make one thing perfectly clear: regardless of what people might choose to believe, he does not get a kick out of firing people. He dislikes it so much, in fact, that he is reluctant even to call it firing. He prefers to describe what happens at Corel as "pruning" or perhaps "weeding." As in, "When people aren't pulling their weight they get weeded out, because if you don't do it the company won't grow." Or, referring specifically to the company's early years, "What I found was that I had to do a fair bit of pruning myself, which I certainly didn't enjoy. But the nice thing is that if you do it right, it's just like a tree—it just grows straight after that. It's self-sustaining, and after a while people get removed at invisible levels, and I don't even see it happening."

Leaving aside the obvious question of whether Corel's former employees appreciate being categorized as undesirable forms of vegetation, the important point is that—in Cowpland's view, at least—he has no choice. As a company expands and evolves, he explains, its needs change. Some employees are capable of adapting to those new requirements, but many others are not. "They may be good, but they may be better suited to an opportunity elsewhere, and our job is not to hold people back from what they can do elsewhere."

Expressed in those terms, of course, the decision to fire someone begins to sound like an act of human kindness and compassion. At last count, something approaching three hundred Corel employees have been "not held back" from other opportunities (of which, it must be said, there are many in the burgeoning software industry). In fact, there is even a multimedia software company in Ottawa whose five founders were all people who had been fired, pushed out or otherwise made to feel unwelcome by Cowpland and his associates. Its name, appropriately, is Future Endeavors. As in, "So-and-so is leaving Corel and we wish him well in his future endeavours."

The single most famous account of a firing at Corel concerns a fellow named Ed Hladkowicz. To many people, the story says everything that needs to be said about the Corel CEO's cold, ruthless approach to business and his insensitivity to the feelings of those who work for him. Others say it simply shows that Cowpland doesn't play favourites—that he is scrupulous about not allowing his personal relationships to interfere with business. It is, of course, entirely possible that both interpretations are correct.

Hladkowicz was a pro at the Rideau Tennis Club in Ottawa when he first met Cowpland in the mid-1970s. His competitive instincts and skill on the court naturally qualified him to join Cowpland's circle of tennis buddies, which at the time also included Glen St. John, Ross Tuddenham and, when he was in town, high-tech investor Ben Webster. They continued to play regularly after Cowpland recruited Hladkowicz to join Corel in 1986 as a commissioned salesman in the systems integration division. By 1991, Hladkowicz had risen to become sales manager.

Then, out of the blue, Cowpland decided to shut down the systems division. Hladkowicz was among eight men and women who were summarily herded into a room by Cowpland's right-hand man at the time, Trevor McGuire, and informed that they were no longer

Corel employees. Keeping watch over them like a prison guard, McGuire ordered the eight to gather up their belongings, turn in their keys and pass-cards and leave the building.

Hladkowicz was stunned, not least because his tennis partner had given him no warning of the shut-down and declined to speak to him personally on the day he was terminated. He was even more stunned a week later when Cowpland phoned him at home to ask when their next game would be. "I wasn't totally jumping up and down about the idea of playing tennis with him again," Hladkowicz told *Canadian Business* magazine in 1995. "I mentioned that he didn't totally understand the severity of the situation."

Perhaps not, but then again, Hladkowicz didn't understand the extent to which his former boss is used to getting what he wants. After a few weeks and several more conversations, Cowpland convinced Hladkowicz to let bygones be bygones. The two men still play tennis regularly, and in 1993 they won the doubles tennis championship at their club. Hladkowicz's brother, John, remains on the Corel payroll as head of investor relations, having been at the company since 1989.

"It was nothing personal," Cowpland says now about Hladkowicz's firing. "The fact is we'd downsized the whole systems group, so there was nothing much that could be done anyway. Those commissioned salespeople were getting big bucks, like a hundred thousand a year, whereas anyone who came in for a non-commissioned position with his qualifications would be lucky to get fifty thou'. He's not going to be happy anyway, so you might as well make a clean break."

Didn't Cowpland hesitate, even for a moment, before inviting his unemployed former subordinate to play a game of tennis? "It was almost the reverse. The business decision was clearly business, so it would have seemed very negative to ostracize him just because he wasn't working here any more. I thought at the time, there could be an issue here but I'll let him make the call, give him the opportunity to say no. I wanted to show that, as far as I was concerned, tennis continues on."

It all sounds quite straightforward and logical, but of course it isn't—at least not for most of the other people who have been fired from Corel over the years. The body count began with the dismissal of Peter Wrage and Les Horn in 1986 and grew to include many of the company's key engineers and marketing stars, whose efforts helped to establish Corel as a software powerhouse in the first place. Many other employees, among them some of the company's most senior managers, quit in dismay or even disgust at the way their colleagues were being treated.

"It got to the point where everyone said you were stupid if you didn't have your résumé in your back pocket," says Merri Lemmex. "And if you didn't have your résumé in your back pocket then you'd darn well better be printing one. I mean, the turnover was huge." She remembers attending a party with Paul Bodnoff, "and we were sitting and talking about how someone had just been let go or walked out or whatever. Paul looked at me and said, 'You know something? If you want to get somewhere at Corel you've got to be a brown-noser.' And we both looked at each other and said, 'We're never going anywhere at Corel!' "

In Lemmex's case, the end came suddenly, in January 1992, only a week after she gave birth to her second daughter. During the two years following the arrival of her first child, she had been working in the marketing department three and a half days a week, an arrangement Cowpland personally approved because, she recalls him saying, he didn't want to lose talented female employees every time one of them gave birth.

Just before Christmas in 1991, after beginning her maternity leave, Lemmex attended a staff party and happened to see a copy of the company organizational chart. Her name wasn't on it. Puzzled, she went to speak to her boss, Paul Bodnoff, who told her not to worry— it must have been an oversight. A few weeks later, she phoned one of her other managers, Arlen Bartsch, to tell him she had just had the baby and it was a girl. Bartsch offered his congratulations. Then, hurriedly changing the subject, he told Lemmex he had a letter in front of him that he wanted to read to her.

"At first I thought it was a letter from one of my [marketing] clients, but then he started reading and it said, 'Further to our discussion today . . .' and it was my termination letter. Someone had typed it up as though we had already had that conversation. It said the company had decided it would no longer allow any part-time positions and since I had agreed I did not want to work full-time, my position had been terminated." The letter was signed by Bartsch, but Lemmex was convinced that it had been dictated by Corel's director of human resources, Valerie McCavour, a woman she had clashed with several times before. When he finished reading, Bartsch calmly told Lemmex she could call back later if she had any questions. Then he wished her luck and hung up.

Devastated, Lemmex contacted the Ontario Labour Relations Board to ask whether her employer had the right to fire her during her maternity leave. Absolutely not, she was told. But while the law was on her side, in practical terms there was nothing she or anyone else could do about it short of filing a lawsuit against the company, which would cost many thousands of dollars in legal fees. And even that was pointless because the standard practice in the province was for companies to give laid-off workers a minimum of one week's pay for every year of service. Cowpland's policy was to pay four times that amount, a month for every year, on the condition that the employee sign a piece of paper promising not to take action against Corel. Even if she declined the severance package and obtained a judge's ruling of wrongful dismissal, Lemmex's lawyer told her, there wasn't a snowball's chance that she would recover more than Corel was already offering. Under the circumstances, her only realistic option was to sign the document. "It's not like I had any choice," she says. "I was only a few days out of the hospital and I needed the money."

Over the following year, more than half a dozen other women were terminated by Corel while on maternity leave, Lemmex says. "Most of the staff were between twenty-five and thirty-five, so you had all these women who were young and just married and having kids. And it was something that just terrified women. There were people who would go on maternity leave and then come back to work after a month because they didn't want to lose their jobs."

For several years, Lemmex remained bitter about the way she'd lost her job, but after a while she became convinced that Cowpland hadn't really meant to hurt her feelings or cause her any harm. Coincidentally, she later landed a position at a company that produced multimedia CD-ROMs for people who wanted to learn how to use CorelDRAW, a job in which she occasionally ran into her former employer. Once, Cowpland was delivering the keynote address before six hundred people at a conference in Atlanta when he happened to notice Lemmex's name on the speakers' list. He promptly interrupted his own speech to introduce her from the podium.

"It was funny because if I was out on the road and bumped into Mike, he would always have a great long chat to me like nothing happened, like I was a real buddy of his and it was no big deal," Lemmex says. "Sometimes I felt like I wanted to talk to him about my dismissal, but then I'd think, 'Well, what's the point?' I was pleased he would still talk to me—I mean, he's an interesting fellow. And besides, he would be totally oblivious to the fact that he had fired me or essentially had me let go."

One thing everybody who works for Mike Cowpland soon comes to realize is that he hates confrontation. Naturally, given his passion for weeding, that created something of a problem in Corel's early days. He needed someone who didn't mind rolling up his sleeves and plunging his hands into the dirt. Someone who, to switch metaphors, would crack the whip now and then and keep the boys in line. Someone who could, when the occasion demanded it, coolly look people in the eye and tell them they had fifteen minutes to remove themselves from the premises.

For a time, men like Andy Nellestyn and Gary Cartwright—two very different men, to be sure—served in that capacity, to some degree. Nellestyn's military background was ideally suited to his role as Corel's senior administrator, the guy who made sure everything happened on schedule and under budget while the boss was off on some crazy tangent, chasing new ideas like they were just so many tennis balls. Cartwright wasn't exactly the big-picture type, but he was loyal to Cowpland, highly ambitious and endowed with plenty of street smarts. He rose to become head of optical disk products simply because Cowpland liked and trusted him. He saw it as his job to keep Cowpland informed about problems in the ranks, and then help to solve them.

Both Nellestyn and Cartwright, however, were pikers compared to the man who eventually came to personify Corel's mercenary management style, Trevor McGuire. Layoffs and firings were so much a part of the Corel culture that, at various times, every senior manager at the company participated in them, if only because Cowpland would tag them as weak and ineffectual if they didn't. But only McGuire actually seemed to relish the opportunity to tell someone he or she was out of a job. He became Cowpland's hatchet man at a time when the company was suffering through one staff purge after another.

"During that whole restructuring period, in '91 and '92, I probably fired seventy, eighty, maybe a hundred people—I lost track after a while," McGuire says. (At the end of its 1992 fiscal year, Corel had 290 full-time employees.) "It was a very demanding place to work. We restructured and restructured and restructured constantly. And people would develop attitude problems. . . . But I mean, there was an incredible amount of turnover." And most people never saw it coming. How could they?

McGuire was all of twenty-two when he started at the company in November 1987. He had a two-year technical diploma from a nearby community college and two and a half years' experience as a junior technician for two local computer graphics firms, Imapro and Bell & Howell. In his first job at Corel, he was responsible for repairing and reassembling a roomful of broken laser printers, using a screwdriver and a soldering gun. He was also somewhat on the pudgy side, not at all the sort of trim-and-fit tennis devotee with whom Cowpland liked to surround himself. He was, in short, the last person anybody would have imagined was destined to become the second most powerful person at Corel.

But McGuire wasted no time in climbing up the corporate ladder. He might have been lacking in higher education, but he was a quick thinker who wasn't afraid to seize the initiative. It didn't matter if the person in McGuire's way was smarter than him or had far more experience; if that person was at all timid or inclined to follow established procedures, he didn't stand a chance. "What I liked about the place was that they were always hiring people, so there was room for growth and advancement," he says. "I grew my own career there largely by seeing things that needed to be done and just assuming responsibility without asking anybody. And all of a sudden, a month or two later, I'd be in that role. That type of initiative was encouraged and rewarded."

The other thing McGuire liked about Corel was the informality. Sure, there were organizational charts, chains of command and so on, but the reality was that Cowpland himself paid little attention to those conventions. His door was always open and he encouraged people to bypass their supervisors and take problems directly to him. One day, soon after McGuire joined the company, Cowpland wandered into his work area and started to complain about the computers some of the other employees had on their desks. He took McGuire over to the accounting department and pointed to a clerk who was typing sales and expense figures into a spreadsheet program. Every time the woman hit the Enter key, the computer, a low-end machine build around Intel's 286 chip, would pause for a few seconds while it digested the new data. Cowpland was annoyed that McGuire's boss, a man named Claude Labranche, had tried to save the company money by purchasing 286-class computers for some of the staff instead of high-performance 386s. "I know you report to Claude, but I write the cheques around here and as far as computers go, I want the top end," McGuire recalls Cowpland saying. For McGuire, the message was clear: at Corel, the chain of command existed on paper only.

By 1990, after two promotions, McGuire held the title of operations manager, a job in which he theoretically reported to Patti Hall, the general manager of integrated PC systems. Cowpland, however, had McGuire in mind for bigger things. CorelDRAW's success had triggered a sudden growth spurt at the company, and Cowpland suspected that some of the employees were not working as hard as they should—or, even worse, were beginning to question his authority. He needed someone to enforce some discipline and correctly perceived that McGuire was the man to do it. "Trevor had a fairly right-wing style, you could say," Cowpland said years later, laughing at the memory. "A bit extreme, even. In some ways that was good in the stage we were at, where we may have been a bit too far to the left, too soft. He kind of firmed things up, you could say."

According to Cowpland, McGuire "just naturally gravitated up the chain of management." In fact, what really happened is that in December 1990, Cowpland decided to reach down and pull McGuire into the senior ranks. Normally, a CEO in his position might have gone out to recruit an experienced chief operating officer, but Cowpland wouldn't dream of taking that approach. There was always the risk that a strong COO would develop an independent streak. He didn't want anyone to challenge the way he ran Corel.

Cowpland's solution was simply to have McGuire and Hall switch places, like two chess pieces on a board. That way, Cowpland would have the benefit of McGuire's "right-wing style" while making it clear that he was still firmly in charge. Immediately, McGuire's salary jumped from $63,833 to $134,166, making him the fourth-highest-paid person in the company. "That's an example of how Cowpland manages," McGuire says. "Those were things that were, like, hard decisions to make that people wouldn't normally make in a company. But he made it in the bat of an eye because it was the right thing to do."

Hall, not surprisingly, saw things differently. She was convinced that McGuire had stabbed her in the back, and she once told Robert Lendvai she was sorry she hadn't fired the one-time technician when she still had a chance. Instead, the tables were turned and it was McGuire who now held Hall's fate in his hands.

With McGuire in charge, the atmosphere around the systems group began to change. It drove McGuire crazy that there were sales-people in the division who, once you added in their commissions, took home more money than he did. He also recognized, as did everyone, that the division's relative importance to the company was shrinking as sales of CorelDRAW continued to soar. In 1991, by Corel's own accounting, the systems group lost $700,000 on sales of $8.8 million. Two years earlier, it had earned $800,000 on sales of $7.6 million. As a percentage of total revenues, the division had fallen to 17 percent from 72 percent in 1988.

The writing, clearly, was on the wall. What is most interesting about McGuire's version of how the division met its end is the way he claims credit for pushing Cowpland to do it swiftly .

"I was in there on a Sunday overseeing the inventory count at the end of the year, and Mike was in there, too, working on something. I went into his office and we talked for a while and we were going over the numbers for the division. There were people in there making insane demands for compensation, and it wasn't even profitable, even though we had grown the revenues quite a bit. So we said, maybe what we should do is toward the end of this year we'll wind it down. So we sat there for ten minutes and I said, 'Well, why wait until the end of the year?' He goes, 'Yeah, that's true. Maybe we'll do it in three months and that will give us time to wind down the inventory.'

"So I go in there Monday and we're having another chat and I said, 'Well, Mike, if we start to wind down the inventory the sales-people are going to complain about not being able to supply cus-tomers with products.' He said, 'Yeah you're right. Maybe we should wind it down quicker—maybe next week.' And we ended up closing it that Wednesday."

On the appointed day, McGuire divided the entire forty-person division into two groups and sent them to separate meeting rooms. The members of one group were told they were going to be re-assigned to other departments. The others, including Ed Hladkowicz and Patti Hall, were sent packing.

"That's the type of thing that just sort of gets ingrained in you at Corel," says McGuire, who left the company in 1994. "Make a decision—act. Make a decision—act."

That had always been Cowpland's style, and McGuire learned quickly what was expected of him. As Paul Bodnoff puts it, "Trevor was willing to do some of the deeds Mike didn't want to do. Mike always wanted to be the good guy, and Trevor was willing to do the other things." Adds Arlen Bartsch: "It was almost like Trevor and Mike had this agreement that Trevor would be the policeman. He had the badge."

Trevor McGuire doesn't deny that his former boss sometimes used him to do his dirty work. He just doesn't want anyone to think that he was responsible for every firing that took place during his tenure at Corel. "As far as doing his dirty work or anything like that, Mike had no problem letting people go himself—people like Mark Charlesworth and John McFetridge."

That said, McGuire makes no secret of his antipathy toward those two former co-workers. As far as he was concerned, both men—Charlesworth in particular—got exactly what they deserved. "Mark was always putting on this attitude, like engineering was superior to everything else. And it caught up with him." Tellingly, perhaps, McGuire refuses to recognize Charlesworth's pivotal role in the creation of CorelDRAW, something even Cowpland is quick to acknowledge. At one point during an interview for this book, McGuire described Charlesworth as "sort of the technical writer for CorelDRAW, the guy who wrote the manual for it. . . . Well, I guess you could say he was sort of the product manager for it, too." For that matter, McGuire maintains that Pat Beirne is often wrongly credited with being the technical genius behind CorelDRAW. "Pat maybe takes a lot of credit for it because he's still there, you know, in terms of history re-inventing itself. But for some of us it was really Michel [Bouillon]."

Perhaps only Cowpland himself knows the real reason he decided to get rid of Mark Charlesworth. Suffice it to say that when Trevor McGuire joined Corel's executive team at the beginning of 1991, his fellow corporate officers—apart from Cowpland and chief engineer Pat Beirne—were Charlesworth, chief financial officer Mike Slaunwhite and Claude Labranche, then general manager of optical technology. Beirne, whose relationship with Cowpland dated back to 1976, was bulletproof. As an engineer, he was the son Mike Cowpland never had. Not only that, Beirne couldn't care less about money and power. He already had as much of the former as he knew what to do with, and as a techie the last thing he wanted to do was manage a large group of people. The other three men, however, were a different story. And one by one, they dropped like flies.

Labranche was the first to go. For years, he'd been known around Corel as one of the company's principal bean-counters—the guy who was always watching the bottom line and questioning whether such-and-such a department really needed so many bodies. Soon after McGuire took over that role, in 1990, Labranche was called into a meeting with Cowpland and Slaunwhite and told that his services were no longer necessary. "It certainly came as a surprise to me," says Labranche. Still, he wasn't entirely sorry to leave. "I joined the company when there were eighteen employees and there was an incredible amount of fun and energy. By the time I left there were two hundred and eighty people there. It was a totally different environment, full of office politics and intrigue."

Charlesworth's removal took longer, in part because of his importance to the CorelDRAW team. Nevertheless, McGuire says his old boss often complained to him about Charlesworth's fondness for working at home and his fear of flying, which prevented him from attending several key industry trade shows. Perhaps more important, Cowpland came to resent the fact that Charlesworth was getting all the glory for CorelDRAW's success. A particular sore point was a feature story on the program's creation that ran in *The Ottawa Citizen* on May 11, 1991. Based on interviews with the original four members of the Waldo team, the half-page piece quoted Charlesworth as saying the product would probably not exist had it not been for Cowpland's willingness to take risks. In an accompanying article, Charlesworth also spoke about Cowpland's "hands-off" management style, saying: "He trusted us. Some guys in his position want to be in there and crack a whip. He's not a whip cracker.... It was all self-motivated, just amongst the team." Referring specifically to the members of the Waldo team, Charlesworth added: "There were no egos or anything like that. It was fun, peer-to-peer and totally apolitical."

Taken at face value, the piece was actually quite innocuous. Its main point was that good products tend to result from teamwork. It even pointed out that Charlesworth and the three programmers "are concerned that they not be portrayed as an elite group that did everything. They repeatedly refer to the dozens of other employees who got involved as the program developed."

When Charlesworth saw the piece in print, he was delighted. He assumed his boss would be, too. After all, he had praised Cowpland and emphasized that Corel was a place where great things happened, thanks to teamwork, talented engineers and supportive management. What was there not to like?

Plenty, as it turned out. In fact, the more Cowpland thought about it, the more incensed he became. To his way of thinking, Charlesworth had made it sound as though the only part the Corel CEO had played in CorelDRAW's creation was the decision to authorize the project in the first place. Hands off? Who the hell had specified that the product should be capable of tracing a bit-mapped image? Who decided it should be compatible with non-PostScript printers? Whose idea was it to go after low-end rather than high-end users? Who decided on the name, the packaging, the pricing—the entire marketing strategy, in other words?

For that matter, Cowpland wasn't too crazy about that "apolitical" comment, either. Was Charlesworth implying that politics was the rule rather than the exception at Corel?

"Mike was real miffed when he saw that *Citizen* article," McGuire says. "There were a number of comments in there he didn't like, that made him look bad. That and a few other things taught him Charlesworth wasn't a guy he wanted to trust and keep."

Around the same time, Charlesworth and some of the other senior managers got into trouble for trying to interfere with one of Cowpland's marketing initiatives. The problem began when Cowpland told Aili Kurtis to design a series of full-page colour ads for CorelDRAW and then buy space for them in the *Citizen*. When the rest of the management team got wind of the plan, they argued that it was an inappropriate way to spend money. In their view, it made far more sense to concentrate Corel's advertising dollars in the United States, where the vast majority of the company's customers lived.

In the past, Cowpland had always seemed open to other people's suggestions. But this time it was different. "It was almost as though Mike's interest in putting ads in the *Citizen* was to make his own image in town more conspicuous," Kurtis says. "At first I argued with some of the other people because I was the advertising manager, and I said, 'Mike really wants this and I'm not sure it's smart to go against his wishes.' But Mark Charlesworth and John McFetridge and the rest of the group—in those days we made a lot of group decisions—all felt strongly that we shouldn't spend money on full-page ads locally, so I went to Mike and told him. Well, he was outraged. He said it was his company and if he wanted ads in the *Citizen* it was going to happen." Kurtis adds, "That was the first time I had ever seen him angry. . . .When he gets that way he doesn't raise his voice, but you can really feel the tension in the air. He gets very stern."

Of course, if it had been nothing more than a single newspaper story or a flap over advertising dollars, it might have been overlooked. What really made Cowpland furious was a growing sense that Charlesworth and some of the others were getting too big for their britches. There was nothing the Corel CEO hated more than being pushed to go along with somebody else's vision, and as 1991 wore on, that was exactly how he was feeling. In his mind, Charlesworth was acting as though CorelDRAW were his personal property—that he knew better than anyone, including Cowpland, how it should be developed and managed.

Ironically, the first sign of internal dissension over CorelDRAW's evolution didn't involve Charlesworth at all. It began when Paul Bodnoff and John McFetridge attended a trade show in Boston in early 1991. While there, they stumbled across a young Taiwanese engineer who was showing a full-featured bit-map editing program called Photo-Styler. Essentially a Windows-based knock-off of Adobe's popular PhotoShop for the Macintosh, PhotoStyler broke new ground among PC-compatible paint programs, just as CorelDRAW had set the pace in the market for vector-illustration software. It was fast, powerful and flexible, with a sharp-looking interface, easy-to-use menus and a wide variety of tools and special effects for displaying, editing and retouching photographic-quality images.

Bodnoff and McFetridge took one look at PhotoStyler and decided that it would be the ideal companion to CorelDRAW. There had already been some discussion to the effect that Corel should develop its own bit-map editing program. Why not save time by licensing one, just as Aldus had wanted to license CorelDRAW? So convinced were Bodnoff and McFetridge that Cowpland would jump at the idea that they promptly talked the young developer— who worked in California for a Taiwan-funded company called U-Lead Systems Inc.—into flying back to Ottawa with them. (Getting him there, however, took some effort, because the developer wasn't carrying his passport and the immigration authorities in Canada weren't wild about letting him into the country.)

Sure enough, Cowpland loved the product and the meeting was a success. Two weeks later, the developer's boss flew in from Taipei to negotiate a sale of the software. Within hours, both sides had agreed on the terms. "There were handshakes and there was a deal on paper that hadn't been signed," Bodnoff recalls. "We all went for lunch to celebrate. It was basically a done deal." Until, that is, Cowpland got cold feet.

McFetridge remembers driving the Taiwanese businessman to the airport, wishing him a safe flight and returning to the office to find out that Cowpland had changed his mind. "All of a sudden we had to renege on the deal. I was so embarrassed. To me a handshake is a deal, especially when you're dealing with honourable people. . . . That was the start of my negative feelings at Corel. It really outraged me."

To this day, Bodnoff remains perplexed by Cowpland's change of heart. "It's still a mystery to me. I think he was afraid of not being able to juggle the multiple products, which is ironic in hindsight. . . . If there was a person behind all that it must have been Trevor McGuire . . . He had Mike's ear. But it wasn't that PhotoStyler was a lousy product. It was a breakthrough on the PC. You could do things with it you couldn't do with any other product." (In June 1991, U-Lead sold marketing rights for PhotoStyler to Aldus Corp., for an undisclosed sum.)

Despite Bodnoff's suspicions, McGuire says he can't even remember the PhotoStyler episode. He does, however, have vivid memories of the controversy that broke out over another potential licensing deal, this one involving a program called Painter from a California software house called Fractal Design. Little wonder—it was the Fractal fight that ultimately cost Charlesworth his job and solidified McGuire's power base at Corel.

The story begins in November 1991, about six months after the PhotoStyler episode. By that point, everybody, Cowpland included, had bought into the argument that Corel needed a bit-map editing and photo-retouching application to sell in combination with Corel-DRAW. The hot new product at the time was Fractal Design Painter, which was already selling strongly in a Mac version and was soon to be introduced for the PC. (An internal Corel discussion paper called Painter "certainly the sexiest" of eight bit-map editors that had been demonstrated at trade shows that fall.) After some debate it was agreed that Charlesworth, Bodnoff and Mike Slaunwhite would fly down to California for two days, meet with the company and find out what it would take to do a deal.

The following Monday, November 25, Arlen Bartsch met Charles-worth on the way into the office. He asked Charlesworth how the trip had gone and Charlesworth, obviously excited, replied that it had been a complete success—they had reached a draft agreement to license the software. "I was surprised so I asked Mark if they had spoken to Mike yet, and it turned out they hadn't. So it was obvious there was a big problem because Mike had been excluded from the negotiations—they couldn't reach him or whatever.

"Mark created enmity between himself and Mike at that point," Bartsch says. "It was a major contributor to [Cowpland's] sense that Mark was getting too big and might have had his own agenda. Mike seemed to feel threatened by the whole process."

Cowpland was livid. He complained to McGuire that the deal with Fractal was far too expensive. The agreement negotiated by the Corel executives would have cost a minimum of $4 million (US) a year in guaranteed annual royalties over three years, in addition to which Fractal's owners were to receive options on $5 million (US) worth of Corel shares. Cowpland also objected to a clause in the agreement suggesting that Corel would maintain the name of the product. That was a problem because, in Cowpland's mind, there had never been any possibility of Corel selling the application as a stand-alone product. His intention had been to bundle the software with CorelDRAW, giving it an equally generic name, such as CorelPAINT. Yet under the proposed Fractal agreement, Corel would have no rights to the source code and would only be permitted to bundle a stripped-down version of Painter—the so-called "appetizer" version—with CorelDRAW.

"There was immediate tension after the Fractal blowup," Bartsch says. "Mark started acting differently. He felt he had lost Mike's confidence and he was aware of the political manoeuvring that was going on. He literally retrenched. You saw fewer face-to-face meetings between Mark and Mike. . . . It was like something had been severed in their relationship."

The final straw for Cowpland was when he got wind of a rumour that Charlesworth was thinking of taking the Fractal matter to the board of directors. Charlesworth won't discuss the reasons for his dismissal, so it is impossible to say whether the rumour had any foundation. But Cowpland heard it and evidently took it so seriously that he decided Charlesworth would have to go. (Even if someone had gone to the board to complain about the way the company was being run, it almost certainly would have been a waste of breath, given that all four non-executive members were personal friends of the CEO.) Oddly, Cowpland displayed no such unhappiness with Bodnoff or Slaunwhite, even though both men had participated in the Fractal negotiations and were known, along with several of the other senior managers at Corel, to be unhappy with Cowpland's leadership. Indeed, Bodnoff actually went so far as to write a letter to the board of directors—a letter he never delivered. "I was furious," he recalls. "I said Mike was being irresponsible. Here were opportunities that were coming and going and being scooped up by other people—smart deals that were being scuttled for no good reason."

For whatever reason, Cowpland decided to train his guns on Charlesworth. "I was with Mike when Mark was fired," McGuire says. "We wanted to let him go in the demo room off the lobby downstairs, to get him out quietly, so we had him paged from reception. Mark's office was on the third floor, and he called the receptionist and said that if Mike wanted to see him he could come upstairs. So Mike was livid. I almost had to run to keep up with him. Mike opened the door to Mark's office and by the time he put one foot in he had fired him."

Chapter Eleven

Trevor McGuire's favourite childhood story involves worms. He was in grade eight or nine—he can't remember which —when he and a friend hit upon what seemed to them a fast, easy way to make money. They would meet on McGuire's front lawn at three or four o'clock in the morning, armed with flashlights and buckets, and wander from yard to yard, scooping up shiny, moist nightcrawlers from the dew. When the sun came up, McGuire and his chum lugged the buckets over to one of the local gas stations in their hometown of Petawawa, Ontario, about an hour northwest of Ottawa near Pembroke. The owner, who had a business on the side supplying bait to tourists and local fishermen, paid fifty cents a dozen for the slithery creatures. On a good day, the enterprising lads could pocket as much as ten bucks apiece.

After a few weeks, though, McGuire and his companion became convinced that they were being ripped off. It so happened that the man down at the gas station was selling their worms for two dollars a dozen—a markup of 400 percent. Overcome with indignation, they spent hours trying to think of a way to get revenge.

One night, while out picking worms, McGuire had a flash of inspiration. He noticed that whenever a worm broke in two—when, for example, it tried to crawl back into its hole—both halves continued to wriggle. Eureka. "We were kids. We didn't know what we were doing. But we thought, 'Hey, that worm's still moving and he's still pretty long.' So we took a bunch of the long ones and we cut them in half. All of a sudden one dozen became two dozen. We figured we could double our money."

There was, however, one very big flaw in McGuire's plan, as any schoolboy must surely know. The worms did wriggle after being split in two, but only long enough for them to be delivered to the gas station. Then they died. And when the owner glanced down into the bucket later that morning and eyed a heap of lifeless, bisected worms, he was not amused.

"That was pretty well the end of the worm business," McGuire recalls, "because when we went back to sell him another batch the next day he started yelling and cursing at us, saying if he ever saw us around there again he'd kick us in the arse."

You can say this about Trevor McGuire: he's honest about what it is that drives him, and it's the same thing that propelled him as a boy. "From the time I was a kid I'd always been very, very money-motivated," he says. "I wanted to make money. I wanted to keep money."

Mind you, McGuire didn't exactly grow up in the lap of luxury. Like Mark Charlesworth, McGuire's father worked in Chalk River, but he was no nuclear physicist. He was a forester, and a tough old guy to boot. To save money on heating oil, he used to buy cheap bush lots and use them as sources of firewood. Every Saturday morning, he roused Trevor and his two brothers out of bed at five or six o'clock and sent them into the forest to cut and stack wood all day. "He instilled a real work ethic in us," McGuire says. "We were almost like a resource, a production factory for him."

After high school, McGuire enrolled in an electronics program at the Algonquin College campus in nearby Pembroke—not because he was particularly interested in the subject, but because one of his cousins had gone through the same program and landed a pretty decent job, bringing in enough to buy a house and a nice set of wheels. McGuire was paying for his own education, so he wanted to make the most of it—and he did. His marks were respectable, and he might even have gone on to study engineering at a university, except that it would have meant moving to a place like Ottawa instead of living at home. As long as he was in school he couldn't afford the rent, and his dad sure wasn't in a position to help.

Instead, he got his diploma and immediately went looking for work. His first job, in the spring of 1985, was an entry-level position at Imapro, which is where he initially crossed paths with Mark Charlesworth. Not that they got to know each other there. McGuire was just a lowly service technician, while Charlesworth was a senior salesman with five years experience at Mitel, a degree from Queen's University and a list of academic honours as long as your arm. Guys like him normally wouldn't give McGuire the time of day.

After a year and a half at Imapro, McGuire switched to a similar job for a bit more money in the Ottawa office of Bell & Howell, a Chicago-based company that sold image-processing equipment. His salary was $20,000 a year. He didn't mind the work, but he was itching to increase his income, so he continued to look around for openings at other companies. "What really spurred me was that I happened to see the pay stub of the guy who was training me. He'd been there ten years longer than me and he was getting, I think, about fifty bucks a week more. And I'm thinking, wow. The other part of it was that it was a branch office and I was there with people who'd been there ten, fifteen, twenty years, and there was nowhere to go, no opportunity for advancement."

A year after joining Bell & Howell, in 1987, McGuire heard about an opening for a service technician at Corel. He applied and got the job, which came with a starting salary of $27,000. He thought he'd died and gone to heaven.

He had no idea.

By his own reckoning, Trevor McGuire made something in the order of $10 million dollars during the seven years he spent working for Mike Cowpland. That's enough to make some of his former colleagues turn green with envy, but it's hard to feel much pity for them. Mark Charlesworth, Paul Bodnoff, John McFetridge, Aili Kurtis, Arlen Bartsch, Mike Slaunwhite, Roger Bryanton, Susan Wimmer, Peter Wrage—the list goes on and on—all became millionaires during the glory years of Cowpland's company. Hell, with stock options, even a secretary could pull in more than a hundred grand in a good year. Anyone who held a senior position at the company when it went public and didn't make several hundred thousand was obviously doing something very wrong.

It's just that McGuire did better than almost all of them. Probably, as he would be the first to admit, because he wanted it more than they did. And it was lucky for him that he was happy to follow Cowpland's party line. Agreeing with the boss was an important step to success. That, and just plain hanging in for the big payoff.

Mike Cowpland never fires anyone without first making sure he has somebody on hand to move into that position. In Mark Charlesworth's case, it was Susan Wimmer. Wimmer had never worked as a product manager before, but as far back as CorelDRAW 2 she had functioned as a kind of part-time understudy to the CorelDRAW team leader, while continuing to perform her marketing duties. She knew graphics and she was in close contact with user groups, so she had an excellent sense of what Corel's customers were looking for by way of upgrades and improvements to the software. Cowpland figured she was ready for prime time.

Besides, Cowpland knew that most of the organizational and design work on CorelDRAW 3 had already been completed. What remained now was to finish coding the product and hustle it out the door—which was another reason why the Corel CEO decided to promote Wimmer to the job of product manager. As valuable as Charlesworth had been to the company, he was a perfectionist, which in Cowpland's book qualified as a serious liability. Charlesworth fretted over every last detail. It was largely because of the engineer's diligence that versions 1 and 2 were such reliable products, not nearly so prone to "bugginess" as many other early software releases. But version 2.01, a so-called maintenance release that added several new features and utilities but was otherwise unexceptional, had taken a full fourteen months to get through testing and quality assurance, and did not actually go on sale until January 1992. There was no way on earth Cowpland wanted to go through that experience again. One of his goals was to complete a U.S. public offering by the end of that year, which meant that it was important to keep driving revenues, and by extension the share price, higher. The best way to do that was to push CorelDRAW 3 out onto the market, fast.

Wimmer did not disappoint. Version 3 shipped in May 1992, only five months after Charlesworth's departure. And, thanks mainly to Cowpland's bigger-is-always-better school of marketing, it proved to be spectacularly successful. He had been looking for a way to build on CorelDRAW's popularity over the previous three years and, in the wake of the cancelled PhotoStyler deal, had come up with the idea of a graphics suite, a product that combined Corel's illustration software with several third-party programs for charting, painting and business presentations. Other companies sold drawing, painting and presentation programs individually for $500 or $600 apiece, but Corel had the audacity to stuff them all into one box for $595 (US), an unheard-of value at the time.

"The idea of having one-stop shopping in the box was ours originally," Cowpland recalls. "The object was to extend the brand. Having come from the silicon chip industry, you always tend to think of pricing your product low, grabbing market share and making it up on the volume. Temporarily you might be losing money, but you always know that the volume is going to save you as long as you're the market leader. In the software business, I felt, well, if we buy all the components in bulk and then give it to customers, it's obviously going to be more efficient than them buying one or two at a time. And because we won't be selling it in bits and pieces, it'll be cheaper to distribute. And it worked. We changed the industry because until then people were selling things piecemeal."

Kim Dixon was one of Corel's product evangelists when version 3 was released, and she was responsible for spreading the word throughout the central United States. She recalls that some industry pundits thought the company was taking an enormous risk by, in effect, driving down prices for all types of graphics software. "That was quite controversial," says Dixon, now Corel's vice-president for marketing.

"People thought it didn't make any sense, but in fact it took the market by storm and we pretty much wiped everyone else out that year. Our sales surged from there."

In other ways, too, Cowpland kept pushing the envelope. In 1992, CorelDRAW became the first graphics product on the market to include, at no extra charge, a CD-ROM disk with more than 250 fonts and 14,000 clip-art images in 60 categories, ranging from agriculture to women. There were even clip-art sketches of such figures as Ayatollah Khomeini, Adolf Hitler and Saddam Hussein. It was almost inconceivable that anyone would ever have any use for most of those images, but to Cowpland that was beside the point. The objective was to give customers everything they could possibly want and more, selling the sizzle—the sheer bulk of the package—as well as the steak. In that sense, CorelDRAW 3 was truly a breakthrough, not because of the engineering that went into it but because of what it represented in marketing terms. In subsequent years the company's critics would accuse it of overkill, but in 1992 Cowpland's strategy looked like a stroke of genius. The only people who weren't happy were Corel's competitors. "We've hit them hard, from so many different directions, they'll have a hard time countering," Cowpland told *The Financial Times of Canada* that June.

"Mike had this intuitive business sense that seemed to carry the day," Bartsch says. "One thing he was always good at was attempting to change the rules of the game. With version 3 he clearly built on the success that Microsoft had been experiencing with its early office suites, combining that with the success and momentum of CD-ROM technology. . . . [The result] catapulted Corel to stardom and market-share dominance beyond any other version."

Version 3 was a landmark product in another sense, as well. It was the first Corel product that consisted to a significant degree of software that had been acquired from other companies rather than developed in-house. One of its components, CorelCHART, a graphing program that automatically converted spreadsheet data into any one of dozens of chart types, was based on code licensed from a

California company called Three D Graphics, which specialized in producing customized graphic modules for use by third-party software developers such as Microsoft and Adobe. As part of the deal, Cowpland had agreed to pay Three D Graphics a small fee for every box of CorelDRAW sold. It was an arrangement he later came to regret. Over the years, the agreement cost Corel so much money that he vowed never again to pay royalties when he could avoid it. "After that, we said the best policy is just to buy the code outright," Cowpland says. "The only time we do royalty deals is if it's a separate product, although we do make exceptions with things like spell-checkers. We've found that if you've got the cash, you can drive some pretty good deals buying the technology because, at the entry level, people are very cash-hungry."

More successful, at least from a financial standpoint, was the arrangement Corel struck in order to include a paint program in CorelDRAW 3. After backing out of the proposed deal with Fractal Design, Cowpland decided to put McGuire in charge of all future software licensing. He gave McGuire a list of three companies that were already selling or were planning to introduce paint programs, told him which one he was leaning toward and asked him to call around and get the best deal. "I did all of the negotiations over the phone," McGuire says. "I wasn't making a choice which one to buy— I felt that was Mike's prerogative. It wasn't my style to go behind his back and try to do crazy deals."

The deal McGuire eventually hammered out was with a Marietta, Georgia, firm called Zsoft Corp., which had been having some success with a $495 product it called Publisher's Paintbrush for Windows. For $1.1 million (US) Corel obtained a non-exclusive license allowing it to distribute Zsoft's code under a different name, Corel Photo-Paint, so long as the program was bundled with CorelDRAW. A year or two later Corel paid another $175,000 for the right to sell Photo-Paint as a stand-alone product, although by then Corel's engineers had substantially rewritten the code. At the beginning, at least, Corel Photo-Paint was clearly inferior to both PhotoStyler (which Aldus was selling for

$795) and Fractal Design Painter, but to Cowpland what mattered most was that it was cheaper. If it needed some improvement down the road, so be it. "What it came down to," McFetridge says, "was that Mike decided to go low-end, not high-end."

The decision galled some people at Corel, including McFetridge, but it should not really have come as much of a surprise. In 1992, Corel achieved one of the highest sales-per-employee ratios of any major North American software company—$330,000 for every engineer, marketing manager, receptionist and customer service rep. Profits fell slightly, to $11.2 million from $11.4 million in 1991, partly as a result of Cowpland's more-for-your-money strategy, but revenues jumped 73 percent to $90.1 million. There was no way you could chalk up numbers like those by targeting the high-end graphics market. "We're not going for the top echelon," Cowpland told his staff. "We're going for a larger chunk of the pyramid."

It was an exhilarating time for Corel and its CEO. The company had been the subject of favourable coverage in the trade press since the release of DRAW 1, but by the spring of 1992 Cowpland's name was also popping up regularly in the mainstream media as an example of Canadian high-tech success—the kind of coverage he hadn't seen since the peak years of Mitel. To top it off, on June 8 that year he and Marlen were married in a simple Rockcliffe church ceremony attended by four of their closest friends: Glen St. John and his wife Trudy, Ross Tuddenham and Marlen's friend Louise Reinhart. The bride and the groom had each been divorced a year earlier, but were having "so much fun not being married," Cowpland says, that for a while they weren't sure they wanted to marry. When they finally decided to go through with it, the ceremony was arranged on four days' notice, leaving Marlen just enough time to make arrangements for her wedding gown, a body-hugging mini-dress with extensive sheer inserts.

"When we got married I just had one condition," Marlen says. "I was scared, because I thought, what if we get married and the excitement goes and he doesn't treat me as a lover any more, he treats me as a wife? So we made an agreement, and that's one thing he never does—he never treats me as a wife. He introduces me as his wife, but he treats me as a lover."

Given his company's financial achievements and his support for a long list of local causes, it was perhaps inevitable that Mike Cowpland would be honoured as business person of the year in 1992 by the Ottawa-Carleton Board of Trade. Yet the impressive sales and market-share numbers reflected only one side of Corel. For many employees, 1992 was also the year Corel stopped being a magical, unbelievably enjoyable place to work.

Granted, there was still much to admire about the way Cowpland ran his operation. Few other bosses were willing to hand inexperienced young men and women so much responsibility, and with the stock flying high nobody was likely to complain about the level of compensation. But as the year unfolded, a creeping sense of fear and insecurity settled over 1600 Carling Avenue. People started to talk about Corel as a place where the biggest challenge was to hang on to your job long enough to pay off your mortgage and put away some cash. You put up with the crap mainly because the money was so good.

For some, the change in atmosphere began with the shutting down of the systems group at the end of 1991. For others, it was the sudden departure of Mark Charlesworth.

"I almost got fired at the meeting to handle Mark's being fired," recalls John McFetridge, who probably took Charlesworth's dismissal harder than anyone. "There was a meeting called to put in place some damage control, and I spoke up. I said I couldn't believe Mike would so callously fire the guy who had given his heart and soul. . . . Pat [Beirne] would never have made the finish line without Mark there to keep the team on track. And yet Mike had decided he didn't need him any more, he didn't need anyone to argue with him. To me, that was when the shift occurred. [Cowpland] went from this open management style, where everyone was encouraged to discuss and argue things, to: 'Man, you had better watch what you say.' "

Aili Kurtis wasn't at all inclined to feel sorry for Charlesworth, but Merri Lemmex's firing briefly shook her faith in her boss's judgment. She'd heard that Lemmex had proposed setting up a daycare for the benefit of Corel employees and that Cowpland had rejected the idea out of hand. To Kurtis, his attitude was old-fashioned and unfair. As far as she could tell, Lemmex had been a competent, committed employee whose only mistake was to be a woman and a mother. After agonizing for a while, Kurtis resolved to question Cowpland about the decision. But when she brought it up one afternoon in his office, his explanation seemed to make perfect sense. The software industry wasn't like any other, he said. Everything was moving at the speed of light, and companies that didn't keep up—that couldn't count on the complete, unqualified devotion of their employees—were finished. He was up for it, but some people weren't, and Merri had been one of them. Cowpland said he was sorry, but there was no room at Corel for people who wanted to come and go on their own schedule. Corel had to come first.

"By the time I left his office he had me convinced this was the way it had to be," Kurtis recalls. "I understood that at Corel, everything was so fast-paced that if someone was here they had to really be here, and that meant full-time. I mean, some people wouldn't even take holidays because it would mean they were out of the picture, and other people would be stepping in and making decisions, and by the time they got back they'd be so far out of the picture they'd be laid off."

Kurtis was far from the only person who bought into Cowpland's corporate vision. Gradually, however, even some of the most fervent believers—people who had been at the company back when its only business was selling computers and printers—began to question the way Corel was being run.

One of the more controversial rounds of layoffs took place in the spring of 1992, when Cowpland decided that the customer service department wasn't processing enough calls and needed to be shaken up. Once again, Trevor McGuire was sent in to do the job.

"We had thirty or forty people in customer service," McGuire recalls. "They had a manager and six supervisors. I used to laugh about it because it was almost like they had more layers of management than GM, where the rest of the company was flat. We wanted to be more aggressive [and] we wanted some numbers to keep track of outbound calls. It was way too relaxed for the kind of company we were. So we restructured that—started by letting go all the supervisors and the manager and some of the other individuals in the group, put some of the others under one person and let a few others go. We ended up with probably a quarter of the people doing two or three times the volume."

A similar cost-cutting drive led to the closing of Corel's production department. Beginning with Headline and Newfont, Corel had always produced and packaged its software products in-house, using a bank of floppy-disk replicators and shrink-wrapping machines in a room off the ground-floor reception area. But as the popularity of CorelDRAW continued to increase, the volume of business began to outgrow Corel's capacity to fill orders. The company could have opted to expand the ten-person department, but to Cowpland it made more sense to shut it down and farm the work out to another company, Saturn Solutions Inc. of Montreal. "Basically, our guys were being paid too much," McGuire says, explaining the decision. "Those types of jobs should be minimum wage, yet we had people in there making thirty grand. The way I see it, if you have somebody doing that for thirty thousand plus overhead and benefits, that's thirty thousand less in [corporate] earnings."

Strictly speaking, McGuire and Cowpland were right—all that "restructuring" did make Corel more efficient and profitable, particularly after the company installed a computerized voice-response system for handling routine customer inquiries. The real problem was the arbitrary and cavalier way the layoffs were handled. Typical of those who lost their jobs was Tina McKay, who had spent three years at Corel, during which time Cowpland promoted her from customer service representative to supervisor. Only two months before she lost her job, she had received a $4,000 raise based on the results of her annual performance review. Financially she had done well at Corel, but the lack of warning that she was about to be let go left her feeling confused and angry. (In her case, the impact was compounded by the fact that her husband, Rick McKay, had lost his job at Corel during an earlier purge of the shipping department.)

Yet on the rare occasions when anyone dared to question the firings, Cowpland didn't seem to get it. He might have tried to explain the business case for the dismissals, pointing out the company's ultimate responsibility to its shareholders and how it didn't make sense to have two people doing a job when one person could do it. Nevertheless, he came across as thoughtless and insensitive, implying the only reason people ever lost their jobs at Corel was that they were lazy. "This is a place where people love what they're doing," Cowpland told *The Ottawa Citizen* later that year. "They love it so much. And if you're in that environment where people love it and are good at it, and you find some people are not getting the job done, [exhibiting a] sloppy, a bad, not-committed attitude, they actually spoil the whole atmosphere. So it's important to get rid of them."

Two of the other people who left Corel during that period were engineers John McFetridge and Paul Chehowski. In McFetridge's case, it didn't come as much of a surprise. His loyalty to Cowpland had been shattered by Charlesworth's firing, and in the spring of 1992 he told his second wife that he doubted he would stay at the company much longer because it was no longer a fun place to work. The end came that summer when Cowpland, without discussing it with him, cancelled a joint marketing deal he had just worked out with IBM. McFetridge was convinced that McGuire was behind the decision. "I ran into McGuire's office and told him what I thought of his tactics," McFetridge says. "He then conspired to get me fired, which wasn't hard because I had been openly disgruntled for a while. It was pretty easy for him to convince Mike I was bad-mouthing everybody, because I was."

Chehowski, too, had become disillusioned with Corel. He believed political manoeuvring was behind a decision to move him out of the optical-drive and CD-ROM business area and on to the CorelDRAW development team. One day in early 1993, he told Cowpland he wasn't happy any longer and that he had lined up a job interview with Adaptec, a California company that was licensing Corel's device-driver software. "He asked me to consider staying and said we went back a long time, that I was one of his top technical guys," Chehowski says. The next day Chehowski's team leader, Eid Eid, gave him a choice. If he went for the interview at Adaptec, he was out of a job. Chehowski resigned.

To this day, Chehowski believes that McGuire was the person who convinced Cowpland to give him an ultimatum. McGuire doesn't deny it. "It was me who pushed for that," he says. "I didn't want the message to get out to other people. 'Oh, you're not happy here? Why don't you take the time to look around at these other places? And don't mind us, we'll be here for you because we're just the country club.' It still seems to me so ridiculous that we as a company would just sit there and take that. I mean, do we look stupid?"

No one who was working for the company at that time will ever forget the morning of Saturday, November 7, 1992. On that day the front page of *The Ottawa Citizen* carried a large colour photograph of John McFetridge standing in front of Corel's shimmering gold head-quarters. Below the picture was the headline, " 'Reign of Terror' at Corel" and a short teaser story flagging a full-page article inside on the recent rash of firings and layoffs at Corel.

"This isn't the Golden Tower. This is the Dark Tower," the 2,300-word piece quoted McFetridge as saying. Based on interviews with ten ex-employees, it stated that fifty of the company's two hundred and fifty employees had been dismissed in the previous twelve months, a turnover rate many times higher than at other high-tech companies in the city.

"It's amazing how hush-hush it's been kept in Ottawa," said Rick McKay, one of the people quoted by the newspaper. "People think Corel is the greatest, but they have no idea what is going on inside."

Cowpland, given a chance to defend his company's employment

practices, insisted that the firings were justified. The only reason people were kicking up a fuss, he said, was that Corel was such a generous employer. "What we really have is people loved it so much here they wanted it forever. And they're really pissed off they can't find similar organizations around town. Otherwise they'd be so busy working at them they wouldn't give a damn about Corel."

Mark Charlesworth was quoted too, but to the surprise of many at Corel he had nothing but good things to say about the man who had unceremoniously fired him a year earlier. "I wouldn't be so quick to criticize," he said. "It's a tough job Mike has in an extremely competitive business. . . . Sure, Mike has high standards. He makes quick decisions. But maybe that's the style you need to succeed in this business." He called Corel "one of the best places to work in Canada."

Cowpland's only comment to the *Citizen* about Charlesworth was that he had a "major attitude fit problem."

For those on the outside, it was hard to tell who was right—the disgruntled former employees who claimed Corel was experiencing a "reign of terror," or the CEO who insisted his critics were just a bunch of whiners who didn't have the right stuff to work at Canada's fastest-growing, best-known software company.

The people who remained at Corel presumably had an opinion on the subject, but they weren't talking. Especially after the *Citizen* piece appeared, Cowpland's staff knew better than to talk publicly about working conditions at Corel, unless they happened to be extolling Mike. The safest approach was to keep your head low, as Merri Lemmex discovered when several of the people she'd known at Corel stopped speaking to her. "John [McFetridge] and I both thought that was pretty bizarre. It kind of drew a line in the sand with a lot of our friends. Some were afraid to talk to us after that." Once she unwittingly arranged to meet a business associate in a downtown hotel where Corel happened to be holding a big event. People she had worked and partied with for four years were walking straight past her in the lobby like she no longer existed.

Two of the most frequently quoted Corel employees during the early- to mid-1990s were Arlen Bartsch, director of sales and marketing, and Fiona Rochester, who had begun as a product specialist and moved up to head spokesperson. Almost as much as Cowpland himself, they were the public faces of Corel. Bartsch was the company's top cheerleader, a one-man pep rally whom Cowpland called upon whenever he needed to whip up a crowd. Rochester played an equally important role in managing Corel's media relations in the boom years of CorelDRAW. A writer for one of the major PC magazines generally wouldn't dream of reviewing Corel software without speaking to her first. Many times, her popularity with the press helped to defuse or soften criticism before it made its way into print. A dedicated employee who wore her heart on her sleeve, she was known to break into tears when journalists told her they were about to hand in a negative story.

Even in Corel's own ranks, Bartsch and Rochester were renowned as Cowpland loyalists. Neither, however, is still working for the company. Bartsch handed in his resignation in November 1996, having decided that it was time to rethink his priorities and spend more time with his wife and eight-year-old son. Rochester left about a year later after a prolonged sick leave for an illness brought on partly by stress. Both continue to speak highly of their former boss as a brilliant businessman, yet both now describe the atmosphere in which they worked as next to intolerable, charged with suspicion and fear.

Interviewed for this book a little more than a year after leaving Corel, Bartsch described the interplay between Cowpland and McGuire as "a fascinating study in human relations." "I don't know what it says about Mike, but it was something I had to live with every day," he said. "Some days the political infighting would drain me of every ounce of energy I had. And through all of this, I had this incredible fear that if I spoke up about it I would be next. I mean, I was attempting to protect my own investment as I was climbing up the corporate ladder. I wanted to be there to enjoy the payoff of what we were creating, the financial payoff. So I had to make sure I was smart enough politically to survive. Because what did Mike do? He killed my mentor—Mark Charlesworth. So if Mike could do that to Mark he could certainly do that to me. And I lived with those thoughts constantly."

Rochester expressed her thoughts in an e-mail message in which she referred to the "senseless" firings of four members of Corel's customer-service and corporate sales departments:

> These four individuals were regarded as devoted, hard-working employees. They had built strong customer relationships. Sure I'm sentimental, but the most hard-hearted practical business perspective would still regard that as a waste of valued company resources. What was worse was the way they were unceremoniously cut loose. We were flabbergasted. We felt a strange powerlessness. We were afraid that it could happen to anyone. The reason feeling powerless was unusual was because most of us felt powerful based on the great things that we accomplished for the company. We knew we made a marked contribution. Nobody had to stroke our egos and tell us. Only a few wielded power for their own personal agenda. We were "pulling together" and oriented toward, "What can I do for the company?" We cared about each other, were kind and respectful with each other. It was a rare environment characterized by unusual warmth. Suddenly all hell broke loose.

More than Cowpland himself, the person people feared at Corel was Trevor McGuire. But McGuire, for all his perceived faults, was really just playing the game by Cowpland's rules. Corel's CEO created an environment in which a twenty-two-year-old service technician making $27,000 a year could aspire to reach millionaire status by the time he was twenty-five, providing he played his cards right. The temptation was practically irresistible.

Besides, Trevor McGuire was far from the only person at Corel who carried out unpleasant tasks because that was what was expected of him. If you wanted to stay on the Corel gravy train, as almost everyone did, you had to make some compromises now and then. Few people could ever bring themselves to walk away.

McGuire, for the record, says he doesn't believe most people at Corel were afraid of him. "I'm sure there were some people who felt that way, but I don't think it was a widely held view. There were some people who were fairly insecure. But I moved up the ladder very fast. People there knew I was very close to Cowpland, had a lot of influence over him. He respected my opinion. So if you happen to have two or three hundred people and all's they see is their friends being let go—all's they know is Trevor McGuire went into a room and suddenly ten people have no job, like there's no loyalty—they think it's because I didn't want them there. They don't understand that with some of these people, we couldn't accommodate them."

Besides, McGuire adds, Cowpland always made sure that fired or laid-off employees were generously compensated. "Some of these people—even guys like McFetridge who badmouth him—if an employer called up and said, 'What's he like?', Mike would say, 'Great guy!' No grudges, no bitterness. And he was generous with options. So maybe you had an unskilled person in production who paid off his mortgage. I mean, how many people have no mortgage?

"But as far as perceptions of me, that was beyond my control. The other factor was, I made a lot of money. So there was a lot of resentment of that."

True enough. In fact, when most former Corel people—those who were in senior positions, at any rate—think back on their experiences at the company, a lot of their emotions are wrapped up somehow with money. For a time, there was just so much of it raining down on them that many people felt conflicted. On one hand, they couldn't help but feel guilty about the huge sums they were taking home. Yes, they worked hard, but the bottom line was that it was all too easy—a consequence of timing and good luck more than anything else. On the other hand, there were plenty of opportunities to feel jealous toward co-workers who happened to be doing even better.

Despite what McGuire says about overpaid employees, the salaries at Corel were not out of line with those at other computer software companies. In 1992, Cowpland's salary was just under $150,000. Mike Slaunwhite, Trevor McGuire and Pat Beirne were one level down from that at about $140,000, followed by Susan Wimmer at $120,000. Senior engineers could expect between $75,000 and $100,000.

Those amounts, however, were inconsequential compared to the money that could be made from stock options. Just before Corel went public in 1989, everyone at the company was granted the right to buy stock for about a dollar a share. A junior employee might be entitled to 10,000 shares. Those in senior positions were often entitled to ten times that number. Each share was $7.50 at the initial offering price which meant that the employees were assured of a substantial gain. (Many former employees, as well as friends of Cowpland, did equally well. At the time of the IPO, Gary Cartwright held 100,000 shares, many purchased for pennies back in 1986 and 1987. His wife, Joanne, had another 19,010 shares. Cowpland's father and two daughters each held 100,000 shares; Ross Tuddenham had 51,000 and Marlen Therrien had 90,833.)

Not long after that, Cowpland began to dole out large quantities of stock options to key employees. It began sometime in 1990, when Slaunwhite and Charlesworth approached him to ask for substantial raises; the two were making about $90,000 a year each at that point and felt they were badly underpaid. Cowpland turned down their request, but agreed to give them each 100,000 options exercisable at the current share price. "As long as you weren't talking about salary, options meant nothing to Mike," Slaunwhite recalls.

And Corel's stock option plan was exceptionally generous. At most high-tech firms, employees have to stay with the company for three, four or five years before they are allowed to exercise their options. It doesn't matter how high the stock goes in the meantime—if the price at the end of the waiting period is below the exercise price, which is frequently the case with software companies that soar briefly only to fall back down to earth, they are out of luck. The system is intended to encourage employees to stay in their jobs and to focus on the company's long-term success rather than short-term share-price fluctuations.

At Corel, however, there was no waiting period. Nor was there effectively any limit on the number of options that could be granted, because as soon as someone exercised his or her options they went back into the kitty to be redistributed. The only rule was that the number of unexercised options at any time could not exceed 10 percent of the outstanding shares. If you were smart, you exercised your options and sold stock as soon as the price went up, safe in the knowledge that you would soon be getting more options. (After McGuire left the company in 1994, the bylaws were changed to give the board more control over the number of options. The ceiling is now 15 percent of the outstanding shares, but options, once allocated, can be used only once. As is the practice at most companies, the board's approval is required for any subsequent option grant.)

By 1991, the art of recycling Corel stock options to generate huge windfall gains had been turned into a science. "Usually, Cowpland, myself and Slaunwhite would get together in Mike's office to divide up the options," McGuire says. "The three of us always got equal amounts. Sometimes we'd each get 100,000 options, sometimes we'd get 30,000, sometimes we'd get 200,000. The thing was, Mike didn't care about options that much because he had so much equity—it was really more to reward us as employees. So, anyway, you added those up and subtracted them from the total available options. Next there'd be a list of ten or twenty employees who might get between 2,000 and 10,000 options each because they were a manager in an area or maybe just because they were really hard-working. After that, whatever was left in the pot was divided up among the rest of the employees based on salary. This happened a couple times a year. . . . Sometimes we'd make sure everybody got options, and others times it was just the three of us."

Counting his salary and stock options, McGuire says he earned "in the hundreds of thousands" during his first couple of years at Corel. "Then I think it went up to around a million one year, and then it was three and a half million and then it was around four million—my last six months there. It was a good half year." By then he and his wife had traded their modest house in west-end Ottawa for a large mansion in suburban Nepean, a pair of luxury four-wheel-drive vehicles, a 60-inch (150-centimetre) television with surround sound and a ski boat. In February 1994, the couple took their first extended vacation together, a month-long trip to Hawaii, Australia, Fiji and New Zealand. Five months after the trip, McGuire resigned from Corel, convinced that he had gone as far as he could go in the company, and no doubt aware that it was only a matter of time before he, too, would be ushered out the door. Pointedly, Cowpland did not try to talk him into staying.

"At the beginning," says McGuire, who now runs a small multimedia software company in Nepean, "it was very, very satisfying. I was twenty-five when I made my first million, and to me that was fantastic. And Mike really took pleasure in seeing people make money off the stock. He'd say that's what it's there for. If you told him you paid off your house, he'd say that's great.

"There were times when your stock holdings would go up over a million dollars in one day and that was kind of neat. But it's funny. At a certain point I knew I'd never have to work again, and I had most of the stuff I wanted. After that it was great to make more and more but it was less of a big deal. That's the funny thing—I wouldn't say I'd give it all away, but I find that after you have it, it doesn't mean a whole lot."

Chapter Twelve

The usual rule in the software industry is that each new release of an existing product is slightly better than the one before, for the obvious reason that the developers have had more time to improve it, and to fix the bugs. Mike Cowpland, however, prides himself on refusing to follow anyone else's rules. And so, without hesitation, he went ahead and released CorelDRAW 4, a product so buggy and prone to crashes that it practically destroyed any hope Corel might have had of making major inroads in the professional graphics market.

Around Corel, people talk about version 4 the way other people might refer to a drunken old uncle—in hushed, embarrassed tones. They'd sooner forget about it, except their customers won't let them, because to some extent version 4 was a harbinger of things to come. Remember the California winery that promised it would sell no wine before its time? If Corel were in the beverage business, you'd probably want to hold its products up to the light before taking your first sip, just to be safe.

What's most interesting about this is that the flaws in version 4 weren't really accidental. They were the predictable consequence of a strategy that was intended to wring as much profit as possible out of CorelDRAW by releasing a new version once a year on schedule, regardless of how much development work was necessary and regardless of whether the latest release was truly ready. Up to then, the practice at most software companies had been to unveil new versions of leading products every couple of years or so, give or take a few months. Corel was the first major software producer to adopt a fixed twelve-month upgrade cycle, thereby forcing users to shell out money once a year if they wanted to stay current. When industry analysts praise Mike Cowpland's talent for retail marketing, that's the sort of innovation they're talking about.

Another major marketing innovation, which coincided with the release of version 4 in May 1993, was the decision to continue selling the previous version alongside the new one. Thus, CorelDRAW 4 was pitched as the top-of-the-line version, priced at $595 (US), while version 3 became the "entry-level" product at $199. The goal going forward was to continue dreaming up new features for the latest releases, while discounting the older versions so as to nab new users at lower price points. "Graphics isn't like word-processing, say, where after you get a spell-checker and a grammar-checker and all the fonts you want, there really isn't much more that you can add," Cowpland told *Maclean's* magazine in 1995. "With graphics, there's almost no end of revision possibilities."

It sounded great in theory, but for Cowpland's two-pronged strategy to work, the engineers assigned to CorelDRAW would have to work harder than most of them had ever worked in their lives. So would their manager, Susan Wimmer, who was in the unenviable position of having to satisfy Cowpland's apparently insatiable appetite for new features. The pressure on her was enormous, because Cowpland had made it clear that he would not under any circumstances consider a delay in the release date. The product had to ship in May because that was when Corel staged its annual design contest gala. Moreover, each new release was planned as the kickoff to a six-month-long sales blitz, which Cowpland was counting on to ensure that revenues would be as strong as possible by the end of the company's fiscal year in November.

Wimmer might have demanded more time, but she knew that if she did she would probably suffer the same fate as her former boss, Mark Charlesworth. Failing to meet Cowpland's deadline was simply not an option.

"The relationship between Susan and Mike was different than

between Mark and Mike," says Arlen Bartsch. "By that point we'd gone from basically four engineers on the product to fifty or sixty engineers, so she was managing a very large organization and trying to keep the whole thing on a schedule, which, according to Mike's agenda, was twelve months. She was dealing with a whole new set of expectations, because Mike had a sense that if we moved quickly and behaved more like the fashion industry or the auto industry, with regular revisions, we could leapfrog our competition."

Wimmer's own view was slightly different. Her experiences as a product specialist, meeting face-to-face with user groups and other CorelDRAW enthusiasts across North America, had imbued her with a deep sense of pride in the product. As corny as it sounded, she was determined to do everything in her power to deserve their respect. "We were riding the high we would get from the awards and the constant feedback we were getting from users," she says. "We honestly thought we were the best team in the industry, really satisfying our users."

At the same time, Wimmer felt torn by the demands Cowpland was making. It had started almost as soon as she took over from Charlesworth in January 1992. The original plan had been to release CorelDRAW 3 in June, but after two months Cowpland had decided to move the launch up to May. Wimmer's team made it, but only just. It didn't help matters at all that Photo-Paint, the bit-map editing module Trevor McGuire had licensed from Zsoft Corp., was riddled with problems, including an inability to save certain types of compressed files and a tendency to freeze when functions such as full-screen preview were selected.

"Mike told me at the last minute it had to go out a month earlier and we all just sweated it," Wimmer says. "Mike would overrule whoever was in senior management at the time. And you'd be begging and pleading with him—'Please don't go with Photo-Paint, the code is crap. Please don't go with it.' And he'd be like, 'Ah, who cares? It's cheap and we're going with it.' And that adds to the dilemma for the programmers because then you're inheriting flawed code."

It was after CorelDRAW 3 went out the door that Cowpland announced his intention to shift to a twelve-month cycle. Wimmer had no problem understanding the business rationale for the decision—indeed, as a stockholder she stood to gain, along with everyone else, by helping to pump up the company's profits. But she also knew that any such move to accelerate the pace of product development was going to necessitate some serious trade-offs. Merely to test and debug a large software suite such as CorelDRAW had become would normally require six months. As a result, she and the engineers were left with only six months at the beginning of the process to draw up the specifications and write the code for all the marvellous new features that would have to be included in the package for it to be worth the cost of upgrading. The work would have to be non-stop.

"I don't know that there was anybody, apart from Mike, who really wanted to go to the twelve-month cycle," Wimmer recalls. "It wasn't really so much the frenzied workload that bothered people as much as our pride of ownership. I'd never worked with a group of people like that before who would really do anything they were called upon to do and give it everything they had. It was a very keen group and a lot of the concern we had was because we didn't want anything tarnishing this ideal that we had all been working toward."

On paper, at least, CorelDRAW 4 lived up to that ideal. In addition to all the features of the previous version, it included a new object-oriented animation component called CorelMOVE that allowed creators of business presentations to design their own characters and animate them onscreen with sound. The six previously existing modules also received a raft of enhancements. Corel Photo-Paint, for example, benefited from a redesigned user interface and the capacity to apply impressionist or pointillist styles to images. The main vector drawing program gained a variety of desktop publishing features, including support for documents of as many as 999 pages. The CD-ROM version came with 750 fonts and more than 18,000 clip-art images and symbols, many of them in colour. Perhaps most important, the package boasted a variety of new pre-press tools, which

Corel hoped would appeal to graphics professionals by giving them the ability to produce colour separations and other high-quality forms of output.

As impressive as all the new features was the launch, which took place at the National Arts Centre in Ottawa in conjunction with Corel's fourth annual world design contest, a black-tie extravaganza complete with a laser light show and a twenty-piece band. Cowpland kicked off the glitzy event with a speech praising the "incredible amount of effort" expended by the CorelDRAW team, whose members "have been working eighteen-hour days, all-night sessions . . . to make all this happen on time." He then turned the podium over to Wimmer, who called the new release "the most exciting upgrade in our history" and summoned the entire team on stage to take a bow. Finally, the lights dimmed and a giant screen behind the stage showed a Star Wars-like promotional video in which the CorelDRAW 4 box hurtled through space like a giant asteroid on its way to earth.

All the hype in the world, however, could not disguise a seriously flawed product. Within weeks of its release, CorelDRAW users jammed the company's customer support hotlines with complaints about system crashes, files that refused to open, repeated printing failures and numerous other shortcomings. Some purchasers reported that whenever a document was closed and reopened, the line-spacing in blocks of text would inexplicably change—a sad state of affairs for a product whose reputation rested to a large extent on its ability to manipulate text.

In July, *PC Week* quoted a longtime CorelDRAW 4 user and volunteer beta-tester who alleged that the company had deliberately released the software prematurely. "My concern was the fact that [I received] two beta releases," said the tester, who wasn't named. "The first one was almost an alpha"—a preliminary version intended only as a proof of concept—"and then, when I received the second, it had incomplete modules that didn't work. Then suddenly they released it a week later." Another tester, quoted by *PC Week* in a follow-up report a month later, said that version 4 was "actually a very fine product and a worthy upgrade, but it needed at least two more builds in beta—the programming folks were clearly under the gun."

Faced with a barrage of criticism, the company had no choice but to make available a seven-disk maintenance release called CorelDRAW 4.0b, which it offered to mail free to any user who called to request it. Publicly, the company took the position that version 4 was actually no more unstable than its predecessor. "We feel that we have improved on the delivery of the product this time over the same time last year," Fiona Rochester told *PC Week*. Yet over the next six months, Corel issued at least at least two more revisions of the product, including an "update" version in January 1994.

Regrettably for Corel's customers, even the company's attempts to fix the bugs produced mixed results. A review published in December by *Windows Sources* magazine began on a positive note by calling version 4 a product whose many new and unique features "will knock your socks off." But after praising many of the changes, the article switched gears and presented a long list of weaknesses, "including inexplicable crashes." Among the problems were several that could be traced directly to the most recent revision, known as Rev B, that Corel was mailing out to customers who complained. "The Rev B program could not load many files created with the original version, and printing a round object with a gradient fill produced a squared-off oval," the magazine said. "We cannot recommend CorelDRAW 4 as a viable illustration program until these problems have been remedied."

Despite such attacks, Wimmer says she cannot remember a single instance in which Cowpland complained or seemed perturbed by the large number of technical problems that CorelDRAW 4 users were encountering. What mattered was that the product had been released on time and was selling well, thanks in part to a multimillion-dollar ad campaign that played up the latest gee-whiz enhancements and the fact that CorelDRAW was the world's most widely used Windows graphics program. "Mike's philosophy from day one was that a certain percentage of bugginess is acceptable," she says.

As for the development team, Wimmer and the members of her

group learned not to take the criticism to heart. "The attitude was like, 'Well, what was it that you expected with only six months of development? I mean, give me a royal break. We worked miracles in six months.' There was a lot of healthy avoidance of the negative."

After a while, the practice of shipping faulty software and then following it up with numerous revisions—"revs," as they were known in the trade—became an ingrained part of Corel's business strategy. While some other software producers, such as Adobe, were famous for holding back new products until they were as clean and reliable as their developers could make them, Cowpland's approach was to damn the torpedoes and fire away. It was a strategy designed in part to lure new users by ensuring that CorelDRAW's feature set always looked more impressive that those of its competitors. And when people complained, he responded that every piece of software had bugs, because the wide variety of PC clones on the market made it impossible to prepare for every conceivable computer configuration.

Unlike Cowpland, there were people at Corel who worried about the longer term consequences of Corel's strategy. One of them was Paul Bodnoff, who left the company in the fall of 1993 at the height of the controversy over CorelDRAW 4. "I remember conversations with people where we could foresee what was coming," Bodnoff says. "You could see that things were starting to get watered down, you could see the company delivering software before it was ready." Even so, Bodnoff is quick to give credit to Cowpland for masterminding the company's rapid growth, an achievement he says might not have been possible had Corel stuck to the slower, more cautious style of development that had produced the first two versions of its mainstay product. "When you're trying to build a company," he says, "two years between major releases of Draw was a long time."

The question was, could Corel keep to Cowpland's schedule without thoroughly alienating its existing customers? Version 5, released in May 1994 under the direction of Eid Eid, after Wimmer and her husband decided to move back to the United States, was significantly more stable than version 4, although there were still enough defects to warrant six revisions. Version 6 had other problems, the most significant being that it was designed to run only on Windows 95, the latest iteration of Microsoft's PC operating system. Originally scheduled for release in late 1994, Windows 95 did not make its debut until August of the following year, which forced Corel to postpone its own launch of CorelDRAW 6 by three months. (Unlike Corel, Microsoft believes in flexible release dates and held back Windows 95 to give its engineers more time—if not quite enough—to work out the bugs.)

The delay in the introduction of CorelDRAW 6, however, did nothing to improve the company's record for reliability. The first 20,000 copies contained what one computer magazine labelled a "major, show-stopping flaw"—a bug that caused it to crash any time an unsuspecting user mixed two fonts in a single word, as Corel had always done with the name CorelDRAW itself. Chagrined company officials admitted that they had inadvertently sent the product off to the manufacturers before distributing it to Corel's beta-testers. As soon as the testers got their hands on the software, they discovered the bug and reported it to the company, which hastily ordered up a corrected version and had it shipped out within a week. A second revision, intended to correct several other problems, appeared in November.

Cowpland, unfazed by the rash of bad publicity, hailed DRAW 6 as "an extremely robust release, the best ever," which might have led some first-time buyers to wonder about all those earlier versions. But no matter—the damage had already been done. Only weeks before the release of DRAW 6, a lawyer in Pennsylvania had filed a class-action lawsuit accusing Corel of lack of reliability, lack of proper programming before sale or distribution and breach of warranty with versions 4 and 5. "When their software is full of bugs, I shouldn't have to ask for an update," said Jeffrey Fishbein, a graphic designer in Selinsgrove, Pennsylvania, on whose behalf the case was filed. "I paid for their program expecting a working version, and I feel I'm entitled to one." His lawyer, Steven Angstreich, added that, rather than addressing the problems of its current users, Corel was in effect forcing them to pay for the latest upgrade.

Although Corel executives claimed not to be worried by the suit—Cowpland said it was proof that unscrupulous U.S. lawyers would stop at nothing to blackmail honest companies—their actions demonstrated that they were taking the complaints seriously. Just in time for the release of DRAW 6, the company announced an expanded warranty for purchasers of the software, including free telephone technical support for ninety days from the date of purchase and thirty days from the user's first call. (Previously, registered owners were entitled only to one free fifteen-minute call, with additional calls costing two dollars per minute.) And to try to head off further criticism, Corel hired a special on-line public relations representative, Mark Lipson, whose job was to surf the Internet and private bulletin-board sites in search of unhappy Corel users. "It's important to manage that because a lot of those people, if they're responded to, they'll tone down right away, whereas if they're left on their own they can go into a real froth," Cowpland told *Marketing Computers* magazine in December 1995. Around the same time, Corel started to pay some of its beta-testers an annual stipend of $2,000, a move aimed in part at demonstrating the company's commitment to more reliable software.

While Corel rushed to placate its critics, Fishbein and his lawyer began a long and ultimately fruitless journey through the U.S. court system. Corel's U.S. attorneys fired one volley of preliminary objections after another, and gradually succeeded in whittling down the suit's original claims. Finally, in December 1997, a Pennsylvania judge threw out the suit after Fishbein himself withdrew, citing an "irreversible" falling out with his lawyers over the firm's handling of the case. In addition, Fishbein said, "I refuse to allow Corel's attorneys to further harass me, especially in light of the fact that they raised stonewalling to a new level."

Corel had won the battle, but in some ways it was losing the war. At the end of 1993, the number of CorelDRAW users worldwide surpassed one million; two years later the figure was well over three million, evidence that Cowpland's aggressive upgrade cycle had achieved its objective of pumping up sales. But in subsequent years, some of Corel's own executives concluded that the strategy had been short-sighted. In the early days of CorelDRAW, Cowpland's engineers could do no wrong in the eyes of their customers. The early-users' love of the product, and their loyalty toward the people who produced and sold it, was on a level rarely seen in the commercial world, let alone the software industry. By the mid-1990s, however, most of those warm-hearted feelings had dissipated, and Cowpland's twelve-month release schedule began to seem like an unnecessary, once-a-year gouge. These days, some of them flatly refuse to upgrade, while others routinely wait until late in the cycle to buy, knowing full well that by that point the company will have issued a maintenance release fixing most of the bugs.

Then there are the people like Susan Wimmer. Now a CD-ROM games developer in Raleigh, North Carolina, she does all of her work on a Mac and hasn't even glanced at a copy of CorelDRAW since version 4. "I designed DRAW 5 and then it was implemented by Eid, but to be honest I never really looked at the product after that—I don't even know how much of the original spec I wrote for version 5 got into the product."

Wimmer, who made several million dollars from her Corel stock options, wants it known that she is grateful to Cowpland, despite his shortcomings as a mentor. ("When I left," she recalls, "he shook my hand and said, 'Thanks, Susan, you've been a good worker,' and I thought, 'Oh brother. I would have liked to have been remembered for more than that.' But that's Mike.") Above all, Wimmer believes that Cowpland's insistence on frequent upgrades is the main reason the company grew as big as it did. Still, she is convinced that Corel's strategy backfired in later years as the market matured and software users began to care as much about reliability as they did about new features.

"I have no access to the sales figures," Wimmer says, "but I daresay it's shifted away from a high percentage of new box sales, which of course represent much more revenue, to primarily an upgrade market. So he's in a position of trying to get the bulk of the users to upgrade each year, which is a totally different game than getting people to buy it the first time. And that's where that historical, through-out-time bugginess is a real negative. Why buy the new one if the last version didn't work?"

When marketing consultant and author Geoffrey Moore talks about high-tech tornadoes, he means the sudden shifts in technology and consumer behaviour that annihilate some high-tech companies and propel others to positions of market dominance. At Corel, however, the most powerful tornado by far is Cowpland himself. Sometimes he works himself into such a frenzy that the entire enterprise is raised up and transported to some new and uncharted territory, like Dorothy in the Land of Oz. Just as frequently, the constant, unpredictable shifts in direction leave people feeling worn out and disoriented. Instead of lifting the company to new heights, he risks driving it into the ground.

That almost happened with another Corel initiative that began to gather force in the early 1990s, an ill-conceived and disastrously executed push—to call it a plan would be misleading—to diversify the company beyond its overwhelming reliance on CorelDRAW.

The reason it can't really be described as a plan is that Corel in those days didn't go in for a lot of planning. (It does now, or claims it does, mainly because companies that are losing buckets of money have to at least appear to be thinking about how they are going to turn things around.) When things were going well and money was cascading through the front door, few people felt much need to ask the boss if he knew what he was doing.

"In all my time at Corel there was no vision, no strategy, no plan," says one former executive who was fired by Cowpland in the glory years. During the first four years of its existence, he added, the board of directors never once thought to question the CEO about where he was taking the company. "Essentially the board looked upon Mike as a god. The senior management never presented a strategic plan to the board and the subject was never discussed. . . . A number of the people in senior positions knew the company wasn't being run well and that, long term, no matter how lucky we were with DRAW, we were going to be in trouble. But who on the outside would have believed that, when, for three or four years, sales were so great?"

The lack of effective supervision by the board, and Cowpland's readiness to bounce anyone in management who challenged his leadership, left him free to run the company in his own mercurial style. That wasn't always a bad thing, but it certainly made life complicated for those around him. They never knew when Cowpland would march in and announce a bold new initiative—only to reverse direction a day or two later when some equally wild and crazy scheme entered his head.

The slender thread that ran through all of these ventures was Cowpland's determination to find something that he could point to as evidence that Corel was not a one-product company. That, and a desire to boost the revenues just before the end of each fiscal quarter by shipping some new product to Corel's distributors and recording the software on its books as having been sold—a practice that finally caught up with the company in 1997, with catastrophic results.

"We were always talking expansion," says Trevor McGuire, who negotiated most of Corel's early software-licensing deals. "A lot of it was analyst-driven. People seemed hung up on what the analysts were saying about us. I always figured that if we generated earnings and increased revenues they'd be happy, but the mind-set was that we were a one-product company, so Mike always wanted to go off in these other areas."

In the beginning, Cowpland and most other people at Corel would have bet good money that the company's optical device drivers were going to take off and become a major source of revenue. The company's first few annual reports were filled with glowing references to the "exciting world market potential" for products that enabled personal computers to communicate effectively with WORM and CD-ROM drives. Hoping to grab an early lead in that market,

Cowpland's engineers produced a line of interface kits—originally called Corel Optistar, but later marketed under the names Corel-DRIVER and then Corel SCSI (pronounced "scuzzy")—that allowed as many as seven different peripheral storage devices to be connected to a single PC. In a further attempt to raise the profile of CD-ROM technology—and hence spur demand for its interface kits—Corel became one of the first major software companies to distribute its programs on CD-ROM. That same year, the company launched a product called Corel Blockbuster, which bundled the CD-ROM version of CorelDRAW with a CD-ROM drive and a Corel SCSI interface pack.

At their peak, Corel's optical disk products never contributed more than about 15 percent of sales. Cowpland's instincts were bang on when they told him CD-ROM drives were destined to become ubiquitous. Like many people, however, he misjudged the extent to which that would drive down prices and margins, particularly for small players. To make matters worse, Corel had signed a software-licensing deal with Adaptec, one of its chief competitors, in which it had promised not to sell its own line of SCSI host adaptor cards. "That board business turned out to be quite good for a lot of companies, but we decided not to go into it because it seemed like a commodity business," Cowpland recalls. "Looking back, I'm not sure if we should have backed out, because it meant that we just concentrated on the software, and then the software business didn't really grow."

In 1996, the remains of the Corel SCSI line, including a promising new software product that made it easy for PC users to create their own CD-ROMs, were sold to Adaptec for $10 million. It was an admission that Corel could never hope to achieve its goal of market leadership in that area. "One lesson I've learned and learned again is that [in the software industry] you want to go for the gorilla niche if you can, the dominant market niche," Cowpland said later, explaining his decision to get out of the device-driver business. "That's where the bulk of the money is made."

Of course, Cowpland was saying exactly the same thing back in

1992 and 1993, when the buzzword around Corel HQ was "focus." Somehow, though, the reality never lived up to the rhetoric. As the company expanded, Cowpland began steering it in a multitude of other directions, most of which made the optical products division seem like a gold mine.

The first major side project actually began as an offshoot of the original work on illustration software. During the development of CorelDRAW 1, Pat Beirne had looked into the feasibility of creating a Windows-based business presentations package that could compete against Harvard Graphics, a popular but outdated DOS application. Code-named Bullet, the product was tentatively going to be marketed under the name Corel Presents, but at the last minute Cowpland and Charlesworth decided to shelve the project to ensure a stronger focus on DRAW.

After the release of CorelDRAW 2, Corel Presents became Corel-SHOW, which was originally going to be bundled with the graphing module that Cowpland had licensed from Elmer Easton of Three D Graphics. Simultaneously, a project manager named Richard Wood-end (later one of the co-founders of Future Endeavors) led a team of engineers working on a software product for small businesses called Desk, a combination word processor, fax machine, telephone dialler and e-mail package. The market for fax software and business suites was then in its infancy, and many Corel veterans believe that Desk, which was ahead of its time in several respects, could have become a significant source of revenue for the company. Once again, however, Cowpland was concerned that the company was spreading itself too thin. In 1991, to the consternation of several developers, he pulled the plug on Desk and gave instructions for both CorelSHOW and CorelCHART to be folded into the next version of DRAW.

Not long after that, Toronto-based Delrina Corp. launched a much more limited fax software package called WinFax. It soon became a huge international success, much to the consternation of the Corel employees who had been promoting Desk. "I remember how upset Richard [Woodend] was about it at the time," Paul Chehowski says, adding that Corel "could have blown Delrina right out of the water" if Cowpland hadn't cancelled Woodend's project. "At Corel you got used to changing directions a lot. There'd be something announced— 'Okay, we're developing a Mac version of CorelDRAW'—and people would be hired and they'd be coding away and then, boom, everything would stop. We'd do a complete ninety-degree turn and head off in some other direction. And we'd say, 'Mike, what are you doing?' And yet he kept making more money, so he did prove us wrong many times." (After several such changes in direction and no end of technical glitches, Corel finally introduced a version of CorelDRAW for the Macintosh in 1996, far too late to have much of an impact.)

For his part, Mark Charlesworth defends Cowpland's decision to cancel the Desk project. "The guys had some great technology going and it looked like a very hot area, but it wasn't all coming together," he says. "This is Mike's modus operandus—to do some experiments and get stuff going, and if it's not looking good just stop and move on to something else. It's not a big bureaucracy where projects take on a life of their own and take years to kill. You can change on a dime which, really, is one of the reasons Corel became so successful."

Adds Charlesworth: "We were always looking at alternatives but eventually we said no, we'll just supercharge DRAW and make it as big as possible. That was a very strong philosophy in those days—'Let's not get involved in a whole bunch of things.' "

A year later, as if to symbolize its determination not to stray from its core products, Corel Systems Corp. dropped the "Systems" from its name. Given the competitive nature of the computer industry, Cowpland told industry analysts, it was essential that the company devote all of its energies to its two key product areas. "From now on, the Ottawa-based firm intends to be known for CorelDRAW and CorelSCSI software—and nothing else," *Computing Canada* said in October 1992.

Times change, however, and so did Cowpland's willingness to go charging off in new directions. The transition began less than a year later, at a time when Corel had more than $60 million in the bank and no debt. "We'd gone up to about $120 million in DRAW revenues but we seemed to be saturating a bit," Cowpland recalls. "And the idea was, where could we expand?"

In the summer of 1993, Cowpland found out that Xerox was hunting for someone to take Ventura off its hands. It was almost too much of a coincidence. Five years earlier, Corel's primary business had been building desktop publishing systems based on Ventura software. Since then, the product had all but vanished from the radar screen, partly because it lagged seriously behind competing desktop-publishing packages in features such as colour support and typographic control, and partly because, like CorelDRAW, each successive release was riddled with annoying bugs.

Yet Ventura still had an estimated 400,000 users across North America and Europe, many of whom were also potential customers for Corel's graphics software. Assuming he could get it at the right price—$10 million (US) was as high as he was prepared to go— Cowpland figured it was a worthwhile addition to Corel's product line. "His exact words were, 'Don't miss this one,'" says Trevor McGuire, who handled the negotiations. "I called Dave Hanna [the head of Xerox's Ventura subsidiary] and told him that Mike really wanted it, but there was no way we could go any higher than $8 million. I felt really good when Hanna accepted because I knew full well that if he said no I'd have to go back the next morning with my tail between my legs and offer $10 million. It was like a personal challenge to get it for the lowest possible price."

The deal, which closed in September 1993, gave Corel ownership of the entire Ventura product line, including the source code and related technologies. But at Corel's end, the celebrations were short-lived. Paul Skillen, who had been at the company for about a year working on CorelCHART, asked to be given responsibility for the product. It didn't take long before he discovered that Ventura was in far rougher shape than either he or Cowpland had imagined.

A few days after the sale went through, Carey Stanton, Corel's business manager, poked his head into Skillen's cubicle and introduced himself. After the two men shook hands, Stanton handed Skillen a large box full of floppy-disks. "Here," he said, "I understand this is your project." The disks, it turned out, held the source code for Ventura.

"It turned out to be a very intense project because it was an old product and we got none of the engineers from the company," Skillen recalls. "As a concept Ventura was brilliant, but they had to get it done in a real hurry so the whole thing was a hack from day one. When you're inheriting a program like that, what matters is how easy it is to keep the program up, but this one wasn't very well documented and there was a lot of sloppy coding. Plus over the years you had people patching it up and actually making things worse."

On the bright side, the engineers at Xerox had just finished working on a revision of the software—the first Windows version of the program that actually did what it was supposed to do. Wasting no time, Corel threw it together with some clip-art and a few other minor add-ons and released it in November as Corel Ventura 4.2. The reviews were lukewarm—*PC Week* noted that "ease of use is not Ventura Publisher's strong suit"—but Cowpland wasn't worried. His main objective was to begin earning some revenue from the product while Skillen and his group began working on version 5, a much more extensive rewrite of the software that Cowpland planned to bundle with CorelDRAW, thus giving Corel's graphics customers yet another reason to upgrade.

The plan made sense, but Ventura 5 quickly turned into the project from hell. Although Corel declined to hire any of Ventura's engineers, it did engage a couple of dozen contract developers who had been working for the U.S. company—one in California, a handful in England and the rest in India. Skillen immediately leased some international phone lines for $18,000 a month and set up a wide-area network so the developers could ship code back and forth to Ottawa while they were labouring on the next version. The original goal was to have the product ready in time for DRAW 5's release the following

May, but the work dragged on right through 1994, finally ending in December. During the last five months, the team worked day and night, several days a week. When things got really bad, Skillen and his engineers even resorted to using time zones in their favour, shipping bugs halfway around the world every night so they could catch a few hours sleep while someone in India or England picked up where they had left off. "We were late, so we had to put a coupon in the Corel-DRAW box and ship the product later to customers who wanted it," Skillen says. "We were a bit disappointed, but the team put in a Herculean effort."

Actually, Ventura 5 might have been released sooner had it not been for the vigilance of the beta-testers. In classic Corel fashion, the company put out a beta version of Ventura 5 in the spring of 1994 that was crawling with so many bugs even the testers threw up their hands in despair. Dan Will-Harris, the San Francisco–based desktop publishing guru, was one of the beta-testers. He was appalled by the company's cavalier attitude toward the flaws in the program. "I had never seen software as bad as that," he says. "It crashed so often it was literally unusable. And yet in the middle of all this Corel announced, 'Okay, the beta is over and we're releasing the software.' And we all said, 'You *can't* release the software—you can't *do* anything with the software.' Finally I sent an e-mail to Mike, pleading with him to try it himself. To Mike's credit, he finally did try it and he realized we were telling the truth. But I thought it was interesting that it had to get to that level before someone would listen to us."

Back in the early days of CorelDRAW, Will-Harris had been among Corel's biggest boosters. But another encounter not long after Corel's purchase of Ventura convinced him that the company had lost sight of the needs of its users. "This actually came to a head because they were making so many changes to Ventura that it was no longer a very good program for long documents," he says. "It got to the point where the beta-testers got really mad and insisted on getting together with someone from Corel. So the company set up a meeting in San Francisco and I went there with about twelve other people, many of whom had been using the program since version 1. The host was Eid Eid, who was the head of software development, and we spent two or three hours telling him how we used the software and what needed to be done to make it a useful production tool. And always his answer was, 'No, no, you're wrong—I know what's best.' " We all just sat there aghast. To me, that was the beginning of the end in terms of the software really falling apart because it seemed like they not only didn't listen to the users but almost disdained them, like they were stupid."

Whatever its flaws, Ventura was at least a logical fit with Corel's core business. The strategy behind another venture launched in 1993 was harder to understand. Corel Professional Photos was a line of almost five hundred CD-ROM titles, each featuring a hundred royalty-free stock photographs. The idea was to cash in on the exploding demand for visual images on CD-ROM by flooding the market, but once again Corel's short-sighted approach wound up costing the company sales.

Cowpland's idea was to deploy several dozen middlemen who would fan out across North America, position themselves in hotel rooms and put out a call to all of the professional photographers in each city. Typically, a middleman might pay $5,000 to anyone who brought in a hundred slides on a single topic. Then he would fly back to Ottawa and sell them to Corel for $10,000. Some of the middlemen made hundreds of thousands of dollars for their trouble.

The problem wasn't the number of photos, it was the quality. At first, the job of selecting the pictures went to Aili Kurtis, who spent hours bent over a light table with her magnifier, painstakingly examining each transparency for composition and colour balance. But when Cowpland saw what she was up to, he chided her for being too picky. After that, Cowpland himself chose most of the shots, along with Tony Davidson, the company's director of multimedia products. The photos arrived in clear plastic sheets of twenty slides per page, and often they would simply hold the sheet up to the fluorescent ceiling light in Cowpland's office and approve them all with a single glance, without bothering to remove the pictures from their sleeves so they could be properly examined. "I was horrified they were making decisions that way," Kurtis says. "The photo CDs were awful, just awful. And the worst thing was that my ads said the photos were crisp and clear and professional, and I knew that was just a bunch of crap. There was no quality control whatsoever. It was just, 'Get them out fast.'"

To save money, the company also tapped every available source of free photography it could find. One example: the disk of wedding photos even included shots of Mike Cowpland and his scantily clad bride Marlen on their wedding day. "Why not? They've already been paid for," Cowpland explained to a subordinate.

When *Macworld* magazine compared three competing brands of stock-photo CD-ROMs in August 1994, the reviewer praised the low cost and wide variety of Corel's offerings while criticizing the pictures themselves. "Most images have noticeable imperfections, and more of these photographs need color adjustment than on the other discs I reviewed."

Cowpland's approach—emphasizing quantity over quality and speed-to-market over careful product design—had been part and parcel of the Corel philosophy since CorelDRAW 3. By 1994, however, Cowpland was pushing things to the extreme.

"There was a lot of technology that was bought and never used in those days," Trevor McGuire says. "As time went on they lowered the bar and started licensing all sorts of crap. Because if you're acquiring a whole slew of products, how many good ones are you going to come across? Not a lot."

Perhaps the most egregious illustration of that was Corel's failed attempt to crack the office-suite market in 1994. According to Trevor McGuire, the project started after Cowpland, for reasons nobody seems to remember, decided to license an inexpensive spreadsheet from a group of engineers in Russia who were doing some freelance coding for Corel. "They had this spreadsheet product that was—well, let's just say it was very similar to another spreadsheet product you might see on the market," McGuire recalls. "It looked very similar to

[Microsoft] Excel. Heck, maybe it was Excel." For a while, the spread-sheet sat on the shelf while people tried to figure out what to do with it. Then Cowpland had a brainstorm: why not bundle the spreadsheet with some stripped-down versions of some of Corel's graphics products and a word processor, and pitch it as an all-in-one solution for the rapidly expanding small-office/home-office market?

Convinced he was on to a winner, Cowpland promptly licensed WordStar for Windows 2.0 from SoftKey International Inc. of Cam-bridge, Massachusetts. A well-known brand back in the days before IBM shipped its first PC, WordStar had fallen on hard times in the mid-1980s and had been given up for dead by most computer users. Cowpland, however, figured a little bit of Corel magic was all it would take to revive the one-time market leader. "We're going to rework the program and add a Corel user-interface," he cheerily told reporters that fall, promising to deliver a "high-end" product, Corel CD Office, for both the Windows 95 and IBM OS/2 platforms. Typi-cally, Cowpland hadn't bothered to discuss the idea with his own sales and marketing department. "They put a press release out at one point and everyone was going, 'What the heck is this?' " Bartsch said.

In reality, Corel CD Office was little more than a patchwork of sec-ond-rate applications—"shovelware," in computer jargon. Even Cowpland seemed to realize it wasn't good enough to go up against the major products in that segment. Just before the launch in 1995, he renamed it Corel Office Companion, the implication being that it was an add-on for owners of traditional office suites. But even that tactic didn't fool software buyers. After shipping more than half a mil-lion copies to distributors, Corel was forced to write off its invest-ment in Office Companion in the first quarter of 1996.

Another major flop was CorelCAD, a computer-aided design pack-age that Cowpland hoped would draw sales away from the number-one product in that segment, AutoCAD, produced by Autodesk Inc. of San Rafael, California. The trick would be to price Corel's entry below AutoCAD, thereby appealing to existing users as well as non-professionals who wanted to incorporate CAD in everyday applications like home renovations. The idea had merit, but Cowpland then proceeded to take the bargain-basement approach of licensing an existing, second-rate CAD program for $3 million and tweaking it slightly to give it a standard Corel interface.

Cowpland assumed that an aggressive marketing campaign would help to overcome the product's numerous shortcomings, but when the initial sales reports came back in 1996 it was clear that CorelCAD didn't stand a chance. Part of the problem, he acknowledged later, was that Corel had acquired the source code to the CAD program but had not hired any of the engineers from the company that had created it, which meant that it was difficult to make any significant improvements to the program. "It was kind of a shot in the right direction, but you have to ask yourself when you're doing that whether you've got a proven winner or just one of the also-rans," Cowpland says. "We were basically taking the low-cost approach of buying technology, but we weren't buying the winning team."

Similar problems hampered Corel's 1995 foray into the burgeoning market for multimedia CD-ROMs. Cowpland had read somewhere that Bill Gates was planning to introduce a hundred interactive titles that year as part of his new Microsoft Home initiative, so on the spur of the moment he announced that Corel would introduce fifty titles. The difference was that Microsoft had invested ten years and close to $30 million building up its Multimedia Publishing division, while Corel tried to accomplish the same thing with fewer than a dozen staff members and a budget of less than a million.

It was an impossible task, but as usual there was no one to tell Cowpland he was making a mistake. In a matter of months, Corel had licensed several dozen titles in the fields of education, entertainment and games, in each case committing to pay the authors a 15 percent royalty on sales. Included in the series were a multimedia biography of Marilyn Monroe, a movie database and collections of card, board and arcade games. By the time they appeared, however, the market was saturated with competing CD-ROMs, many of which were of substantially higher quality. "We tend to be speedy, but that one surprised us," Cowpland says. "Our first titles were the kiddie ones because they're the quickest to develop. But even they were almost obsolete when they came out because everyone else was jumping in so quickly." Company lore has it that one title, a children's electronic colouring book called "Blue Tortoise," sold seven copies worldwide.

Part of the problem was that Corel was simply trying to do too much with too little. By the end of 1995, Corel's lineup included more than forty separate products, not counting at least a dozen other projects that had been launched with great fanfare and then unceremoniously shelved. To Cowpland, it made sense to exploit Corel's existing distribution channels by jamming new products into them and seeing what sold. But the result was a parade of mediocre software, dressed up with so much hype and garish advertising that even the few truly impressive products tended to get lost in the shuffle. Meanwhile, Corel's own sales reps were focusing most of their efforts on the main CorelDRAW product line, because that was where the big margins were. "We had salespeople who never even knew Corel carried some of these products," one former executive says.

Cowpland's tendency to issue wildly unrealistic forecasts about the potential revenues from new ventures only made matters worse. In a conference call with analysts in the summer of 1995, Cowpland suggested that third-party multimedia publishing was on track to become a $50-million annual business for Corel. CorelCAD was forecast to reach a similar level in two years. (In fact, insiders say the company lost money on both projects.)

The overly ambitious marketing strategy and constant barrage of product announcements led one high-profile industry observer, Jesse Berst, editorial director of *Windows Watcher* newsletter, to label Corel "the whatchamacallit company." Added Lawrence Aragon in *PC Week*: "It's almost as though Corel forgot to take off the gloves before drawing up its new strategy. Analysts just plain can't figure it out."

Cowpland's high-pressure, turn-on-a-dime strategy also took its toll on Corel employees. Around Ottawa, stories abounded of Corel programmers who had no discernible life outside the company, who coded all day, dragged themselves home at two in the morning and then came back in at nine to pick up where they had left off.

One of the more famous examples was a software developer named Kiko Sato, who now works for Accelerix, an Ottawa company that makes silicon chips for graphics processing. "This guy was amazing," says Kevin Rheault, a former product specialist and marketing rep who worked at Corel from 1990 to 1995. "He actually used to keep a sleeping bag under his desk. He'd work all night, pull out his sleeping bag, get some sleep and then start coding again. And he wasn't the only guy who worked like that." Sato remembers spending a solid week at the office during the crunch period leading up to the release of DRAW 4. At the time, he viewed the punishing pace as a kind of personal challenge. "When I started at Corel I was working with the most talented group of people I've ever known. The funny thing is, within a year every single one of them had quit, because they were burnt out."

For many Corel workers, that kind of regimen just went with the territory. Being young and, in most cases, unattached, their social lives revolved around their jobs. When they weren't glued to their computer monitors they were often playing softball or volleyball with friends from work. To keep people motivated and in high spirits, Cowpland set up a committee he called the Fun Squad, which met once a week to organize parties, picnics and regular outings after work. Largely because of those events, the high-tech community in Ottawa is now littered with married couples who met while working at Corel. "The spirit was unbelievable," Rheault says. "Part of it was the team atmosphere and the fact that Corel hires a lot of people right out of school and gives them tons of responsibility and freedom. . . . Eventually I got let go, because the turnover is unbelievable, too, but I wouldn't trade it for anything. It was a great experience."

Kiko Sato, too, has fond memories of his time at Corel, particularly the period he spent working under the direction of Susan Wimmer. "The people who reported to her felt a powerful sense of loyal devotion," he says. "Susan was a visionary, and because of that she had an ability to get an incredible amount of work out of the people below her. It wasn't the same after she left. Eid Eid was really more of a taskmaster. He didn't have that vision of the product, and neither did Mike."

As time went on, Cowpland's unforgiving pace and frequent shifts in direction took an increasing toll. Employees either learned to roll with the punches or found themselves looking for new jobs. "Cowpland summed it up at a press conference once when he said he wasn't disturbed about the turnover as long as people kept applying," says Greg Owens, a former documentation manager for CorelDRAW. "As long as he has a supply of fresh meat, he doesn't care."

Owens, who grew up in Ajax, Ontario, and studied political science at university, was twenty-five when he started at Corel. Before that, he earned minimum wage at an Ottawa consulting company that churned out corporate reports and user manuals for several high-tech companies. In many ways he is typical of the twentysomething microserfs who pass through Corel on their way to more stable careers at other companies. "For the most part I enjoyed the job, not because I was at Corel but because of the people it attracted," he says. "The average age was about twenty-five when I started. Most people had been out of school three or four years and weren't really sure what they wanted to do. It was a really good group of people, very social. And when you work that hard you tend to get close to people. You'd work non-stop for about seventy hours a week for two or three months before the product went out, and then you'd have two months without much to do—sort of compensation for what you'd done. Then the cycle would start up again and you'd start getting into the longer hours again. It all depended on what you did—some people were always on overtime mode."

During his three years at Corel, Owens's salary jumped from $34,000 to almost $60,000, in part because "every time you made noises about leaving they'd just dish out more cash." He made another $8,000 in total from stock options. But in spite of the money and the myriad little perks—free tennis club membership, Nintendo machines in the staff lounges and catered meals when his team was working late—Owens eventually became fed up with the long hours and constant turnover. In mid-1997 he quit to take a similar but lower-paying job at Northern Telecom. "I went to Nortel for a 10 percent pay cut, no stock options and I took a demotion. I'm just a writer now where before I was a team leader. And I don't care. I don't work overtime and I don't have to deal with the headaches."

Then there were the people who were run so ragged they either collapsed on the job, suffered a nervous breakdown or found themselves on the brink of divorce. The Corel culture demands total commitment to the company. If an employee feels torn between his or her job and family relationships, sooner or later there is bound to be trouble, particularly if that person is unlucky enough to be assigned to a project that Cowpland has declared to be a top priority.

Typically, these are what are known in the high-tech industry as "death march" projects—projects that seem doomed to fail because of impossibly aggressive timetables, ridiculously tight budgets or because the project manager, desperate to impress his or her superiors, promises more than mere mortals can deliver. Death march projects occur at every software company, but at Corel they are the normal state of affairs, simply because Mike Cowpland wouldn't have it any other way. Like Bill Gates, the Corel CEO firmly believes that nothing worth achieving in life can be accomplished by working eight hours a day. "The analogy I like is that when people train for the Iron Man competition in Hawaii they've got to torture their bodies for twelve hours a day and most of them don't even get a prize," Cowpland says. "But it's a challenge. Some people like a challenge, and if you provide a good team-working environment there's nothing more enjoyable."

Self-serving though that rationale may be, Cowpland is right: many software developers do enjoy the intensity of death march projects. The problem is that, even at a company as notoriously chaotic and deadline-driven as Corel, there are some people who have no desire to participate in Iron Man competitions. They'd much rather settle for a job, a paycheque and a realistic challenge.

Josh Korn fell into the latter category. An Australian-born engineer, married with two young boys, he was working for another software company in Ottawa in 1984 when that firm ran into financial trouble and closed its doors. Intrigued by a newspaper article that portrayed Corel as an innovative, exciting place to work, Korn went for an interview and met Pat Beirne. Beirne was impressed with Korn's engineering skills and immediately drafted him for his most recent pet project, a proposed desktop video-conferencing system that soon became known as CorelVIDEO.

CorelVIDEO proved to be an expensive dud, but it started out hopefully enough. In the early 1990s, Pat Beirne's younger brother, Garry, was the senior research associate and director of field studies for the Ontario Telepresence Project, a three-year government-sponsored consortium that was studying the use of advanced computer and telecommunications technologies "to support collaborative work between geographically separated individuals." In everyday language, that meant two-way video communication in the workplace, an idea that has been floating around for decades but has never caught on—in part because of privacy concerns and in part because, in the real world, nobody can figure out why they would possibly need it.

In any event, Garry Beirne told Pat Beirne what he was up to and Pat Beirne told Mike Cowpland. In a flash, Cowpland decided that video-conferencing was the Next Big Thing. He signed Corel up as an industrial partner of the Telepresence Project and asked Pat Beirne to put together a prototype.

That was in January 1994. On May 3, Corel issued a press release vowing to become "the world's first company to implement video on every desk by the end of 1994."

For the first six months or so, the project operated as what engineers call a skunk works—a small, loosely structured unit formed to encourage innovation. (The term originated in the 1950s with a legendary group of aerospace engineers at Lockheed Corp., whose research facility was frequently subjected to the overwhelming stench of burning plastic from a nearby factory.) There was a positive, good-natured spirit about the enterprise. Beirne worked mainly on the hardware, along with an engineer named Rick Hill. Korn led the software team, a diverse band of programmers from Iran, Bulgaria, Poland, Romania and Hong Kong. On one particularly glorious day in December 1994, the team actually managed to make its first end-to-end call—an achievement no less momentous for the fact that the two PCs happened to be sitting next to each other on a desk. It looked as if things were beginning to come together, although Korn and most of the others assumed it would be years before the technology would actually be ready for commercial rollout. There were still plenty of unsolved technical problems, not to mention the fact that nobody at the company had yet established that there was a market for the system.

The research probably would have continued at that pace for at least another year were it not for two things. First, Cowpland was getting desperate to find another "killer app" that he could wave in front of the investment community as proof that Corel was more than just CorelDRAW and a motley collection of recycled software and budget CD-ROMs. Second, the CorelVIDEO product manager, a woman named Trudy Eisele, had made the mistake of presenting her boss with an overly ambitious list of proposed features. Among the promised goodies was an electronic phone book composed of thumbnail images of every person on the network. To put in a call to someone, all you had to do was click on his or her picture. Cowpland thought it was a brilliant idea and decided to push it even further. Rather than photos of the people on the system, he wanted the menu to display freeze-frame video shots of their offices, updated automatically every two minutes. That way, people who worked in groups would be able to check up on one another's whereabouts just by glancing at the screen.

Cowpland was so enthused that he scheduled a press unveiling for March 1995, ignoring the fact that the hardware still didn't behave reliably over long distances and the system was vulnerable to noise and distortion. In addition, the engineers couldn't figure out how to make the freeze-frame technology work properly without causing the entire network to crash. Even if it did work, there was the obvious question of whether people would actually want their employers to be able to keep tabs on them by means of a strategically placed video camera.

None of that mattered, however, because Cowpland wanted his video-conferencing system and he wanted it fast. All through January, February and most of March, the engineers worked seven days a week, usually until one or two in the morning, surviving on take-out pizza and Chinese food. Once, on his way home from work, Korn bumped into a friend on the bus. The friend assumed Korn was heading into the office because the time was 6:15 in the morning.

After three months of killer hours, the system still could not be made to work as planned. The press preview, for which twenty journalists were scheduled to be flown in from around the world, was first postponed and then cancelled to avoid a major embarrassment. In its place, Corel decided to invite a reporter from *The Ottawa Citizen* to view the product, a demonstration that almost blew up in the company's face when the technicians had a hard time getting the system to function. "There's the odd glitch in the video and the network crashes occasionally," the paper reported. "Overall, the broadcast quality is good for a developing product that was conceived only a year ago."

A couple of weeks later, Corel showed the system to columnist Bob Metcalfe of *InfoWorld* magazine, who in the 1980s had invented Ethernet, the most popular technology to enable computers to communicate with one another. This time, Cowpland couldn't resist piling on the hype. He promised that Corel's system would be ready to ship by the time of the next CorelDRAW gala in August—a suitable kickoff for a product Cowpland was claiming would soon be bigger than CorelDRAW itself.

Facing another impossible deadline, the engineers continued to work long hours through the spring and summer. But regardless of what they did, they couldn't get the system to work properly beyond the confines of a single building. It was fine as long as everyone on the system was hooked up to the same local area network, but whenever the signals were transmitted between buildings the video quality became unacceptably poor. Either that, or there was no signal at all.

"It looked fairly cool in small demonstrations, and there was a sense that something major was about to happen, but it didn't," says Korn. "When it was formally unveiled [in August] there was a lot of hype, but the first thing our customers said was that they wanted to be able to go beyond one building. That was a rather rude awakening because it meant, basically, we had nothing to sell."

Immediately after the unveiling, Korn's manager tried to enlist him for another three-month blitz in order to work out the remaining bugs. Around Corel, the process of drafting engineers for such projects is called a sign-up.

"A sign-up means you have to get so much work done in a certain period of time, and it's going to require working around the clock. It means, 'Are you in it, come hell or high water?'"

This time, Korn wasn't. All those late nights and weekends had taken an enormous toll on his wife and children. He was convinced that if he kept working at Corel's punishing pace, his and his family's mental health would be seriously harmed. "What I told them, and it was true, was that my family had basically disintegrated because of the long hours," Korn says. "I simply couldn't do it any more." On August 21, a day after he told his supervisor that he would be unable to continue working so much overtime, he was fired for refusing an assignment and given three weeks' severance pay, the minimum under the law. "Nobody cared in the slightest about my situation. They were completely callous about it."

The abrupt manner of his departure left him seething with anger. A month after leaving the company, he sent a registered letter to Corel's human resources manager, Sandra Gibson, demanding to be paid for all of the undocumented overtime he had worked between

January 1, 1985, and the date of his firing. When the company resisted, his lawyer, Denise Workun, filed a claim for compensation with the Employment Standards Branch of Ontario's Ministry of Labour. The claim was supported by internal Corel records showing, as Workun put it in a letter to the branch, that Korn "had an excellent performance record, that Corel actively pressured its employees to work long hours both at home and at work, and that the deadlines imposed by Corel could only be met by working an extensive number of overtime hours."

For more than a year, Corel fought to have Korn's complaint dismissed, arguing that the onus of proof fell on each employee to keep a detailed log backing up any claim for overtime pay. On January 21, 1997, however, an adjudicator rejected that position, saying it was the company's legal responsibility to maintain records for each member of staff. In a tersely worded, two-page decision, employment standards officer Karen Perkio-Bryans ordered Corel to honour the full amount of Korn's claim—a total of 404 hours of overtime and statutory holiday pay, worth $30,758.77.

"I've been in the software industry for twenty years and Corel is not like any other company," says Korn, who now works for Simware, the company founded by John McFetridge. "At Simware, the products are the commodities and the people are the assets. At Corel it's the other way around."

Chapter Thirteen

One cold winter morning in 1988, Mike Cowpland was driving his Chevrolet Corvette toward Ottawa from Kanata. Barrelling down a long hill on the Queensway, the car struck a patch of black ice and Cowpland lost control. The rear-wheel-drive Corvette spun around once and hurtled nose-first off the right shoulder of the highway, toward a fence consisting of three thick steel cables stretched tightly between heavy wooden posts. As luck would have it, the front end of the Corvette was so low it slipped underneath the guard wires, and the car continued to plow forward at high speed. Cowpland somehow managed to duck just in time to avoid being decapitated as the cables came ripping up the hood of the car, slammed into the windshield and tore off the pillars and roof as cleanly and efficiently as a giant can-opener.

The car was a total write-off. For an instant, Cowpland assumed he was, too. When it finally dawned on him that he was alive and unscathed, he clambered out of the wreckage, waited for the police to show up and then hitched a ride to the office.

By the time he got there, the Corel CEO was late for a meeting. Yet he didn't utter so much as a word about the accident. When someone asked what had taken him so long, Cowpland merely smiled and shrugged.

"I had a bit of car trouble," he said.

Cowpland tells that story to explain why he switched from Corvettes, his favourite brand of sports car during the 1980s, to an all-wheel-drive Porsche 911 Carrera, which, in addition to its numerous other attributes, happens to be much better suited to the snow and ice of an Ottawa winter. But Cowpland's refusal to let a near-fatal car crash spoil his day also fits in perfectly with the image he likes to project to the world: that of the fearless, high-octane businessman who stays cool and collected in situations that would reduce any halfway normal person to a quivering wreck. The 007 of software, if you will— neither shaken nor stirred.

At times it might seem like an act, but then Cowpland goes ahead and does something so outlandish that it proves he's either off his rocker or has nerves of steel. Such as? Well, such as buying Word-Perfect for $170 million and proclaiming to the world that he's out to crush the undisputed king of the software business, Microsoft supremo Bill Gates.

Risky isn't the word for it. At the time of the WordPerfect takeover in January 1996, Microsoft's annual revenues were thirty times greater than Corel's. According to the high-tech research firm International Data Corp., WordPerfect's share of the $3-billion Windows office-suite market was an embarrassing 5 percent, its sales having fallen by at least two-thirds in the previous two years. Even if Gates wasn't the richest man on the planet and one of the most focused and aggressive competitors in the history of capitalism, the idea that Corel was going to beat Microsoft at its own game would have seemed so far-fetched as to be unworthy of consideration. There was no way on earth Microsoft was going to let Corel overtake it in one of the software industry's most profitable product niches, as anybody who had even the slightest understanding of the business already knew.

Except Mike Cowpland. The Corel CEO, as one former colleague puts it, "doesn't know what he doesn't know." Sometimes that's a good thing. Back in 1987, common sense would have said there wasn't a chance in hell that an Ottawa-based systems integrator with fewer than fifty employees was going to outgun an established giant like Adobe in the PC graphics market. When Cowpland turns out to be right, his obstinate refusal to listen to common sense looks like sheer genius. When he's wrong, he quickly puts it out of his mind and marches on to the next great technological battleground. No excuses, no regrets.

Cowpland's unwillingness to consider the possibility of failure is both his greatest strength and his biggest weakness. The WordPerfect acquisition illustrates both sides of that equation. How it will eventually play out is still unclear, but people who owned stock in Corel at the time of the transaction can be forgiven for wishing it had never happened.

It wasn't that WordPerfect, the software, wasn't very good, because it was. The real problem was that WordPerfect, the company, had grown fat and complacent after more than a decade at the top of the PC word-processor market. When the market began to shift, the company mistakenly assumed it was strong enough to hold back the tide. Its own history should have taught it the folly of trying to dictate changes in customer buying habits, but like a lot of once-proud software producers, WordPerfect chose to ignore the lessons of the past and wound up paying a heavy price.

The WordPerfect story begins back in the mid-1970s, when a computer science professor at Brigham Young University in Salt Lake City named Alan Ashton hooked up an organ to a computer in order to analyse the linear structure of music. In the process of doing that research, he realized that the file-management structure he had developed might have other uses, perhaps as the basis of a word-processing system. Hoping to make some money on the side to support his wife and rapidly growing family, he spent the summer of 1977 designing a word-processing program that boasted a number of innovative features, including the ability to scroll through a document rather than viewing only one page at a time and the elimination of different modes for typing. (Earlier word processors had a "create" mode, for typing new text at the end of a document, an "edit" mode, for making changes to existing text, and an "insert" mode, for adding text in the middle of a document without erasing what was already there.)

To help him write the program, Ashton enlisted a promising master's student named Bruce Bastian, the director of the BYU marching band, who was working on a 3-D graphics application to choreograph the band's step-by-step formations around a football field. It took them two years to complete the word processor, during which time they formed their own company, calling it Satellite Systems Inc. because they liked the sound of SSI. Together they improved and expanded Ashton's original design, to the point where they were selling two or three copies a month. "When we made a sale, we got to eat that evening," says Bastian, who was so hard up he had to borrow money from his father to continue working full-time on the project.

At first, Ashton's and Bastian's word processor could run only on Data General minicomputers, because that was the machine they had access to when they were writing the program. Early on, however, they resolved to create versions for a wide variety of computing platforms, to provide superior customer support and to pay close attention to the comments of secretaries and others who used the application. By 1982, WordPerfect had become an underground hit, with sales cracking the $1-million mark. Ashton and Bastian were delighted, since all they had really wanted to do was earn a few thousand dollars a month to supplement their academic incomes.

Their big break, however, came two years later. Up to that point, the dominant word-processing program had been WordStar, introduced in 1979 by MicroPro. But at Comdex in 1984, MicroPro shot itself in the foot by introducing an entirely new program called WordStar 2000. WordStar 2000 was bigger, better and used a nicer interface than its best-selling predecessor, but it had one major flaw: its file format was incompatible with that of the previous version. The result was that millions of existing WordStar users were forced to choose a replacement, and while some chose WordStar 2000, many others shopped around and settled for one of the competing products. As often as not, they bought WordPerfect, which was superior to WordStar 2000 in several respects and seemed to have more momentum than the other products in the category. A glowing review in *InfoWorld* that year was the crowning glory, helping to push sales of WordPerfect to $29 million.

Before long, WordPerfect supplanted WordStar as the top-selling DOS word processor. Under the day-to-day leadership of W.E. (Pete) Peterson, Bastian's brother-in-law and the former manager of his family's small drapery business, WordPerfect Corp. (the company changed its name in 1986 to avoid confusion with Utah's growing community of aerospace contractors) became one of the world's fastest-growing companies, doubling its revenues every year during the 1980s. By 1991, sales stood at $622 million, and the installed base of users was 15 million, earning it the distinction of being the world's most widely used PC application.

Along the way, however, WordPerfect fell victim to its own success. It was making so much money from DOS software that it tried to resist the growing pressure to rewrite its product for Windows. Convinced that Microsoft would have an unfair advantage in creating applications for Windows, WordPerfect instead threw its support behind OS/2, a rival interface from IBM. In effect, Peterson and his colleagues were betting that their refusal to introduce a Windows version would convince the market to adopt OS/2 instead. The strategy failed, and by the time WordPerfect finally got around to launching its Windows version, in early 1992, Gates already had a two-year head start with Microsoft Word. To make matters worse, the first release of WordPerfect for Windows was slow and somewhat buggy, giving rise to lukewarm reviews.

"The mistake was that we didn't put our best people on Windows from the start," recalls Peterson, the company's former executive vice-president. "We were so successful in the DOS market that a lot of people didn't see the urgency. We felt that if Windows won out, Microsoft was going to be in a very powerful position, and so as a company we threw our support behind IBM because we felt we'd be in a better position if OS/2 were successful. I mean, you have to play the cards you're dealt, and we did not want to bet on Microsoft."

WordPerfect's other big problem was its nice-guy corporate culture. While Microsoft fought tenaciously for every percentage point of market share, Ashton and Bastian, both Mormons, always felt uncomfortable bragging about their products or attacking competitors. They ran their company on a foundation of strict Christian principles, to the point, in the early days, of sometimes quoting Scripture during meetings. "They saw themselves as an honest, hardworking, and great service company, and thought people would be automatically drawn to it," Dan Lunt, the company's former vice-president of marketing, said in 1993. Ashton, who banned liquor and cigarettes from WordPerfect's hospitality suites at trade shows, liked to say that the company's "clean work environment adds to health and vitality."

Perhaps it did, but another result of WordPerfect's paternalistic culture was a conservative and somewhat lackadaisical management style. Job security was all but guaranteed, overtime was frowned upon, and employees enjoyed salaries that were well above the industry norm. "Many people work 8:30 a.m. to 5 p.m., then bolt home to their families," an amazed reporter from PC Week wrote in early 1994 after visiting WordPerfect's headquarters in Orem, Utah, half an hour south of Salt Lake City. "It's as though the company had been preserved in a time capsule from the comfortable 1950s." Unlike Gates—or, for that matter, Mike Cowpland—Ashton hated to see his employees spend so much time at the office that they neglected their families. "We want them to work wisely and hard," he said in 1992, explaining his earlier decision to postpone the introduction of WordPerfect for Macintosh because of the toll it was taking on the developers. "If they spend too much time on something, they can burn out."

Things began to change after WordPerfect's disastrous attempt to resist the Windows onslaught, but the new strategy only seemed to make matters worse. The first person to be pushed out was Peterson, who had alienated many insiders with his attempts to conserve marketing dollars and put more resources into product development— not to mention his strategy of ignoring Windows. Ashton and Bastian then brought in a professional sales and marketing manager, Adrian Rietveld, who set about trying to transform the company into a leaner and more aggressive competitor. Rietveld's efforts to slash spending included everything from cutting out unlimited free tech support for WordPerfect users to abandoning the company's long-standing policy of providing complimentary soft drinks to employees.

None of those efforts, however, addressed WordPerfect's most serious shortcoming: the absence of a product suite to compete against Microsoft Office, which by 1993 accounted for 60 percent of Microsoft's Word sales. WordPerfect had toyed with the notion of selling its own spreadsheet, database and presentations package as early as 1990, but Peterson and others shot down the idea, insisting that suites were just a price-cutting gimmick. "The ultimate legacy of Pete Peterson's reign at WordPerfect is that he left the company without an applications suite, a situation which is today sapping the company of its strength," editor David Coursey wrote in the April 1993 edition of *PC Letter*, an industry newsletter. Eventually WordPerfect did manage to cobble together an office suite, but only by forming a partnership with another large software producer, Borland International, which produced a spreadsheet called Quattro Pro. The product, marketed under the name Borland Office, was nowhere near as tightly integrated as Microsoft's offering, forcing owners to become familiar with a different set of tools and a different user manual for each application. In 1993, Borland Office sold 167,000 copies worldwide, compared with 244,000 copies of Lotus Development's SmartSuite and 1.9 million copies of Microsoft Office.

On January 1, 1994, Rietveld took over from Ashton as Word-Perfect's CEO, determined to reduce the company's bloated payroll of five thousand employees and to launch a more aggressive campaign of product development in the office software suite market. He also moved firmly to quash speculation about a possible merger with either Borland or one of its Utah neighbours, Novell Corp., the leader in PC office networking software. "A merger's not on my agenda," Rietveld told reporters, adding that WordPerfect was well positioned to succeed on its own.

But Ashton and Bastian, each of whom still owned 49.9 percent of the company, clearly felt otherwise. The two men had always taken pride in WordPerfect's image as one big happy family, and neither had any desire to preside over the massive layoffs and top-to-bottom restructuring that would be necessary to transform it into a disciplined, numbers-oriented company. Only three months after installing Rietveld in the chief executive's office, they turned around and sold the company to Novell for $850 million. For good measure, Novell also bought Borland's Quattro Pro for $150 million. Novell chief executive Ray Noorda was itching to take a run at Microsoft, and figured that his company's expertise with office computer networks (also known as local-area networks, or LANs), allied with WordPerfect's strength in word processing, would be an unbeatable combination.

It didn't turn out that way. For one thing, Noorda retired as CEO shortly after the purchase, leaving Novell in the hands of a bunch of senior managers who weren't anywhere near as enthusiastic about the prospect of challenging Bill Gates. Early on, the company made a huge mistake by announcing that it would no longer upgrade WordPerfect's DOS word-processing software, a decision that forced millions of veteran users to switch over to Microsoft. Even worse, Novell had no experience at selling software to consumers. Its networking software had always been aimed at business users and distributed through resellers rather than retail stores, which put Novell at a distinct disadvantage when it came to trying to out-market Microsoft. As a result, sales of WordPerfect and PerfectOffice, the new name given to the suite, dropped like a stone. "There was no real leverage there," explained Jeff Waxman, executive vice-president of Novell's applications group. "The customer never bought the idea that the networking vendor would have better applications because they would be network-enabled"—in other words, simply because they would be customized for network use. Added Waxman: "We sell infrastructure —the wiring, the plumbing—not shrink-wrapped stuff."

Indeed, the marriage of Novell and WordPerfect was troubled from the start. The company tried to save money by merging the sales and marketing forces of the two operations, which led to a clash of cultures and a dramatic drop in employee morale. "We felt strongly about that, including having our own sales and marketing force," David Moon, former vice-president of development at WordPerfect, told *The Deseret News*, one of Salt Lake City's two daily newspapers. Moon was one of several senior managers who argued in vain to have the division split off as a separate business unit. "The fact that there was less support within Novell for the original merger than we thought was disappointing and led to distrust," he said. Other employees complained of feeling like unwanted stepchildren, to the point where workers from Novell's networking and business applications divisions were getting different Christmas bonus cheques and pay increases.

One incident seemed to symbolize the strained relations between the two sides. During a meeting with a large group of WordPerfect developers, a senior executive of Novell stood up and declared herself a devoted fan of the product, adding that she and her family used the Macintosh version of PerfectOffice at home. In reality, no such version existed. "For some people, that was the last straw," says one Word-Perfect manager. "We knew darn well that upper management did not have a clue what we were doing. And what's more, they obviously didn't care."

Novell's executives were in no mood to listen, in part because WordPerfect was not the company's only problem. Its core networking program, Netware, was also losing market share to Microsoft's new networking product, Windows NT. Novell's new CEO, Bob Frankenberg, clearly considered the task of revitalizing Netware to be a much higher priority than salvaging WordPerfect.

After eighteen months of heavy losses, Frankenberg threw in the towel. On October 30, 1995, he announced that Novell was looking to dump its entire business applications division, saying sales of the products had not lived up to expectations, and that Novell was already talking to several "mystery suitors" in hopes of completing a sale by January. The reaction from investors was immediate. On the day of the announcement, Novell's stock rose $1.25 to $16.13. "This is the right thing for them to do," said Amy Wohl of Wohl & Associates, a computer industry research firm. "Could you turn [WordPerfect] around? Probably. Could you turn it around in a couple quarters? I don't think so."

Frankenberg's comment about "mystery suitors" naturally gave rise to a great deal of speculation. Some analysts thought IBM was the logical best fit, while others placed bets on Computer Associates, an Islandia, New York–based software giant that had a history of buying up other companies' castoff products and restoring them to profitability. Still others speculated that a financial firm might try to buy WordPerfect with the aim of whipping it into shape for a share offering a year or two down the road.

It didn't occur to anyone that Corel might be interested in making a bid. As recently as that summer, Cowpland had told *Maclean's* magazine that he wasn't the slightest bit interested in taking on some other software company's problems, since it was easier and far cheaper simply to buy the source code. Besides, he said, word processors were low-growth products compared to things like video-conferencing systems and multimedia CD-ROMs. Corel already had WordStar and Ventura—what more did it need?

To anyone who didn't know Mike Cowpland, that seemed to settle it. To those who did, Cowpland's professed lack of interest in takeovers was about as meaningful as a child's wide-eyed promise not to raid the cookie jar when mom and dad aren't looking.

One of the reasons Cowpland changed his mind was that WordStar was proving to be much more of a problem that he or anyone else had bargained for. Paul Skillen had assumed responsibility for the project after completing his work on Ventura. He joked among co-workers that his unofficial job title was Demolition Man—the unlucky person whom Corel called on whenever it licensed some clapped-out piece of software that was in desperate need of renewal.

"Actually, the WordStar code was not in nearly as bad shape as Ventura, so for a while we were hopeful," Skillen says. "We still wanted to get into the business [applications] market, so I was given the job of trying to revive it. In four months I hired almost a hundred people to work on the team. After six months we started realizing that, yes, we were getting somewhere, but no matter what we did we were still going to come in late with a product that was weaker than the competition."

Corel Office Companion finally went on sale in May 1995. Coincidentally, only a few months later Bob Frankenberg put WordPerfect on the market.

At first glance, the idea that Corel might be big enough to swallow the Utah-based word-processing giant would have struck most people as ludicrous. As successful as it was, Corel was just coming off a year in which its sales hit a record of only $196 million. WordPerfect, on the other hand, had done $600 million in sales as recently as 1991. Even after several years of drift and mismanagement, it was still a far larger company than Corel, with three times as many employees and an installed base of 20 million users, compared to fewer than 3 million for CorelDRAW.

What few people outside Novell knew was that Frankenberg was getting desperate. The speculation about IBM and Computer Associates wasn't far-fetched: representatives of both companies had flown in to Orem to have a look around. IBM, however, decided to pass, in part because it was still in the process of completing a hostile $3.5-billion takeover of Lotus Development. The intentions of Computer Associates were less clear, but even if the company had tendered an offer for WordPerfect it is doubtful whether Novell would have accepted it. CA's modus operandi in such cases was generally to slash spending to the bone by cancelling all new development activity and refusing to invest any more money than was absolutely necessary to retain a core base of existing users. Novell knew that if that happened, many of its networking customers—those who also depended on WordPerfect—would be furious, and they would blame Novell for allowing the once-proud product to fall into the wrong hands. In addition, Novell was worried that its reputation in Utah's political circles would suffer if the vast majority of WordPerfect's engineers suddenly found themselves out of work.

Another rumoured bidder was Bain Capital, a Boston investment company with interests in several technology companies. But it, too, seemed less interested in preserving WordPerfect than in turning it around for a quick profit.

What it came down to was that Novell was trapped. It couldn't just shop around for the best offer for WordPerfect; it had to make sure that the product went to a good home. Whoever purchased the company would have to commit to continue development of the software and would have to agree to take many, if not all, of the employees. It would also have to be capable of providing ongoing customer support to WordPerfect's existing users. "Novell was a massive company and the sale was really just a rounding error for them, but they were very, very concerned about their reputation," said one person who was familiar with the company's thinking. "Financially they knew they were going to take a bath no matter what happened, so it was the right thing to do to preserve the image of the company."

By December, Novell's investment bankers at Morgan Stanley were running out of options. That's when George Boutros, one of the firm's San Francisco–based senior partners, picked up the telephone and called Cowpland. He knew that Corel had plenty of money in the bank, no debt and aspirations to become a player in the lucrative market for business applications.

At first the talks went nowhere. Boutros told Cowpland that Novell wanted something approaching $500 million for WordPerfect—equivalent, he said, to a year's worth of revenues at the current rate of sales. Cowpland did a quick back-of-the-envelope calculation and decided that was too rich for his blood. He also flew the idea past his board of directors. Joe Cohen, a Wall Street investment banker who had joined the board in May 1993 and had loads of experience in such matters, felt strongly that the price was too high. Cowpland's answer to Boutros was blunt: thanks but no thanks.

Then something happened to make Cowpland rethink his position. At the same time that Novell was hunting for someone to take WordPerfect off its hands, SoftKey International, of Cambridge,

Massachusetts, negotiated a takeover of children's software maker The Learning Company, for which it paid $606 million cash and $470 million in stock. Plus, SoftKey dished out another $106 million in stock for another educational software producer, Compton's New Media Inc. Most analysts accused SoftKey of paying too much, but others said the acquisitions made sense in view of the company's long-term strategy to establish itself as one of a handful of international software giants. "The home computer market is going global," said Richard Zwetchkenbaum, director of brand research at International Data Corp. in Framingham, Massachusetts. "Distribution-oriented companies like SoftKey . . . realize there's only so much property out there, and they go out and get the good ones."

To Cowpland, there was something to that argument. The software industry *was* entering a period of consolidation, at the end of which there would likely be only a handful of major players. The same kind of process had taken place earlier in the century in the North American car, consumer electronics and fast food industries. In each case, what distinguished the giants from everyone else was the quality of their brands. And in software, WordPerfect was right up there with the best in terms of worldwide recognition, arguably second only to Microsoft.

On a more pragmatic level, Cowpland was struck by the fact that The Learning Company and Compton's had about $150 million in combined revenues. SoftKey, in other words, was paying roughly eight times annual sales for the two companies. "When I saw that, it did get the wheels spinning," Cowpland says. "I thought, 'Hmmm, that's amazing. Maybe I'm missing something here.' Frankly, it made WordPerfect seem not that expensive, because supposedly they were talking about a price of one-times sales. We weren't in the habit of buying companies so I wasn't really in that frame of mind, but I thought maybe I should keep an open mind here. So I gave it more serious thought and bounced it around again with the board members."

By mid-December, Cowpland was sufficiently intrigued that he decided to send a team of three Corel managers down to Orem to take a closer look. The scouting party consisted of software director Eid Eid, business manager Carey Stanton and Lisa Kenkel, Corel's in-house lawyer. Kenkel, who had been with the company since March 1993, understood better than most how Cowpland's mind worked. She knew that he was still desperate to prove Corel was more than a one-product company.

"We'd gone through the experience of trying to do multimedia products, trying to do the peripheral stuff, even trying to do a whole office suite on our own by licensing WordStar and other non-best-of-breed applications, to put it kindly," Kenkel says. "We'd gone down that path and tried different things and finally pulled back because that just wasn't going to be competitive. So the choice was to either start again from scratch or do it by acquisition. To do a huge chunk of revenue from scratch is always extremely difficult. And to do it by acquisition—how many times are you presented with a target company that happens to be available and has that much revenue associated with it? That doesn't come along every day, so when it does you have to take a very hard look at it."

There was no question Cowpland was interested—the only issue was the price. He had no real problem with paying an amount equivalent to the company's annual revenues, or "one-times sales," but what exactly was the current level of sales? The closer he looked at the numbers in Morgan Stanley's deal binder, the more uncomfortable he became with Novell's figure of between $400 and $500 million. In reality, the sales in the most recent quarter were only about $50 million, and falling fast. Everything seemed to hinge on Novell's prediction that revenues would rebound sharply as soon as WordPerfect released version 7, the first version designed specifically to take advantage of Windows 95. Version 7 was due to go on sale in April, but in the meantime WordPerfect was losing valuable market share to Microsoft, which had released a Windows 95 version of its suite months earlier. It was anybody's guess as to whether WordPerfect would ever be able to regain that business. If it couldn't, WordPerfect was at best a $250-million business, maybe less.

The issue came to a head during a two-hour conference call on December 27 involving representatives of Corel, Novell and Morgan Stanley. Cowpland, who was spending Christmas and New Year's at his beachfront home in Boca Raton, started off by telling Boutros that he was ready to make a deal, but not at the asking price. Boutros responded that Novell would never consider selling WordPerfect for less than one-times sales, and according to their calculations that was at least $400 million.

Cowpland wasn't getting anywhere with Boutros so he turned his attention to one of the other Novell people on the line, Glen Mella, general manager of the applications group. Mella, Waxman's second in command, was the least senior Novell person involved in the talks, but he actually knew more about the division's finances than anyone else.

"It was one of those cases where everyone was talking and not getting anywhere, and then all of a sudden Mike just focused in on the issue," Kenkel recalls, still marvelling at her boss's persistence. "He started asking very, very specific questions on the current sales levels, the returns and all that sort of stuff. It was like this beautiful cross-examination, you know? He knew where he wanted to end up and he was talking fast, with this sense of urgency that comes through even over the telephone. Meanwhile the other guy was sounding weak and vague, and Mike obviously sensed that because he just kept going. Every time the fellow from WordPerfect said something that was inconsistent or hedged a little, Mike was right on top of him. He just kept grilling him and got him to admit it was basically a $50-million-a-quarter business, and who knows what the future would hold? After that, there was dead silence from their end. It was hilarious."

The call had gone well from Corel's perspective, but Boutros still wasn't budging, so there was no point in talking any further. "I said, it's clearly not selling $400 million, so thanks and goodbye," Cowpland recalls.

That probably would have been the end of it had not Jeff Waxman called a few days later to plead with Cowpland to reconsider. Waxman was a twenty-five-year veteran of the computing industry who had been hired by Novell only seven months earlier to replace Adrian Rietveld as head of the business applications group. An outsider at Novell, he had been brought in for the specific purpose of handling the sale. (Waxman left the company in November 1996 and now runs Secure Computing Corp., a network security firm based in St. Paul, Minnesota.) The fact that he had not been part of the original decision to buy the company, and had no real emotional stake in its sale, made him, from Cowpland's point of view, the one person at Novell he could deal with openly and directly.

Waxman's take on WordPerfect was simple: the company had been so poorly managed and was so overstaffed that anyone with half a brain should be able to turn it around and run it profitably. Novell, which knew nothing about the retail software market, should never have bought the thing in the first place, but for a company like Corel it was a perfect fit.

Cowpland agreed, but repeated that the price was too high for a company the size of Corel. If he went to the bank and borrowed several hundred million dollars to finance the purchase, he'd be taking a huge risk.

Waxman, however, wouldn't give up. And he made it clear that Novell was prepared to be flexible. Says Cowpland: "He basically said that of all the companies they were talking to—and I had the impression there were at least half a dozen serious contenders—he said, 'You guys have the right fit, you have the engineering ability, you have the ability to execute, so why don't we find a way to make it work?' I think they had other offers on the table but they were keen to have it find a good home, as opposed to something like a leveraged buyout where they'd milk it, because Novell did have a reputation to keep with their ongoing customers. So then I thought, well, in that case, there is an opportunity here because WordPerfect is a world franchise. They'd almost created the industry. I thought, let's come up with something creative where we wouldn't use any cash, because if we don't use any cash we're not really betting the company.

"That's when I guess they told their investment banker to forget about the $400 million because it wasn't realistic. It went from $400 million cash to, well, 'Name the ticket provided you guys are serious about carrying the product forward.'"

So there it was. Novell was hell-bent on getting rid of WordPerfect, and yet so fixated on leaving it in good hands that it was prepared to accept any reasonable offer. From what Cowpland could tell, Novell's foremost concern was to minimize the inevitable embarrassment it was going to suffer if and when a sale was announced. The deal had to at least look good from a distance, regardless of the way it was structured.

From that point on, the sale of WordPerfect to Corel was practically a foregone conclusion. But while Cowpland and Waxman appeared to see eye to eye, there was still a healthy degree of suspicion between Corel and Novell's other executives. Kenkel and Stanton were convinced that the Utah company was trying to pull a fast one by under-reporting the number of WordPerfect boxes that had been shipped to distributors or retailers but hadn't actually made into customers' hands. That was a potentially serious problem, because if there was too much unsold inventory, it would hamper efforts to sell the next version of WordPerfect. In all likelihood, the distributors would simply refuse to take delivery of Version 7 unless Corel agreed to buy back unsold copies of the older version, an expense that could easily run into the tens of millions of dollars.

The solution proposed by Corel was to apply a holdback on a portion of the purchase price. Every time a box came back, its value would be deducted from the amount Corel had yet to pay. That way, Corel would be spared the expense of all those returns.

Novell wasn't sure it liked the sound of that, but it was far more concerned about another issue. To be blunt, a number of Novell executives and advisers were convinced that Cowpland was untrustworthy. They were especially annoyed after Cowpland flew down to Orem for a meeting with Novell CEO Bob Frankenberg on

January 11. At that time he outlined Corel's offer, which consisted of $10.75 million in cash and just under 10 million Corel shares, worth about $100 million (US). There were still a number of unresolved details, but Novell considered the meeting a success. "I was confident that there had been a clear meeting of the minds, and a firm hand-shake between Michael Cowpland and Bob Frankenberg," David Bradford, Novell's legal vice-president, later told *Upside*, a San Francisco–based magazine that covers the technology industry. Yet when Cowpland returned home the next day, he gave an interview to *The Ottawa Citizen* in which he all but denied rumours that Corel was in the hunt for WordPerfect. The likelihood of Corel purchasing the Utah operation, Cowpland said, was "a stretch," a "one in a hundred" chance. "Nothing is currently planned."

Even Lisa Kenkel was caught off guard by Cowpland's comment. She was on a plane, flying back from a short vacation in Palm Springs via Vancouver, when she saw her boss's quote reproduced in *The Financial Post*. "I read the story and I said to myself, 'Gee, I wonder if I missed a conference call?' I was trying to figure out what was behind this. Had Mike really said he didn't want to do the deal? I mean, he makes very quick decisions. He can go one way and then completely reverse himself. Did I miss something? I'd been travelling for a couple of days, so I called in and, no, everything was on track."

If that was the case, why had Cowpland gone to such lengths to quash speculation about a purchase? Asked about the incident later, Cowpland insisted he was only being conservative, and that as far as he knew Novell was still carrying on negotiations with several other possible suitors. But that explanation fails to take account of Cowpland's earlier discussions with Jeff Waxman, in which Waxman had plainly indicated Novell's desire to secure an agreement with Corel. Nor does it jibe with the very clear impression on the part of Kenkel and others that Cowpland, by early January, was strongly of the view that a deal with Novell could and should be worked out. "Mike was really, really excited," Kenkel recalls. "I think he had already made up his mind that he would really like to do the deal. He had started to visualize that this could really happen, that he could have this product in his stable."

As much as Cowpland denies it, it seems likely that his comments to the *Citizen* were actually aimed at stabilizing Corel's stock, which had been on a sharp downward trajectory since trading in the $25 range in mid-November. The most immediate problem was a sudden and unexpected drop in revenues from CorelDRAW. The latest version, DRAW 6, was compatible only with Windows 95, and with sales of Microsoft's new operating system falling short of expectations, DRAW 6 sales were nowhere near forecast levels. Several analysts, in fact, were predicting a loss in Corel's 1995 fourth quarter.

The other reason the stock was in decline was that investors were wary of speculation that Corel was negotiating to buy WordPerfect. Indeed, when rumours of a purchase surfaced just before Christmas, the shares fell $2 in a single day. The price continued to fall through late December and early January, dropping below $15 on the day Cowpland was meeting with Bob Frankenberg in Utah. (Compounding the problem was the disclosure that same day that four top Corel executives had cashed in stock options during November, just before the shares went into freefall. To many investors, it looked suspiciously as though the Corel insiders had sold shares knowing that fourth-quarter earnings were going to be affected by poor sales of DRAW 6—information that was not publicly available at the time.)

In any event, Corel's falling share price represented a serious impediment to Cowpland's hopes of acquiring WordPerfect. He had already decided that Corel would pay for the purchase largely by issuing new shares, but the company's bylaws specified that the board of directors had discretion to issue new stock only in quantities up to 20 percent of the existing number of shares. Given that in January 1996 there were 49.8 million shares outstanding, the maximum number of new shares Cowpland could offer Novell was just under 10 million. Anything more and he would be obligated to call a special meeting of shareholders, which would delay any purchase by several months and allow WordPerfect to continue losing market share.

For that reason, Cowpland was under pressure to do everything possible to prop up Corel's flagging share price. His public declaration that a deal with WordPerfect was a "one in a hundred" chance might well have been intended to do just that. And on the same day that Cowpland spoke to the *Citizen*, Corel announced that it was considering buying back as much as 10 percent of its outstanding shares. The intention was clearly to prevent the shares from falling so low as to preclude a WordPerfect purchase.

In the following few days, the share price did dip lower, but then it recovered slightly and stabilized at around $14, enough to make the deal work. Meanwhile, the negotiations were moving ahead at full speed in hopes of meeting Novell's self-imposed deadline of January 31. Kenkel, Eid Eid and Carey Stanton packed their bags and flew to Utah to look after the nuts and bolts of the deal—exactly which pieces of software would be included, how many employees Corel would take on, how much Corel would pay to lease Word-Perfect's old buildings, and so on. They were accompanied by Paul Skillen and one of the other senior engineers, Lucien Mustatea, who were there to give advice on the technical side. A thousand kilometres away in California, a separate contingent led by company treasurer Paul Labarge and Gordon Davidson of Fenwick and West, Corel's U.S. law firm, looked after the legal aspects of the negotiations. By coincidence, Fenwick and West's offices were just across the street from Novell's law firm in Palo Alto, the heart of Silicon Valley.

With less than three weeks available for Corel to do its due diligence and hammer out all of the complex details of the agreement, the atmosphere went from tense to ugly. Novell's people were convinced that Cowpland and his employees were a bunch of sharp operators, willing to say or do anything—even mislead their own shareholders—to achieve their objective. At the same time, Corel's negotiators thought that Novell was trying to take advantage of them by withholding critical information about WordPerfect's operations and finances. There was a dispute over how much Corel would pay toward the cost of providing customer support during the sale's month-long transition. And there were countless arguments over which assets were to be included in the deal and which ones would be made available to Corel only if it paid an additional licensing fee.

"Either they were disorganized or they were consciously trying to cheat us by holding back information," Kenkel says. "It was pretty adversarial, but we just had to go and slog it out. We were pushing them hard to get as much information as possible because, in an asset deal, if you don't list the asset, you don't own it. For us, it was *buyer beware*. There were disagreements on every front. It was a really, really weird dynamic."

Fortunately for Corel, it had one very big advantage as the negotiations went down to the wire—the belief on the part of Novell's senior management that Mike Cowpland was liable, if pushed, to change his mind at any time.

"That was the good thing about that article in the newspaper," Kenkel says, "because they didn't believe a word he said at that point. We knew that Mike's only concern was to close the deal, but luckily they thought he was wingy enough that he might just completely reverse direction on a whim. . . . They were tied to us and thinking, 'Jeez, I don't know about this Cowpland guy. He seems a little unstable.' In hindsight, I don't think they thought they had any leverage."

The final deal was announced at a press conference on January 31 at the Provo Park Hotel in Provo, Utah, not far from WordPerfect's headquarters. The event almost didn't come off as planned. The night before, some kind of mechanical problem had delayed the arrival of Cowpland's chartered jet in nearby Salt Lake City. According to a Corel employee who was on the plane, the pilot wanted to land the aircraft halfway to its destination, but the CEO insisted that he keep flying. (Cowpland says he doesn't recall the incident in detail but that if there was a problem with the plane it could not have been important. "I think they were working on one of the lights, nothing serious.")

There was more trouble on the ground in Utah. On their way from the hotel to a local auditorium for a get-acquainted session with several hundred employees, Cowpland and the three executives who were travelling with him missed the exit from the interstate and were forced to drive several kilometres out of their way before doubling back. By the time they arrived, the event was already underway. "This was not an auspicious start to a merger designed to propel Cowpland's modestly sized software company into the big leagues," journalist Paul Kedrosky wrote later in *Upside* magazine.

Indeed it wasn't, but WordPerfect's staff—relieved finally to be out from under Novell's long shadow—didn't seem to mind a bit. "I counted about twenty standing ovations," said one engineer who attended the event. Another worker, from customer support, said, "I'm feeling good today. I've been told I have a job. It'll be good to work for a company that believes in me."

Arlen Bartsch kicked things off with a rousing speech about how Corel's young, energetic workforce was looking forward to building on the strengths of WordPerfect's existing product line. Then Cowpland himself strolled up to the podium, to loud cheers and sustained applause. After an MTV-style video featuring a jester giving a tour of Corel's Ottawa headquarters, he welcomed his new employees with jokes and confidently predicted that WordPerfect would capture fully half of the entire office suite market within three years. It was a brash prophecy that Cowpland, not to mention the rest of Corel's senior management, would soon come to regret.

The WordPerfect purchase may have been a gamble, but it wasn't an outrageous one given the terms of the deal. On top of the $10.75 million (US) in cash and 9.95 million new shares it had offered in mid-January, Corel had agreed to pay Novell 2 percent of its annual revenues to a maximum of $30 million and an additional $8 million a year for five years for the right to license two Novell products, GroupWise and Envoy. All told, the price came to about $170 million based on the stock price at the time of the purchase. For that, Corel obtained ownership of the entire WordPerfect family of software as well as Quattro Pro, a business graphics application called

Presentations and a personal information management program called InfoCentral. Corel also gave Novell a seat on its board, a token gesture considering that most of the other directors were unswervingly loyal to Cowpland.

Even many of the stock market analysts had to admit that the Corel CEO had done an admirable job of bargaining Novell down from its initial asking price. "It seems, even using conservative numbers on WordPerfect, like the deal will add earnings to the company," said David Wright, research director at Marleau Lemire in Toronto. Robert Kugel of Seidler Cos. in Los Angeles, who had been among the most outspoken opponents of the WordPerfect purchase when it was still only a rumour, told *The Globe and Mail* that his opinion had moved up a notch to "let's wait and see." He predicted that the deal would "have at least a modestly positive impact on earnings this year, but that's not to say whether over the long run it will pay off." Jean Orr of H.G. Edwards in St. Louis, meanwhile, noted that WordPerfect was a solid product that had lost ground mainly because of poor marketing, and that Corel's expertise in that area was exactly what was needed to turn it around. "I think on balance it will turn out to be positive," she said of the acquisition. Investors seemed to concur: in two days of trading in the wake of the announcement, Corel shares jumped $1.62 to close at $16.25. "I am more optimistic than I thought I would be at this point in WordPerfect's life," said David Course of *PC Letter*. "Of all the people who were likely to buy WordPerfect, Corel is the best."

So much for the good news. Less well received was Cowpland's bizarre assertion that WordPerfect would soon lay claim to 50 percent of the office suite market. What was the guy smoking? It was one thing to believe that Corel, with its merchandising savvy, would be able to restore a bit of lustre to a long-neglected product, but quite another to think that Mike Cowpland was somehow going to roll back Microsoft's gains in one of that company's most important product segments. The mere suggestion might be enough to incite a counter-offensive from Bill Gates.

"If they try to get 50 percent of the market share, they'll get hurt," said David Wright, adding that a wiser approach would be settle for about 10 percent and pray that Gates was in a tolerant mood. Added analyst Richard Piotrowski of Levesque Beaubien Geoffrion: "They have walked into Microsoft's sights . . . and they will be targeted with both barrels."

While the rest of the industry debated whether Cowpland had completely lost touch with reality, Corel went to work repairing what was broken at WordPerfect. Of the 1,300 people employed at the Orem head office as of January 1996, Corel agreed to keep 600, half in product development and half in technical support. The rest, mainly in administration and marketing, were to be offered jobs at Novell or laid off. Cowpland figured those functions could be handled by his existing staff in Ottawa, saving many millions of dollars in salaries and overhead.

Paul Skillen, whom Cowpland put in charge of the new division, was the only Corel employee to relocate to Orem. Although the newspapers in both Ottawa and Salt Lake City were full of articles about how the Corel and WordPerfect cultures were remarkably similar, that was far from true. One of Skillen's first acts was to fire six senior WordPerfect managers, including Glen Mella. Over the following three months he got rid of more than a dozen more, wiping out two of the company's five layers of management. "When I went in there, the company had quite a rigid management structure, with a lot of people who were really just professional managers—they might as well have been selling soup cans," Skillen says. "At Corel, we tend to favor junior managers who have strong technical backgrounds and more of an entrepreneurial spirit."

The description applied equally well to himself. Skillen was all of thirty-five when he took charge of WordPerfect, a self-taught programmer and veteran of sixteen years in the Ottawa-area high-tech industry. His career had begun at nineteen when he finished high school in Carleton Place, half an hour west of the city, and started his own company, Xitek. The firm, which grew to about fifteen employees, manufactured assorted electronic devices for a number of local companies, including Telesat Canada and Atomic Energy of Canada Ltd. One of Xitek's clients was a company called InstanTel, which made digital seismographs. InstanTel's owner was former Digital of Canada president and Mitel director Denzil Doyle, who was so impressed by the young man's initiative that he struck a deal to buy Xitek and make Skillen his director of R and D. It was there that Skillen met and hired Eid Eid, who later became his partner in the unsuccessful venture to develop and sell high-end imaging workstations for hair salons.

Skillen's low-key, modest style, so at odds with Cowpland's flamboyance, made him the ideal person to oversee WordPerfect's rehabilitation. To ease the transition, he organized a series of town-hall meetings with groups of fifty or a hundred employees at a time. At first there was a fair amount of nervousness about the new owners, some of which resulted from a concern—understandable under the circumstances—that Corel might not be planning to stick around for the long haul. Within weeks of the takeover, however, Corel showed its intentions by spending $10 million to equip its new employees with state-of-the-art Pentium computers, a new local-area network and a new phone system. Skillen had been shocked to discover that some WordPerfect developers still spent their days hunched over 286-based computers, machines so antiquated that they were incapable of running the software the engineers were supposed to be producing. The arrival of new computers by the truckload—many employees received one for the office and one for home—did much to convince WordPerfect's engineers that Corel was serious about reinvigorating the operation. So did Cowpland's announcement, during a visit to the Orem offices on March 1, the day the purchase closed, that every employee, no matter how junior, would receive Corel stock options. "It all feels so comfortable," one programmer told *The Deseret News*. "This is the kind of direction we were looking for."

Skillen's willingness to listen and his obvious concern for the people who worked under him made it easier for him to institute some of the changes he felt were necessary at WordPerfect. Nevertheless, he was surprised by how difficult it was to break down the old, hierarchical way of doing things and replace it with Corel's style of quick, on-the-spot decision-making.

"You hear about corporate culture and how big an issue it is and you think, 'Oh, it can't be that bad.' And I really did experience that it was tough to deal with. Sometimes they welcomed change, but other times I had to drag people kicking and screaming. The biggest thing is that they were used to working in a linear fashion. We would have, say, ten versions of WordPerfect—different languages, 16-bit, 32-bit, the suite, the pro version, those kind of things—and they would work on them one product at a time, which in the software industry these days just won't cut it. At Corel, you always have several projects moving along in parallel.

"Also, they were very rigid in the sense that an engineer might have spent years working on one particular feature of a product. You'd ask them to do something else and they'd say, 'No, no, my expertise is here.' So what I did was I deliberately assigned them to a project at which they had no expertise. They really didn't like it at first, but after a while they thought, 'Wow, that is great.' It took a year and a half to get there, but eventually we got to the point where people could move around freely—not quite as much as in the Ottawa office, but pretty close."

Hard as it was, the task of overhauling WordPerfect's internal operations was nothing compared to the challenge of strengthening and increasing the product's customer base. Early on, Cowpland scored some notable victories, but the cost in marketing dollars was horrendous, driving Corel deeply into the red and putting the company's very survival at stake.

The offensive against Microsoft began with the release of Corel WordPerfect Suite 7 at a splashy black-tie extravaganza in Salt Lake City on May 29, 1996. Veteran Corel-watchers recognized it as a virtual clone of the annual CorelDRAW gala, complete with enthusiastic speeches to employees, a colourful Corel hot-air balloon hovering over the city and $1 million in prizes for ten WordPerfect users who were judged to have made original and creative use of the product's features. "The energy and the enthusiasm is back," gushed Bruce Bastian, who was given a special "Hero of WordPerfect" award to the obvious delight of longtime employees. "It's really good to see Corel interested in the product. Novell never was."

Backing up the hype was a planned $100-million marketing campaign, a thirty-six-city road tour of meetings with journalists and retailers and, most important of all, steep discounts. The suite's list price was $260, but users of earlier versions or competing products—the definition was so broad that almost anyone qualified—could upgrade for $99, less than half the cost of upgrading to Microsoft Office. (The only requirements for obtaining a competitive upgrade, one reseller joked, were "a pulse and a dial tone.") For corporate users, WordPerfect was even more of a steal. Initially, Corel charged $235 for each person using the software, roughly the same as Microsoft. But within months Corel threw out the old pricing structuring and replaced with a flat rate of $807 for each Windows NT server hooked up to a local-area network. "Whether you have fifty or five hundred users per server, the price is the same," a Corel spokeswoman explained.

By mid-summer, the approach seemed to be paying dividends. At the Comdex Canada trade show in Toronto, Cowpland boasted that Corel had taken half the retail market for office suites in June, measured by units sold. The announcement was not quite as momentous as it sounded, however. For one thing, Corel's drastic price cuts meant that Microsoft still had a commanding three-to-one lead in dollar-volume sales. In addition, analysts were quick to point out that retail sales accounted for no more than 15 percent of the total market, with the rest made up of bundling deals with PC vendors and direct sales to corporate customers, two areas in which Microsoft's leadership remained unchallenged. Desperate to show some momentum, Cowpland inked a bundling deal with Packard Bell Electronics Inc., the world's third-largest PC vendor, to put the top-of-the-line version of WordPerfect's suite on all that company's new machines. "This deal is huge in marketing value alone," Cowpland said, ducking questions about how much revenue Corel could expect from the contract. In fact, the agreement was almost a straight giveaway, meant to raise Word-Perfect's profile and, with luck, increase the likelihood that Packard Bell owners would buy Corel's upgrades in the future.

Unfortunately for Cowpland, his mass-market strategy was having little success in the corporate arena. Early in the summer, Corel lost a competition to supply 40,000 copies of its office suite to Canada's Department of National Defence, a deal estimated to be worth about $8.5 million. Cowpland complained loudly about the government's decision to go with Microsoft, but his appeal to the Canadian International Trade Tribunal fell on deaf ears. The problem was not discrimination, as Cowpland had charged, but compatibility. Having established itself as the de facto industry standard, Microsoft Office was, plainly and simply, the preferred software for those to whom exchanging files with other users was more important than up-front expense. Another factor working against Corel was the reluctance of corporate purchasing managers to buck conventional wisdom. Back in the heyday of the mainframe computer, there was a saying that "Nobody ever got fired for buying IBM." By the mid-1990s, the same was true of Microsoft's business applications. It didn't matter whether another product was cheaper or arguably even better—the manager who chose a competing suite over Microsoft was taking a risk.

As much as Cowpland complained about that wall of resistance, the reality was that his decision to shut down the marketing department at WordPerfect headquarters had only made matters worse. "After the WordPerfect acquisition, people came up from Orem and said, 'Mike, we've got to have people to talk to those large customers about the WordPerfect product,'" says Arlen Bartsch, who quit Corel in late 1996. "In those meetings we decided we weren't going to do that—we were going to manage everything from Ottawa. And that was the wrong strategy, because you can't do it remotely. Corel thought it was about price, but these guys don't care about price, they care about service. We didn't see that. We thought, 'Great brand. Retail? We can do this.' I know I failed to see it because I had no experience in the enterprise market."

Thus, Corel's efforts to claw back market share in the corporate sector were doomed from the start. And even the retail sales were something of a dubious achievement, since most of the gains could be traced to a high-volume advertising campaign that Corel could not possibly afford to sustain. In just one year, Corel's cash reserves plummeted by 93 percent, to $7 million from $82 million. (In contrast, Microsoft was sitting on cash reserves of $7 billion, a thousand times Cowpland's resources.) The company finished 1996 with $334 million in revenues, up from $196 million the previous year. But 1995's profit of $14.8 million had been transformed into a loss of $2.8 million, the first in the company's history. If Bill Gates really was "running scared," as Cowpland kept insisting, it was hard to understand why. "No one has deeper pockets than Microsoft," said Ann Stephens, president of the market research firm PC Data in Reston, Virginia. "They're not being hurt by Corel."

Much, much worse was in store for Corel in 1997. Forced to cut back on advertising spending, the company watched sales of both WordPerfect and CorelDRAW drift steadily lower. Its share of the retail word-processing market fell to 25 percent, pushed down in part by an aggressive price-cutting strategy by Microsoft—Bill Gates's answer to Cowpland's brash talk about taking on the world's biggest software company.

"It's been tougher than we thought, because I don't think we anticipated quite the—if you like—brainwashing mentality some people have toward Microsoft now," Cowpland admitted in an interview late that year. "They'll buy Microsoft just because it's Microsoft. And that's got worse over the past two years. Back when we were negotiating to buy WordPerfect, Microsoft wasn't quite so all-powerful. But two years is a long time in this business."

And the losses kept piling up. In June 1997, Corel took a $105-million write-down on the value of WordPerfect and related software, a move intended to improve the company's finances going forward by eliminating the need to amortize those expenses at the previous rate of $9 million a quarter. In the third quarter of 1997, the company reported a $31.4-million shortfall after deducting $42 million for unsold inventory—fall-out from a long-standing policy of stuffing its retail sales channels with as many boxes as possible and then counting the software as sold, even though most of it was still piled high in distributors' warehouses. Then, in December, Corel stunned investors with the news that it would declare a fourth-quarter loss of $95 million on sales of just $44 million. The loss included a write-off of $12-million for discontinued versions of CorelDRAW, a $50-million reduction for returns of unsold software and a further $28-million write-off related to the cost of acquiring certain Java programming technologies.

The flurry of accounting changes, write-downs and inventory adjustments left most investors reeling. Amid all the numbers, however, the bottom line was painfully obvious. In its first seven years as a publicly traded company, Corel had reported a total of $92.5 million in profits. In 1997 alone, it lost $231.8 million, almost one dollar for every dollar it reported in revenue that year. Meanwhile, Corel's shares had fallen from a peak of $26.63 on the Toronto Stock Exchange in 1995 to a mere $2.05 at the end of 1997. More than a billion dollars in shareholders' equity had disappeared into the ether.

And Mike Cowpland was brimming with confidence. "While the results for the 1997 are disappointing," he said in a press release announcing fourth-quarter results, "the company remains strong and well-positioned for a successful 1998."

Chapter Fourteen

Think of the software business as a powerful narcotic and you'll have a pretty good idea of what Corel was going through in the early 1990s, and why it is in so much trouble now. When CorelDRAW hit the market in 1989, its effect on Cowpland's company was like that of a hit of cocaine. First came a powerful rush, in which anybody and everybody associated with the company was swept up in a frenetic whirlwind of long hours, passionate commitment and money—more money than most of them had ever seen before or likely would again. After a while, though, the intensity and the sense of exhilaration wore off. When it did, many of Corel's most valuable employees—those who had not already quit in disgust or been fired during the chaos of the early years—felt exhausted and even sullied. They longed to get back home to their families, their lives, the quiet routines that had been sacrificed for the sake of Corel's explosive growth.

Mike Cowpland, however, still craves the next hit. At a stage in life when most other people, including many CEOs, are thinking of slowing down and cutting back on their commitments, he is every bit as determined to keep proving himself as he was thirty years ago, when he was an enthusiastic young engineer at Bell Northern Research. The exotic cars, the lavish houses and his blond-bombshell wife—all are Cowpland's way of proclaiming to the world that the little boy from Bexhill-on-Sea has made it in the world's most competitive and fast-moving industry. Yet beneath the blustery, hey-look-at-me exterior that so many people find off-putting, Cowpland is still driven by an engineer's boyish love for the latest gee-whiz technology. The prospect of packing it all in and retiring to a life of leisure is no more appealing to him than his own lifestyle of long hours, constant stress and unpredictable fortunes might be to most other people.

"If I spent four hours just doing nothing I'd be exhausted, I'd find it very tedious," Cowpland says. "There's nothing more energy-sapping than doing nothing. Like, I'll play golf occasionally because it's social, but you never get those endorphins at the end of a golf game. You feel kind of frustrated. So to my mind, activity—be it tennis or business—is a form of relaxation. The ability to create. Stuff like this is really thrilling to me, because you're playing on the global scene, you're doing something different and you're working with people to make it happen. Not every day is perfect. You're going to have your tough days. But on the other hand you have a goal and a challenge, as opposed to just sitting back and doing nothing."

The nature of that goal matters less than the simple fact that it exists as a kind of high-tech Holy Grail into which Cowpland can pour his abundant energies. One moment it might be multimedia CD-ROMs, the next it's video-conferencing, or the all-consuming battle against Microsoft in office suites. People who have worked closely with Cowpland over the years often describe him as an opportunist, meaning that his approach to business is to jump on the latest trend and ride it for as long as it seems promising or profitable. That's true, but what sets him apart from most run-of-the-mill opportunists is the degree to which he honestly believes in whatever happens to be the latest enterprise—until, that is, he finds something else to take its place. It drives people around him to distraction, but Cowpland can switch allegiances as easily as other people change their shirts. It's what allows him to get charged up with enthusiasm for the latest hot technology even if his last half dozen can't-miss ideas have turned out to be costly failures. Odds are that the next one will be a flop, too, but in the computer business you simply never know. And when the next big wave comes along, Cowpland intends to be the one riding it. Either that or he'll drown in the attempt.

These days, Cowpland's greatest enthusiasm is reserved for the concept of the network computer (NC) and the as yet unrealized potential of the Java programming language. Leaving aside the technical details for a minute, suffice it to say that Cowpland's investment in the NC is, bar none, his biggest bet ever. If he turns out to be right, Corel's recent failures will be forgotten in a millisecond and investors will once again embrace Cowpland as a prophet of the new technology. If he's wrong, the company, its shareholders and its CEO will be many millions of dollars poorer. If Corel survives at all, it will likely have to slash R and D spending to the bone and settle for being a much-weakened purveyor of two increasingly aged software applications. The chances of Cowpland sticking around under those circumstances—or, for that matter, of being allowed by shareholders to remain in his current position—seem at best remote.

In typical Corel fashion, the gamble on network computers and Java did not come about as a result of careful planning and a strategic assessment of future trends in computing. It happened more or less by accident (some would say whim) and gradually picked up momentum, pushed along by Cowpland's own excitement and a ceaseless river of hype about the huge market that supposedly lay waiting just around the corner.

Mind you, Corel is far from the only company to be seduced by the magic of Java. To understand how it happened, the best place to start is probably 1995. That was the year when the entire computer industry—not to mention the news media, large chunks of the business community and any number of public policy wonks—suddenly caught Internet fever. The cause of the epidemic was a service called the World Wide Web, which gave computer users a simple, user-friendly means of navigating what up to then had been a no-frills digital highway dominated by academic researchers. Until the Web came along, the Internet was used mainly for exchanging e-mail and hosting on-line, text-only discussion groups. The Web made it possible to combine text and graphics, and to jump easily from one document to another—regardless of whether the content you were searching for was stored at the same Internet site or halfway around the world—merely by clicking on a highlighted word or phrase. To view the millions of documents, or pages, on the Web, all you needed was a software product known as a "browser," the first of which, Mosaic, was developed by a undergraduate student named Marc Andreessen at the University of Illinois in 1993. A year later, Andreessen helped found Netscape Communications Corp., which introduced a more advanced version of Mosaic called Netscape Navigator. Suddenly, the Internet boom was on.

By the end of 1995, there was hardly a software company anywhere in North America that wasn't trying to figure out how to make money off the Internet or, more likely, how to keep from being crushed by the Internet juggernaut. Corel was no exception. Its entire business—the profitable part of it, anyway—was founded on desktop publishing and the idea that people could use computers to create graphics and text documents that, once completed, could be transmitted to a printer and distributed on paper. The Web made possible a new kind of desktop publishing, one that allowed anyone who was hooked up to the Internet to distribute documents electronically. To avoid losing ground in this new era, companies such as Corel would have to embrace the Internet as a fundamental part of their business models. Publishing a document on the Web would have to be as easy as publishing it on paper.

To Cowpland's credit, Corel was one of the first major publishing software firms to recognize the growing importance of electronic delivery. Ventura 5, which shipped in November 1994, included a filtering tool that allowed users to import documents created with the Standard Generalized Markup Language (SGML), an authoring technology suitable for editing and storing material in a variety of electronic formats, including CD-ROMs and on-line files. By that point, the early growth of the World Wide Web was fuelling demand for products that supported a related format known as Hypertext Markup Language, or HTML. In January 1995, Corel announced plans to add SGML and HTML document publishing capabilities to Ventura, using technology licensed from two smaller Canadian software firms, Microstar Software Ltd. of Ottawa and InContext Corp. of Toronto. Unfortunately, Cowpland's engineers soon realized that Ventura needed a full-scale rewrite to support all of the major new additions. The massive overhaul proved so time-consuming that Ventura 6 fell far behind schedule and did not appear until August 1996. By that point, Corel had decided to call the product Ventura 7 so as to synchronize it with CorelDRAW 7 and WordPerfect 7.

While that was going on, Cowpland was sniffing around for a way to enter the Web-publishing market with a stand-alone product that would combine desktop publishing tools and multimedia capabilities. He soon discovered he was in a race with several deep-pocketed rivals, among them Bill Gates. In January 1996, Corel struck an informal deal with a Cambridge, Massachusetts, firm called Vermeer Inc., under which the Ottawa company would acquire a non-exclusive license to Vermeer's HTML editing and page-layout technology for about $1 million (US). The deal was worked out over the phone on a Wednesday, but a snowstorm forced Corel's executives to postpone their flight to Boston for the final paperwork. Over the weekend, Microsoft swooped in and bought the entire company for $132 million. "That was a case where we moved very quickly, but another couple of days would have been even nicer," Cowpland says ruefully.

Microsoft incorporated Vermeer's code in a Web-authoring package called FrontPage, which quickly became the market leader. That forced Corel to do a deal with its second choice, iband Inc. of Campbell, California, which shortly thereafter was acquired by San Francisco-based Macromedia. Macromedia used iband's technology as the basis for its popular Backstage product line of HTML editing tools.

Corel, as usual, couldn't seem to make up its mind on a marketing strategy. First it took iband's code and packaged it, along with some pre-designed page templates, backgrounds and images, under the name CorelWeb.Designer. After two months that product became part of Corel's Web.Graphics Suite, a rough-and-ready assortment of page design and editing tools licensed from third parties. (*Windows Sources* magazine remarked that the suite was "eerily reminiscent of the Web itself: a semi-navigable mishmash of the good, the bad, and the ugly.") Then, in early 1997, the product was refined and reintroduced as Corel's WebMaster Suite. Despite the name change, it never made more than a small dent in what, by then, was a very crowded market.

The product manager at Corel who helped to pilot the company's early efforts in the Web-authoring market was Chris Biber. A native of Germany, Biber immigrated to Canada in the mid-1980s and joined Corel in the fall of 1988 as a part-timer responsible for translating CorelDRAW into German. Six months later he became the full-time marketing manager for Europe, reporting to Arlen Bartsch. Biber left Corel in June 1994 to become vice-president of sales at Microstar Software but returned a year later, around the time that the company was getting serious about on-line publishing and the Web. "Those were the gold-digger days of the Internet," Biber recalls. "We knew we wanted to enter the HTML editing and page-creation market, and we could either create something ourselves and bring it out nine months later, or acquire something and build it up over time. Mike wanted to move fast, so I was tasked with sourcing technology that would allow us to get into that market quickly." Biber enjoyed the work but was frustrated by Corel's chaotic management style and frequent changes of direction. "The products did reasonably well, but I don't think they ever got the attention they deserved, either at Corel or outside."

All that thrashing around in the Web-authoring market, however, did have one lasting consequence. Toward the end of 1995, while hunting for new features that could be added to Corel's Web product line, several of the engineers began experimenting with an Internet-friendly programming language from Sun Microsystems Inc. of Mountain View, California. Dreamed up by a Calgary-born Sun engineer named James Gosling in 1990, the new language enabled all kinds of computerized devices to run simple programs distributed to them over a network. Code-named Oak, Gosling's invention sat around unused for several years, a solution in search of a problem. But when the Internet began to catch fire, Sun CEO Scott McNealy realized that Oak—which he renamed Java—was ideally suited for the new world of Web-centred computing. Using it, a developer could write a program once and it would theoretically run on any kind of computer, regardless of processor and operating system, as long as the machine was equipped with a simple interpreter program known as a Java Virtual Machine (JVM). In its simplest form, Java could be used to create small programs, or "applets," that could be downloaded from a Web server and run on a client workstation, the fancy term for a computer hooked up to a network. Down the road, a Java application could conceivably take the place of any traditional PC application, including a word processor or a spreadsheet.

McNealy's decision to throw Sun's enormous weight behind Java was driven as much by personal resentment as by hard-headed business logic. Since its founding in 1982, Sun has earned most of its profits by selling high-end servers and software to corporations. By 1994, however, that business was coming under attack from Windows NT, a network-capable version of Microsoft's popular operating system. McNealy was desperate to break into a new market and even more desperate to strike back at his archenemy, Bill Gates. Java looked like the ideal weapon to loosen Gates's control over desktop computing, for the simple reason that it did not depend on Microsoft's flagship operating system. McNealy, who is famous for his public attacks on what he calls "Bill Gates's centrally planned economy," recognized that if Java became the dominant standard for how software was written and distributed over the Internet, there would no longer be any need for Windows. For that reason more than any other, Java has drawn support from a growing number of computer and software companies that feel threatened by Microsoft—IBM, Oracle and Netscape among them.

It wasn't long before Corel joined the squad of Java cheerleaders. At the outset, however, Cowpland's engineers saw Sun's new programming language mainly as a tool for adding animation capabilities and enhanced formatting features to the company's planned stable of

Web publishing applications. "A number of engineers were playing around with it," Biber says. "It was eventually decided that we could put together a fairly interesting addition to our products by doing Java animations. They started to work on it, and in about three months they had a demonstratable version, which we called Barista." In simple terms, Barista was a small program that could be used to translate text and graphics into Java applets so they could be displayed on any Web browser that incorporated a JVM. Combined with Ventura, it allowed publishers to put documents up on the Web with much richer formatting than was possible with HTML, in essence by displaying a snapshot of the original document based entirely on Java. (Many Web site developers were already doing something similar with Adobe Acrobat, but the drawback was that files written for Acrobat could be read only with a special program known as a plug-in that had to be downloaded from the Internet and installed on the client computer's hard drive. With Java, the plug-in—or JVM—was already built right in to the browser.)

By the time Corel's engineers had come up with a working version of Barista, word of the project had reached Sun Microsystems. Sun was anxious to prove to the rest of the industry that Java was more than just a toy, so it sent two representatives of its Javasoft subsidiary to Ottawa to find out what Corel was up to and see what, if anything, Sun could do to help out. The two visitors were Lou Tucker, Javasoft's director of corporate relations, and Nazila Alasti, an independent software consultant who had been hired by Sun as a Java evangelist. In effect, her job was to convince software developers to support Java by writing applications for it—the more the better.

In late March 1996, Tucker and Alasti had a fateful, two-hour meeting at Corel's head office with Cowpland, Eid Eid, Carey Stanton, Chris Biber and Vincent Lin, the engineer who had first taken an interest in Java and had led the work on Barista. Tucker and Alasti started by congratulating Cowpland and his staff on their work, which, in only a few short months, had established Corel as a leader in the rapidly growing community of Java developers. Then they got down to business. Now that Corel had acquired some experience with the programming language, Tucker asked, why not put it to good use by creating a full-blown business application in Java? Indeed, since Corel had only just purchased WordPerfect, the obvious next step would be to write a complete Java office suite, a software package that could be downloaded from the Internet or distributed over a local-area network and run on virtually any kind of computer. If it worked, it would not only place Corel at the forefront of the hottest trend in computing, it would give Cowpland a clear shot at overtaking Micro-soft in the market for productivity software. The likely reward would be billions of dollars in revenue, not to mention the distinction of being the first man to humble Bill Gates. "The message from Sun was that it would really be in our best interests to move this way, to counter Microsoft," Carey Stanton recalls. "They told us, 'What would really make Java go would be if you guys had an application for it, and if you do that we'll commit to giving you the spotlight.'"

Cowpland was intrigued by the possibilities, to say the least. Despite his public bravado about overtaking Microsoft in traditional Windows office suites, he knew as well as anyone that the chances of that happening were between nil and nonexistent. Microsoft's position in the office-suite market was similar to Corel's in the Windows graphics market: having established a strong user base, it was practically unassailable. Corel's only real hope was to redefine the battle, to open a new front, as it were. In the same way that Microsoft had trounced WordPerfect when the PC world migrated from DOS to Windows, Corel would have a chance to beat Microsoft if and when Java became accepted as the new computing standard. "At the time we thought, 'Why should we be trying to fight Microsoft where we do not have a level playing field?'" Eid Eid says. "Here was an opportunity with a whole new platform, and we could be first in developing apps for that market. Why spend the effort to be number two when we might be number one?"

Soon after the meeting with Tucker and Alasti, Cowpland convened another brainstorming session with his senior engineers.

Vincent Lin, it turned out, had already done some preliminary work on new Java tools for Corel applications. One was a small charting program; another was a Java-based interface for a spreadsheet program that would run over a network. After being briefed on those projects, Cowpland asked Lin if the idea of a Java office suite really was feasible. According to Cowpland, Lin went away and thought about it for a while, then came back and said yes. The resulting software package would clearly not have all of the power and features of a regular Windows suite, for the simple reason that a Java rewrite of WordPerfect would be too big and bulky to operate efficiently over a network. Nevertheless, Lin said, the basic concept was perfectly sound.

That was all the encouragement Cowpland needed. Before the end of the day, he gave Lin the go-ahead to design a working prototype of what would be called Corel Office JV, and later Office for Java. Cowpland wanted the prototype ready to show at Sun's inaugural Java developers conference, JavaOne, which was scheduled to take place in San Francisco's Moscone Convention Center from May 29 to 31. Lin would have a team of about a dozen developers at his disposal, and all the pizza and Cokes they could consume. With less than two months to go before the unveiling, there were going to be plenty of all-nighters.

"Basically," Cowpland recalls, "I said, let's put some resources into this and see how far it could go. And the more we did it, the better it looked."

Down the road, when it became obvious that Office for Java had become a colossal waste of money and manpower, almost everyone connected with the project would try to shift blame to someone else. The real problem was that, in the rush to embrace a promising new concept, nobody ever stood back and asked three simple questions. First, what exactly was Corel trying to achieve? Second, if it worked, would there be a market for it? And third, was the underlying technology at a stage where it could support such an ambitious undertaking? The answer to the first question might have seemed obvious, but it wasn't. There were, in fact, several different agendas at play. Even at that early stage, the objective in Cowpland's mind was to create a marketable application, and get it out there as soon as possible before anyone else had the same idea. The guys in engineering were equally enthusiastic, but for another reason: like most software developers, they got their kicks out of working with new technology, and Sun's Java language was far and away the hottest thing in the business. To some of them, at least, Corel Office JV was really more of an experiment, a "proof of concept" rather than the first step toward a viable product. Whether it actually ever brought in any revenue was beside the point. "I never had the intention of developing a full suite," Lin insisted later. "The whole department was clear on this."

According to Chris Biber, the aura of excitement surrounding Java clouded everybody's judgment. "At that point it wasn't hashed out what it would really mean. The idea was to see what an office suite in Java would look like, and the verdict from on high was to see if we could have something done by May of that year. It crossed everyone's mind that it was a very ambitious undertaking, but at the same time there was general euphoria—and not just at Corel—that Java was indeed going places and was going to make a huge impact in the market. What was undertaken was seen as an engineering challenge more than anything else, to put together a working prototype in an incredible short period of time."

To Lin's credit, he and his skunk works team pulled it off. On May 30, 1996, a day after the launch of WordPerfect Suite 7 in Salt Lake City, Mike and Marlen Cowpland flew into San Francisco, accompanied by Paul Skillen, Eid Eid, Carey Stanton and Chris Biber. They carried with them a three-and-a-half-inch floppy-disk on which was stored a copy of Lin's Office JV prototype, a barebones (it occupied less than a megabyte) demo of what Corel's PR staff were touting as a fully functional Java office suite. The demo version couldn't actually be used to do anything, but it was good enough to convince most developers that the idea held merit.

If Cowpland had harboured any remaining doubts about the

promise of Office for Java, they would have been erased by his experiences at JavaOne. Sun's executives were so impressed by Corel's little demo application that they treated Cowpland and his group as honoured guests, seating them at the front of the convention hall. At a news conference arranged to discuss Corel's Java strategy, Scott McNealy himself dropped by and introduced Cowpland to the press. Cowpland basked in all the attention and was amazed by the turnout for the conference. The organizers had expected about 2,000 developers to show up, but instead there was a capacity crowd of more than 7,000—incontrovertible proof that Java had caught the industry's imagination. Analysts and Silicon Valley hotshots who had never even thought of Corel before were milling around the company's display like groupies at a rock concert.

"To me, JavaOne was the real turning point in terms of our strategic focus," Stanton says. "Before that trip, Mike was interested in seeing what Java could do, but there wasn't really a full-scale commitment. All of a sudden we were being escorted to the front row at the Moscone Center and it's like, 'Holy shit, look at all these people—this is bigger than a Windows developers conference!' And we were treated like stars. The Corel logo was flashing up there on stage on the big video screen, we were being written up in *PC Week*. . . . What it came down to was that we were getting more mileage out of this little Java project than we got from the launch of WordPerfect 7. So right then and there, you could see there was a dramatic shift in our thinking. In Mike's mind it was, 'Okay, boys, we're going with Java.'"

Biber, too, got swept up in the excitement of JavaOne: "Without overstating it, Corel was literally the sensation of the show. Up to then Java had been used mainly for things like stock-tickers and other types of animation on the Web—cutesy little things. And here was a fairly well-recognized company saying, 'We can do this,' and people went, 'Wow!' They saw a running spreadsheet and a running word processor. They saw a running business graphics app, which definitely caused a huge stir."

As soon as he returned to Ottawa, Cowpland gave the authorization to turn Office JV into a commercial product, the world's first integrated Java-based application package. Almost overnight, Lin's team quadrupled from about a dozen developers to fifty. An article in the June 10 issue of the *Seybold Report on Desktop Publishing* said that the first component of the suite would be WordPerfect 7, followed by Java-powered versions of the Quattro Pro spreadsheet and Corel-CHART. "Essentially, Corel has rewritten these applications in the Java language," the newsletter said, "thereby picking up both platform independence and network access. A beta version of Corel Office JV will be ready by the end of 1996, by which time we believe that many of Java's performance problems will have been solved." The same article noted that Java, in its initial release, suffered from prolonged downloading times, problems with cross-platform compatibility and occasional security glitches, but that all of those flaws were in the process of being corrected. "All in all, by the time the snow flies, we can expect Java to be much faster, cleaner and safer."

It all sounded quite straightforward, but the view from the trenches was nowhere near as encouraging. The ugly truth was that Java, despite all the hype, was still an exceedingly rudimentary medium, somewhat like the early versions of Windows, only worse. The difference was that Microsoft had, by the fall of 1987, assembled a well-stocked, if poorly documented, library of authoring tools—sections of code that help developers and designers build other software programs by performing routine tasks, such as opening a dialog box on the screen or activating the program's search engine. In the case of Java, most of those tools had not even been designed yet. Rather than relying on Sun for most of the primary authoring tools, Corel's engineers would have to write most of the basic code themselves, practically doubling their workload.

The developer who was given responsibility for creating those tools was Claude Montpetit, a talented senior programmer who had been reassigned to Lin's group after his own Windows-based project had been cancelled in the wake of the WordPerfect acquisition. "It was right after the JavaOne announcement," Montpetit explained to

Electrical Engineering Times. "I was just back from a week's vacation and we had to come up with a whole design and develop everything from scratch. It was a huge task." Added Montpetit: "No one had a 'mind' for Java. We all came from a background in using Microsoft Foundation Classes [a set of developers' tools for Windows]. We thought there was a need to develop a similar framework for Java so we could share all the Office components. In Java, everything was very basic." With the help of several other engineers, Montpetit created what became known as the Corel Application Framework, a basic library of routines on which any application could depend. As soon as CAF was ready, other groups began writing applications on top of it.

By the fall, the project had progressed far enough that Corel decided to post a preview version of Office for Java—the company described it as a "pre-beta" release—on its Web site. That way, Java devotees and the merely curious could examine and play with it for themselves. The early feedback was by and large favourable, which wasn't a surprise considering that only confirmed technology enthusiasts were likely to take the trouble to download the product and run it on their desktops. Consultant Geoffrey Moore defines such people as "the gatekeepers for any new technology," adding that because they appreciate technology for its own sake they represent an ideal testing ground for new products. "They are the ones who will spend hours trying to get products to work that, in all conscience, never should have been shipped in the first place," Moore wrote in his 1991 book *Crossing the Chasm.* "They will forgive ghastly documentation, horrendously slow performance, ludicrous omissions in functionality, and bizarrely obtuse methods of invoking some needed function—all in the name of moving technology forward."

The big problem with technology enthusiasts, as Moore himself is quick to point out, is that their love of innovation frequently blinds them to serious flaws in design and execution. To some degree, that's what happened to Office for Java. The techies were so bowled over by the concept that they were slow to appreciate the product's major shortcomings.

A case in point was an article posted on the Internet on November 4, 1996, by Michael Cullison, a columnist for an Ohio-based on-line magazine. "Imagine running WordPerfect or Quattro Pro on any platform that has a Java-enabled browser," Cullison wrote after downloading Corel's new office suite. "Check this one out. It requires a pretty high-speed connection and some patience, but it's worth the wait just to say you were one of the first to try a spreadsheet or word-processor written in Java."

Around the same time, *PC Week* ran some tests on the software and published an approving if not entirely positive review. "Corel Corp.'s Corel Office for Java, the first suite of office applications written entirely in Java, proves that it can be done and paves the way to plat-form-independent computing.... Although containing only a few of the planned features at this point, the product we examined had a working version of the WordPerfect word processor and Quattro Pro spreadsheet and gave a good indication of the suite's potential." On the downside, the magazine noted that Office for Java was sometimes "painfully slow" when running in a standard Web browser, and that many of the program's functions, including the ability to save and print documents, were not working.

Clearly, a enormous amount of work remained to be done. Yet Cowpland's public pronouncements were unfailingly upbeat. He repeatedly promised that Office for Java would be ready to ship in the first quarter of 1997, backed by a "multimillion-dollar" ad campaign. And at Comdex that fall, Cowpland declared Corel's intention to enter the hardware business by launching a network computer with enhanced video capabilities called the Corel Video NC. In effect, Cowpland had decided to rip the guts out of Corel's money-losing video-conferencing unit and reposition it as a stripped-down computer suitable for corporate networks. Realistically, Cowpland knew he could never expect to make much money from hardware, but he hoped that the availability of such devices— similar machines, known in the industry as "thin clients," were beginning to appear from companies such as IBM, Oracle and

Sun—would benefit Corel by stimulating demand for Java-enabled software.

All this time, however, Corel still hadn't stopped to consider whether its goal of an integrated office suite was the right one for the dawning era of network-centric computing. If office workers throughout North America were going to start accessing their key business apps from some central server, those programs would have to be as light and nimble as possible to avoid lengthy downloads and sluggish performance. Yet the further along Corel got with Office for Java, the larger the application became, and the more it came to resemble a monolithic Windows office suite, with all of the standard bells and whistles. From inside and outside the company, there was pressure to add all of the functions of the existing WordPerfect suite, as well as file compatibility with a wide range of popular PC programs so that users could import documents and work on them in Java.

"Collectively, I think we all got carried away with the fact that we had already shown something working," Biber says. "Especially because the press and crowd reaction was so incredible. Rather than stepping back, reviewing our experiences and starting again from ground zero, we just charged ahead with the same fundamental architecture. And what made it worse was that we had a number of pilot users and early adopters saying to us, 'This is great—now, can you add this feature and this feature? Can you do a spell-checker, and how about something like revision control?' Everybody in the organization got swept away by that. So over the longer term, what was beginning to emerge was exactly what we had been trying all along to avoid, namely a rewrite of WordPerfect."

Corel's developers had to contend not only with the increasing scale and complexity of the project but also with changing technology. In 1997, Sun introduced a new Java development kit, JDK 1.1, that was better than the original version but also very different in the way its components interacted with one another. Corel was among the first major software companies to begin using JDK 1.1, but instead of making things easier, the switch necessitated an enormous amount of recoding for little perceived gain. Worse, the early releases of 1.1 were maddeningly unstable. Looking back, Biber believes it was a mistake for Corel to have jumped on JDK 1.1 when it did. It would have been better and far cheaper, he says, to have waited several more months while others discovered all the bugs.

Having been widely hailed as one of the pioneers of Java, however, the last thing Mike Cowpland wanted was to slow down and allow his competitors time to catch up. Like everyone else in the Java universe, he knew that IBM's Lotus Development division was hard at work on its own Java suite, code-named Kona, which was due out in September 1997. (In contrast to Corel's all-in-one strategy, Lotus's efforts were aimed at creating several smaller Java apps to handle basic functions such as e-mail and database connectivity.) In addition, there were persistent rumours that Microsoft itself was working on a collection of Java business applications. If those reports were true—Gates and his officials would neither confirm nor deny the stories—Corel had not a moment to lose. It was crucial to continue moving forward at full speed, both to avoid being overtaken and to maintain Corel's image as a leading-edge Java developer. "Being first to market with one hundred percent Java software has, if nothing else, gained the company incredible mindshare," reporter John Spooner observed in *Marketing Computers* magazine. "Cowpland has the attention of the press, analysts, Java developers, even companies such as Sun Microsystems that never even thought of Corel before. . . . What Larry Ellison [the chairman of Oracle and a vocal proponent of network computers] has mostly talked about, Mike Cowpland seems on the verge of delivering."

It was largely to maintain that aura of leadership that Corel posted an updated version of Office for Java on its Web site on April 2, 1997, coinciding with the start of the second annual JavaOne developers' conference in San Francisco. Speaking to reporters at the conference, Cowpland boasted that Office for Java was the first such application to be certified by Sun as "100 percent Java pure," and he brashly predicted that it and other Java-related products would generate

$40 million in revenue for the company that fiscal year. "We're out of the gate," he added. "It does establish us as the front-runner in Java applications." For good measure, he announced that Corel's goal was to become the premier Java applications provider, the "Microsoft of Java," as he put it.

Unfortunately for Cowpland, much of the novelty of Office for Java had worn off by that stage. Out in the real world, testers were beginning to judge the product not by its potential but by its practical utility. They were not impressed. Although Corel described the new release as a beta version and promised that the finished product would be ready to ship by the summer, Office for Java still fell well short of the mark. Critics panned it as being too slow, too big—the portion of the software designed to run on a network computer had ballooned to almost 10 megabytes—and rife with bugs. "I think this was a case of shoot first and then aim," said Jeffrey Tarter, editor of *Softletter*, a computer trends newsletter based in Watertown, Massachusetts. "It's not clear why anyone would want a Java version of Office."

Finally, after a year of hype, the reality of Java development was starting to sink in at Corel. As a programming language, Sun's creation held great promise, but it was still evolving and clearly not up to the challenge set by Cowpland. What's more, Corel had erred badly in trying to use Java to recreate a monolithic office suite loaded with features and built on tons of code. It was undoubtedly true that Java represented a significant advance in computer programming, but to get the most out of it would require a new, more modular approach to software development. In some ways, the learning curve for Java recalled the pioneering days of television in the 1940s and 1950s. Because few people back then understood the full potential of the new medium, most of the early programs were really just radio with pictures. Only later did producers and directors figure out how best to exploit the technology's visual dimension. Similarly, the engineers at Corel—not to mention their bosses—were slow to appreciate the unique properties of Java, and the extent to which they demanded a rethinking of traditional software design. "There was too much code,"

Montpetit complained, referring to the bloated beta version of Office for Java. "It was too big and it took too long to download."

Inside the company, there were growing tensions over the future of the project. On paper, the fifty-member Office for Java development team in Ottawa reported to Vincent Lin, who in turn answered to Paul Skillen at WordPerfect headquarters in Orem, Utah, several thousand kilometres to the southwest. But geography wasn't the only thing separating the two men. Lin complained that the word-processing software for the suite, which was being Java-coded by a separate team of WordPerfect veterans under Skillen's direction in Utah, was poorly written and so slow that it made the rest of the project look worse than it was. Meanwhile, Skillen, who in March had succeeded Eid Eid as vice-president of engineering, was becoming increasingly convinced that Lin's whole approach to Java architecture was wrong. "Paul eventually convinced Mike that we needed to change direction," says Carey Stanton. Rather than designing a full suite, Skillen favoured a new, network-friendly paradigm known as "distributed computing," in which applications are broken up into collections of small components that can be shipped quickly and efficiently across a network and reassembled as needed on the user's desktop. "The analogy I like is that we had been trying to stuff an elephant down a garden hose," says Stanton. "With distributed computing, it's more like a bunch of ants."

The growing animosity between Skillen and Lin finally came to a head in the summer. On June 30, Corel put out a press release announcing that it was centralizing development of its Java office suite in Orem. "We're talking about cranking up a team in Utah to be a Java powerhouse," Cowpland said. A Corel spokeswoman explained that the decision meant that twenty-two positions would be transferred to Orem. Oddly, however, none of Corel's Ottawa-based Java engineers were being asked to relocate. Instead, the Orem jobs would be filled by existing WordPerfect staff and some new employees.

The newspapers reported it as a straightforward reorganization, but in fact the announcement was the first hint of an abrupt change in direction for Corel's Java strategy. Vincent Lin, who only two months earlier had been profiled in *The Ottawa Citizen* as the driving force behind that strategy, was being pushed out. And with Skillen now firmly in control of the project, Office for Java was for all intents and purposes dead. One by one, about twenty developers defected from the company over the following two months, disillusioned by the power struggle and uncertain whether their contributions mattered any longer. "It was a weird situation," Montpetit, who resigned from Corel in July to work on his own Java start-up project, told *Electrical Engineering Times*. "Everybody felt sort of lost and discouraged. We had worked so hard for a year and now we felt we had to go a different way. A lot of people left the company."

Meanwhile, Paul Skillen faced the unenviable task of trying to explain to Java's supporters, the media and Corel's investors why the company had suddenly dumped a project in which it had invested so much time and money. After much internal discussion, it was agreed that he and Corel's media relations director, Cindy Scott, would spend a week on the road meeting with industry analysts at several of the big technology consulting firms, including The Gartner Group in Stamford, Connecticut, and Forrester Research Inc. in Cambridge, Massachusetts. Scott knew that as soon as the news of Corel's strategic shift got out, mainstream journalists would be calling the analysts to seek reaction and ask what it all meant. By getting to those people ahead of time, Corel would have a better shot at spinning the story to its advantage, or at least minimizing the damage. The official line was to be that Corel, far from having lost its way, was gearing up to leapfrog the competition by applying its detailed knowledge of Java to a new, more sophisticated business plan.

The analysts' tour was scheduled for the first week in August. Coincidentally, just before it began, Scott got wind of the fact that an influential trade publication based in Redmond, Washington, *Windows Watcher*—the newsletter that had labelled Corel "the whatchamacallit company" in 1995—was preparing to run a damning article about Office for Java, reiterating the charge that the company's Java-based software was too fat, too slow and offered no significant advantages over existing PC business apps. In what must have seemed at the time like a brilliant tactical stroke, Scott managed to talk the writer of the piece, Robbin Young, into postponing the article until she and Skillen could drop by the *Windows Watcher* office in person. Scott hoped that a face-to-face session with Young would yield a more sympathetic assessment of Corel's Java initiatives.

She was badly mistaken. Moreover, for reasons that are still unclear, Corel neglected to make sure that Young signed a non-disclosure agreement, a standard commitment sought by companies when discussing new products and business strategies that are still under wraps.

As a result, the first public indication of Corel's decision to abandon Office for Java came in an article posted on the *Windows Watcher* Web site on Wednesday, August 13, 1997, under the heading, "Cowpland skids Corel into yet another high-speed turn." Needless to say, it did not portray Corel or its founder in a favourable light.

"Picture a bumper car going 64 mph," Young wrote. "It hits a wall. The driver steers hard to right, and floors it again. He hits another wall. Another 90 degree turn. This time he dodges two or three slower cars, till he hits another wall. He cranks hard to left, and floors it again. Presumably he'll keep going till he runs out of power, the car is destroyed, or he breaks through the wall in search of a bigger arena. After hearing about Corel's latest strategies, that's the image that pops into my mind of Corel CEO Mike Cowpland."

There was more. Young quoted Skillen as saying that Corel did not believe "Java is the centre of the world," a strange assertion coming from a company that had been hyping the programming language at every opportunity. The piece went on to attack Corel's new product plans as "fuzzy," adding that until the company provided more details it was "impossible to say if Corel's version of component-based computing stands a chance."

As soon as Chris Biber saw the article, he knew what to expect. Having served as the company's chief Java spokesman for the previous eighteen months, he had been unhappy about being left out of the analysts' tour and believed strongly that the change in strategy had been mishandled from a public relations standpoint. In his view, a strategic shift of that magnitude needed to be backed up with supporting documentation—in effect, a white paper—that would explain, for the benefit of people both inside and outside the company, exactly what the company was doing and why. Since that wasn't done, it was inevitable that the move would be interpreted by Corel's critics in the worst possible light. Robbin Young's colourful portrayal of Cowpland as a madman in a bumper car was a perfect example of what he feared most.

And now that the news had slipped out, it was inevitable that there would be people with their noses out of joint. Sure enough, within twenty-four hours of Young's piece appearing on the Internet, Corel started fielding calls from angry writers at rival trade publications, demanding to know why they had been left out of the loop. For more than a year they had dutifully reported on Cowpland's Java strategy, mistakenly assuming that the company knew what it was doing. Suddenly Corel had switched direction and the first publication to find out about it was a newsletter well known for its previous attacks on the company. It just didn't add up. "The first reaction," says Chris Biber, "was that a lot of other journalists wanted to know why they were not told about this. So what we ended up with was a whole angry horde of pissed-off people."

And it got worse. In the same week that Robbin Young had torn a strip off Cowpland, the company's shares jumped 7 percent in unusually heavy trading. Investors, financial analysts and business reporters were all clamouring to figure out why, so Corel's director of investor relations, John Hladkowicz (brother of Ed, Cowpland's tennis partner) scheduled a conference call for the following Monday. "The message from Mike during the conference call was, 'We believe the future is bright, our products are moving well and—by the way—some of you may have heard about our Java shift and we want to take this opportunity to explain our plans to you,'" Biber says. In fact, it was the first that most of the participants in the call had heard about the change. Several of them pushed for more detail, but Corel had no background documentation to give them. Indeed, Biber himself had only been told about the conference call half an hour before it started. "It was a badly organized and badly supported call," Biber says. "In typical Corel fashion it was shoot from the hip—let's just do it. And that just doesn't always work, because the media are left to draw their own conclusions."

Which they did, most egregiously in the lead story in the next day's *Globe and Mail Report on Business*. Under the headline, "Corel ditches Java initiative," reporter Patrick Brethour left the impression that the company had all but given up on Sun's programming language. "Until yesterday, Corel's Java-based office software was the centre of the company's efforts to displace Microsoft," Brethour wrote. "No more. Corel said yesterday that it will instead focus on selling office software that is based on Microsoft's Windows NT, an increasingly popular operating system. . . . A Corel spokeswoman said surging corporate demand for Windows NT was a factor in the decision to change directions."

The *Globe's* story was, if not wrong, certainly incomplete. In recognition of that, the paper ran a shorter, follow-up piece a day later noting that Corel actually planned to increase spending on Java research as part of what Cowpland was referring to as "Phase Two" of the company's Java strategy. But the damage had been done. Taking their cue from the earlier story, newspapers across North America were reporting that Corel had dropped Java—full stop. And down in Redmond, Washington, legions of happy Microsoft flacks were faxing off copies of the *Globe* article to technology writers around the world, determined to make sure that some of the negative publicity rubbed off on Sun and its loud-mouthed chairman, Scott McNealy. Corel's stumble was by far the most embarrassing setback in Java's two-year history, and Bill Gates was milking it for all it was worth.

In the months after the Office for Java cancellation, Corel's reputation suffered one heavy blow after another. On September 10, the company warned investors that it would report a third-quarter loss of $32 million on sales of $54 million, primarily because of weaker than expected sales of CorelDRAW and the WordPerfect office suite. The announcement drove the shares down 27 percent to a four-year low of $6.50. After the close of trading on September 24, chief financial officer Chuck Norris jolted investors again by predicting a loss of as much as $20 million in the fourth quarter. The next day, Corel's stock gave up another 20 percent, falling to $5.45.

It was hard to conceive of things getting any worse, but they did. On October 3, the Montreal *Gazette*, citing insider trading reports filed with the Quebec Securities Commission, broke the news that Cowpland had sold 2,431,200 Corel shares—26 percent of his personal holdings—in ten separate transactions between August 11 and 14. The obvious question was whether the Corel CEO had known that the company was going to fall far short of its third-quarter financial projections at the time of those transactions. If so, it would have been a clear violation of securities regulations against trading on inside information.

Cowpland insists he did not know—that when he sold his shares he still believed the company was on track to meet its targets for the three months ending on August 31. Yet the fact remains that he knew his company was losing market share to Microsoft and other competitors. According to PC Data Inc., a market research firm based in Reston, Virginia, Corel's market share in the business software category, which includes both CorelDRAW and WordPerfect, had fallen 32 percent in terms of units sold in the twelve months ending June 1997. In dollar terms, the sales were down 19 percent. Interviewed by *The Ottawa Citizen*'s Andrew McIntosh in October of that year, Cowpland acknowledged receiving the PC Data report before he sold his shares but said the figures in it were "irrelevant" and didn't influence the timing of his decision.

Technically, that might be true—after all, PC Data's findings related only to retail software sales. As previously noted, Corel counts its products as having been sold when they are shipped to a distributor, a method of accounting for sales that gives it a significant degree of control over its reported revenues in any one quarter. (By allowing the unsold inventory in the distribution channels to rise, Corel could claim an increase in sales even when the actual number of boxes purchased by customers stayed the same or declined.) In the third quarter of 1997, the company shipped $96 million (US) worth of software to its distributors. Had Corel followed its normal procedure for reporting sales, it would have used that figure for its third-quarter revenues. Instead, it booked only $54 million in revenues, implicitly acknowledging that the level of unsold inventory had gotten way out of control.

According to Chuck Norris, the fundamental difficulty was that sales of WordPerfect 8, which had been released in June, were nowhere near as strong as the company had projected. Normally, there was anywhere from 60 to 90 days' worth of unsold software in the hands of distributors; at some point during the summer, the company realized it had risen above 120 days. "The problem essentially is that a bunch of product got shipped into the channel in anticipation of [customer demand] and it didn't happen," Norris says. "We were left with inventory in the channel which was really too large for us to treat, from a conservative accounting point of view, as sales. Based on what we were seeing from distributors—their reports of what they were carrying—at the end of the third quarter we had to acknowledge there was really too much there. People weren't upgrading from version 7 to version 8 as fast as sales and marketing had anticipated they would."

Norris added that Corel's financial staff and its sales department initially disagreed over the appropriate way of responding to the shortfall. The sales department—and, apparently, Cowpland himself—took the view that the problem was a temporary one, that in time the level of unsold product would fall back into line with the industry's accepted range of sixty to ninety days. Norris, however, felt strongly that the company had to own up to the problem by reducing its reported sales. "There was obviously some discussion of that, because part of the calculation is what you anticipate future [retail sales] to be. There was a lot of research done on that by sales and marketing and by us, a lot of back and forth, but in the end we basically said, 'This is what we have to do.'"

The key question, then, is: when did Corel realize that it had a serious problem with unsold inventory? Norris says he only found out in early September, when the sales department handed him its regular month-end report. Based on figures supplied by nine or ten of the biggest North American software wholesalers, the report provided a detailed breakdown of shipments from Corel to its distributors, and from the distributors to retailers, mail-order firms and resellers. "Some of the distributors report [to Corel] weekly, some report monthly," Norris says. "The numbers would come into sales and they would monitor it. Then the sales department would consolidate those reports and report to me once a month." Norris adds that he does not know whether Cowpland became aware of the problem before he did. "He may have had other numbers and he might have have been talking to other people, so I really can't comment on what he had available versus what I had available."

For the record, Cowpland says he sold the shares when he did because he needed the money to pay debts that had come due. It should be noted, however, that the stock sales took place soon after a series of closed-door meetings between Corel managers and financial analysts from Canada and the United States. One of those analysts was Eliot Glazer of the New York firm of DuPasquier & Co. Inc., an adviser to several large U.S. mutual funds. Glazer declined to be interviewed for this book, but one of the Corel managers who met with him in Ottawa, Chris Biber, says that Glazer seemed impressed by the company's prospects over the longer term: "Fairly shortly thereafter we saw some consistently higher volumes of Corel shares being purchased, so my suspicion is that Glazer was behind that."

Another person who was bullish on Corel was David Kramer, a Montreal-based technology analyst for RBC Dominion Securities, one of Canada's largest brokerages. A former software programmer and small-business consultant, Kramer had been with the brokerage for only a year at that time and had never written a report on Corel prior to the summer of 1997. On August 12, shortly after a meeting with Cowpland, Norris and John Hladkowicz at which Cowpland spoke enthusiastically about the company's latest sales figures, Kramer initiated coverage of the company with a "buy" recommendation, the first from any major investment house in several months. His report placed a twelve-month target of $12 on the stock, adding that the company's earnings were "nearing a turning point" after two years of volatility.

Corel's shares, which had fallen almost 14 percent since the start of the year, immediately jumped 55 cents to close at $8.70. Obviously, a number of investors had taken Kramer's recommendation to heart and were rushing to acquire the shares, unaware that the principal seller was none other than Cowpland himself.

Like Glazer, Kramer declined to be interviewed about his recommendation, citing a company policy that bars RBC Dominion analysts from speaking to reporters. Speaking privately, however, a representative of the firm says Kramer feels he was misled about the company's financial position. "Either Cowpland had a feeling for what the third-quarter results were going to be, or if he didn't he definitely should have," the RBC Dominion staff member says. "Either way, he's damned if he did and damned if he didn't."

Chapter Fifteen

orel's near-death experience in the second half of 1997—the huge losses and the collapse of its stock—forced Mike Cowpland to make some long-overdue changes. He brought in a new senior vice-president of sales, a no-nonsense former Dell Computer sales manager named Don Sylvester. Sylvester immediately set about establishing a network of six U.S. corporate sales offices, a move Cowpland himself had always resisted for fear of having to delegate authority to managers in the field.

Next, Cowpland resigned from the boards of two Toronto-based companies, Geac Computer Corp. and Hummingbird Communications Inc., both of which had received venture financing from his old friend and tennis partner Ben Webster. Cowpland told associates that he wanted to give his undivided attention to Corel, but that was only part of the story. The other reason was that Webster, himself a former director of Geac and Hummingbird, was dying of cancer. Without his presence on the two boards, Cowpland no longer felt much of a connection to either company.

There were even signs that Cowpland was prepared, perhaps for the first time in his twenty-five years as an entrepreneur, to listen seriously to outside advice. *The Ottawa Citizen* noted that he had approved the purchase of subscriptions to software industry reports by high-profile U.S. consulting firms such as The Yankee Group and The Gartner Group. In the past, Cowpland had sneered at such outfits, viewing them as too far removed from the front lines of high tech to be of much use. But Corel's dramatic loss of retail market share over the previous year had underscored the folly of trying to sustain the WordPerfect brand without a significant base of corporate customers. And whether he liked it or not, Cowpland had to acknowledge that big American companies tended to look to organizations like The Gartner Group for advice on purchasing new technology. If Corel really was serious about trying to crack the corporate market, its CEO would have to learn a little humility.

Most astonishing of all, Cowpland hired an outside consultant, Robert Shereck of the Tanev Group, to train Corel executives in the ways of participatory management and team-building. Shereck, whose client list includes such blue-chip companies as Molson, Nesbitt Burns and TrizecHahn, is a Montrealer who spent fifteen years in the electronics industry before deciding that his true calling lay in teaching people how to achieve better results through improved communication and more sensitive leadership.

Although Cowpland does not remember the encounter, Shereck says he first met the Corel founder in 1987 when he was a volunteer fundraiser for the Children's Wish Foundation, a national charity that helps children with life-threatening diseases. Cowpland made a generous donation, and Shereck never forgot it. A decade later, in November 1997, Shereck was driving home from his office in St.-Adolphe d'Howard, an hour northwest of Montreal, when he heard a report on the radio about Corel's plummeting stock price. He phoned the company the next morning and left a message for Cowpland. "Ten years ago you listened to me and trusted your instincts," Shereck said. "Please trust yourself again and call my office, because this time I'd like to help you."

Under normal circumstances, Cowpland would have ignored Shereck's message. But in the fall of 1997 he was close to despair—so worried, as he told Marlen, that he found it difficult to deliver his annual pep-rally speech at the company gala marking the release of CorelDRAW 8. He dialled Tanev's number and was sufficiently intrigued by Shereck's pitch to ask for references. "Pretty soon I got all these sound bites coming in to my voice-mail from different companies saying that Tanev's advice had helped them increase performance by as much as 1,000 percent. The numbers were just irresistible, so I thought, well, what's to lose?"

"It was twelve hours a day for three days, for all the VPs and a few levels down, like some of the directors of engineering and sales people," Cowpland said after the initial round of seminars, in April 1998. "I'd never done that before because I'm not a great believer in consultants as a category. I think if you're not careful they can take away internal initiative. But it turned out to be really worthwhile. What I found was that, although I believe very much in consensus, other people don't necessarily see it that way because of the amount of perceived power you get in my position."

By interviewing each of the eighteen participants individually and then observing how they interacted in a group, Shereck and his associates began to get a feel for the problems that, in their estimation, were preventing the company from achieving its potential. At the top of the list was Cowpland's kinetic, top-down management style, which invariably left other people at Corel scrambling to keep up with the boss's latest strategic shift—and feeling that their own opinions hardly mattered.

At the end of that first, three-day encounter, Shereck gave each of the managers a project to work on before the next session. Cowpland's project was to come up a new way of conducting meetings that would encourage his subordinates to speak their own minds. "For example, we have an executive meeting every Thursday, and as far as I'm concerned it's always been a level playing field—99 percent consensus—but the thing is other people see it differently," Cowpland said, as though recognizing the problem for the first time. "If I was saying one thing, they might be too intimidated to put forward another strong opinion. So my specific objective is to create a platform for other people—whether we institute votes or minutes, or get someone else to run the agenda—so that each individual or group within the company feels it's being represented."

As an illustration, Cowpland pointed to the launch in April 1998 of a new version of WordPerfect that incorporated voice-recognition technology licensed from Dragon Systems Inc. of Boston. The software makes it possible for people to dictate letters and other written documents into their computers, rather than using a keyboard. "The type of thing that tends to happen is that we would get the Dragon software, for example, which was an idea I helped pioneer and steer, and nobody would disagree with it, but there'd still be a ripple effect when it got down to the engineering team in Orem. They might be working on the Swedish version of WordPerfect 8, so you'd say, 'Okay, drop that because we're going to work on Dragon.' And people would say, 'Well, that's just Mike's pet project,' so there wouldn't be any real buy-in. What I'm learning is you have to have transparency so people can see that, yes, someone from their group—Paul Skillen, for example—has been fully involved with this decision so, yes, it's good. That's an interesting thing. And it's quite a challenge, because it means you have to get people feeling involved in the process from the beginning as opposed to feeling jerked around on the end of the string."

Mike Cowpland as a sensitive, New Age manager? The idea was far-fetched to say the least. Next thing you knew, a guy like Trevor McGuire would be getting in touch with his inner child.

Fortunately for those who actually enjoyed watching Cowpland's high-wire act, the Corel CEO had lost none of his appetite for speculative ventures. That much was obvious from his next big initiative, which was intended to establish Corel firmly in the top ranks of companies supplying computers and software to North America's largest corporations. A skeptic might say that it was a bit like Hyundai, the Korean car company, setting its sights on the Formula One championship, but Cowpland was clearly relishing the challenge. By early 1998 he had taken to describing Corel as "a very big start-up company," which might not have been much comfort to investors (whose shares had surrendered almost 90 percent of their value in two and a half years) but spoke volumes about Cowpland's own attitude toward the company. Once again, he was preparing to dive in at the deep end. In time, Corel's shareholders would find out whether there was any water in the pool.

The game plan was vintage Cowpland, right down to the pivotal role played by Pat Beirne. In September 1996, only four months after Corel had made a splash at the first JavaOne conference in San Francisco with its plan to create a full Java office suite, Beirne sat down and began to design his own network computer—his first major hardware project since leaving Mitel in 1985. At its core was Motorola's Power PC microprocessor, chosen because, at the time, it seemed to offer the best combination of price and performance, while consuming much less power than a comparable Intel chip. That was important, because the less power the computer required, the less heat it would give off—and less heat meant that it could be housed in a smaller box.

"The smaller you make something," Beirne explains, "it might be a little more expensive to manufacture at the beginning but in the long run it's cheaper. A typical desktop computer today uses a lot of metal and plastic—you're probably talking fifteen or twenty dollars' worth of raw material, plus all the wires and fuses and other things that are associated with high power. If you can get rid of all that you're going to save money." (One of Beirne's objectives, in fact, was to ensure that his network computer would fit inside the sleek, textbook-sized plastic case that had been designed for Corel's desktop video-conferencing system. That way, at least, the millions of dollars invested in CorelVIDEO would not go entirely to waste.)

Beirne spent six months designing and building his computer before discovering that the Power PC simply wasn't up to the challenge—it was too slow and awkward to program. Fortunately, by then Corel was able to get its hands on a much faster processor manufactured by Digital Equipment Corp. under licence from a British company called Advanced RISC Machines (ARM). RISC stands for reduced instruction set computing, a technology that is cheaper and more efficient than traditional computing because it relies on a simplified chip architecture and fewer instructions. The Power PC microprocessor was a RISC design, too, but Digital's StrongARM chip was superior to it in almost every way. The version Corel decided to use, the 275 megahertz SA 110, was almost as fast as a top-of-the-line Intel Pentium chip, while drawing less than one-twentieth the electricity. The price was far lower, to boot: about forty dollars per chip compared to several hundred dollars for a conventional Pentium processor. (In February 1998, in conjunction with a planned acquisition of Digital's semiconductor division, Intel signed a licensing agreement with ARM to manufacture microprocessors based on the StrongARM technology.)

Switching to the new chip forced Beirne and his team—by that point he was overseeing three other hardware engineers and about fifteen software developers—to make a number of other changes inside the box. While they were at it, they also opted to introduce a new operating system. Originally, they had planned to use a proprietary operating system called netOS, from Neoware Inc. of King of Prussia, Pensylvania. But every time Corel's engineers altered the computer's hardware specifications, they found themselves having to wait for Neoware to made corresponding changes to the operating system. The process was time-consuming and expensive, because Neoware charged extra for each revision.

Finally, a Corel engineer named San Mehat approached Beirne and proposed that the team consider using a free operating system called Linux, a stripped-down version of Unix that originated as part of a programming experiment in 1991 by Linus Torvalds, then a twenty-one-year-old student at Helsinki University in Finland. Instead of trying to sell his operating system—which would have meant competing against Bill Gates, among others—Torvalds began to give the source code away over the Internet, on condition that anyone who altered or made improvements to it had to agree to make those changes freely available to the public. (These conditions were laid down in something called the General Public Licence, the basis for what has become known as the open-source software movement.) Within a few months, there were more than a hundred developers working on Linux improvements; after several years, there were tens of thousands of them in user groups all over Europe, North America and Asia. Thanks to their contributions, Linux was evolving in a kind of Darwinian process of natural selection. Changes that made Linux more powerful, more flexible or more efficient tended to be adopted quickly by developers around the world; everything else was simply discarded and forgotten.

Mehat himself was a member of the Ottawa Carleton Linux User Group, and like most Linux supporters he shared Torvalds's idealistic, anti-Microsoft vision of a freely distributable operating system, one capable of running on virtually any hardware, with an infinite capacity to be customized. So compelling was that vision, in fact, that by 1998 there were an estimated 5 million Linux installations around the world, including, according to one study, more than half of all the servers connected to the Internet. The number of users was doubling every twelve months, making Linux the only operating system in the world, aside from Microsoft Windows, that was increasing its market share from year to year. More and more, Linux developers saw their mission as being not merely to provide an alternative to Microsoft Windows but to defeat Microsoft in what—in their minds, at least— was shaping up as a kind of holy war for the desktop.

For Beirne, the distant possibility that Linux might one day supplant Windows was of less importance than the fact that the source code was readily available and it was free. Indeed, a young British engineer named Russell King had already spent several hundred unpaid hours adapting Linux to the ARM microprocessor, the core logic inside the StrongARM. By collaborating with King, the engineers at Corel Computer were able to solve the remaining problems more rapidly and far more cheaply than if they had had to do the work on their own.

In June 1997, while Beirne and his colleagues were still hard at work on the machine, they and about three dozen other engineers and marketing personnel moved out of Corel's golden tower on Carling Avenue and into a new set of offices a couple of kilometres closer to Parliament Hill. It was the headquarters of Corel Computer Corp., a newly created spinoff of which Eid Eid was president. The announced goal was to launch Corel's network computer by the fall of that year, but that deadline, like so many others before it, came and went with no public explanation of the delay. Instead of a splashy product introduction at the annual company gala in October, Cowpland had to settle for a modest Corel Computer display off to one side of the main convention hall. The exhibit was staffed by none other than Pat Beirne himself, looking slightly uncomfortable in a jacket and tie. "We had to delay the launch for a bunch of reasons, mostly to do with the software," he said later. "In hindsight, though, it all worked out for the best, because all during that period we kept finding all sorts of hardware problems, too."

By the beginning of 1998, the glitches had been pretty well fixed and Corel's NC was ready to be sent out for testing. Beirne didn't pretend to know whether there would be a market for the computer—it would be up to Cowpland to figure that out—but he had no doubt at all about the machine's technical virtues. Compared to the other network computers that were beginning to appear on the market, Corel's NC was faster and more flexible, in part because it incorporated a hard drive that enabled the machine to keep working even when there were problems on the network to which it was connected. The inclusion of a hard drive—the technical term for it was a "persistent cache"—solved one of the most notorious shortcomings of network computers: the fact that they could be rendered useless in the event of a network crash or slowdown.

Beirne's characteristically cool engineer's exterior melts away as he speaks about the attributes of his team's creation. He calls it "our little beast" and happily runs down the list of its features, which include half a dozen independent processors to look after the keyboard, the screen display, the hard drive and other components. He is most proud of the machine's built-in communications capabilities, which in many ways harken back to his experience as a designer of Mitel phone switches; in addition to being used as a computer, Corel's NC can provide a full range of digital telephone and video-phone services. Once it is installed on someone's desk, the communications signals can easily be routed through the existing local-area network (LAN), eliminating the need for a separate internal telephone network that in many cases can cost hundreds of dollars per employee to install. "That way," Beirne says, "you could wire up an office of, say, twenty people simply by putting a LAN connection at each person's desk and then wiring the LAN to Bell. Five years ago it would have been tricky, but today it's a piece of cake."

Realistically, however, Beirne knows that it might take years before computers such as Corel's NC are in widespread use. "The thing is, there isn't a market for this kind of all-in-one device yet," he says. "When you go into any company, the guys who run the telephone system and the guys who run the LAN are two different departments. We've got to beat down the door and point out to them that it doesn't have to be that way—there can be one group providing one reliable LAN and all the telephone services anybody would want. If we come across companies that already have that vision we'll be able to walk right in and say, 'Here's the solution, here's the peg that fits in that hole.' But in most companies right now those functions are performed by two different groups, and there is bound to be a lot of resistance. Because what this box will do, it will eliminate jobs."

To have any chance at all of commercial success, Beirne's little computer needed two things. The first was software. After axing the Office for Java project in the summer of 1997, Corel switched to a new strategy that implicitly recognized what everyone in the PC software industry already knew: most companies, and most workers, did not want to have to give up their Windows applications. By developing a new technology it called jBridge, Corel hoped to make it possible for an NC—indeed, any computer equipped with a Java Virtual Machine—to access Windows programs from a central server. The concept was similar to a product introduced in 1996 by Citrix Systems Inc. of Fort Lauderdale, Florida, under the name WinFrame, which was later licensed to Microsoft for sale as the Windows Terminal Server. The difference was that Citrix and Microsoft had taken a relatively simple approach in which the server itself performed all of the processing work. As a result, only changes to the graphical interface—in other words, the look of the screen—were sent to the local terminal.

In contrast, Corel's jBridge technology was designed to take full advantage of the processing power of the client computer. In effect, the entire application would be broken down into reusable Java components—JavaBeans, in the fanciful language dreamed up by Sun Microsystems—that were downloaded to the client as needed. The user would then work independently of the network until another software component was required. The arrangement, Corel said, dramatically improved the performance of applications while reducing network traffic and placing fewer demands on the server.

Of course, all of that assumed that jBridge could be made to work as advertised and would be both stable and fast enough to satisfy large corporate customers. Among the many skeptics was Chris Biber, who quit Corel in September 1997 after becoming convinced that the company had lost its bearings. He now works for an Ottawa start-up called InterNetivity. "I try to look at things from a longer-term perspective," Biber said, "and when I looked at Corel I saw a company that was doing all kinds of different things on software and then suddenly they also started doing hardware with Corel Computer. So I thought, 'Excuse me? What do we think we are doing in the hardware business?' And trying to bridge that gap and explain to financial analysts and industry analysts with a straight face, 'We know exactly what we're doing,' just wasn't me. Personally, I couldn't even explain it to myself."

It wasn't just the repeated changes in direction that troubled Biber. From what he could tell, the technical challenges surrounding jBridge were going to be horrendously difficult to overcome. "Microsoft and Citrix are both working on platform-specific implementations of this and they still have huge problems—instability, speed, performance and so on. So here's the company that owns the operating system trying to put this together and having huge problems with it. What makes us think at Corel that we can implement a Windows NT terminal program on a non-platform-specific implementation, with all the vagaries of Java and all the speed problems with Java, and succeed where Microsoft and Citrix are not succeeding?"

Apart from software, the other thing Corel badly needed to vindicate its client-server technology was the endorsement of at least one high-profile corporate user. In marketing, such companies are known as "reference customers." By taking a chance on some new and unproven technology, they allow its creators to gain valuable real-world experience. If all goes well, the relationship can be a stepping stone to wider market acceptance.

For a while, Cowpland was confident that he had found his reference customer. His old employer, Northern Telecom, was thinking of using Corel's Java-based software in order to modernize all of its in-house applications. Cowpland had been speaking about the idea with David Niles, Nortel's Ottawa-based vice-president of advanced technology and infrastructure, who in turn had discussed it with Nortel CEO John Roth. Under the terms of the proposed deal, Corel would rewrite Nortel's internal applications for free in return for the right to sell the software to other large enterprises. As an additional incentive, Corel would pay Nortel a royalty on future sales of 6 percent in the first year, declining to 1 percent over four years.

"Pretty soon we should have a very major agreement with Northern," an excited Cowpland told me during an interview in late November 1997. "We've got a meeting tomorrow with about fourteen people. This is going to be probably the biggest thing we've ever done. We're looking at modernizing all of their in-house applications, and the beauty is that we can then sell that to the rest of the world. And we'll have the scalability of something we know works in a 70,000-person organization. We've been talking to them for three months or four months and it's now actually getting to the point of signing. I think we'll sign it before Christmas." He added that Niles himself had initiated the discussions. "He called me up. He's the IT [information technology] guru, and he said, 'We're very interested in what you're doing, let's talk some more.'"

Interestingly, rumours of a major deal between Corel and Nortel had been circulating on Bay Street since August. It looked suspiciously as though someone at Corel had been leaking word of the discussions in a desperate attempt to breathe life into the company's flagging stock price. But if that was the case, the strategy failed miserably. And as the stock price continued to drift lower, investors waited in vain for any confirmation of a contract with Nortel. Nortel officials, including Niles, refused to speak publicly about the negotiations. The telecommunications giant was clearly having second thoughts about aligning itself so closely with a money-losing software company that had a reputation for unpredictability and virtually no track record in the corporate market.

Finally, in April 1998, Cowpland admitted that the Nortel deal was off. "We've actually kind of put that on ice, because we found they were not moving fast enough," he said. "Between us, the deal was a real sweetheart deal for them, which we initiated early on when we thought they could do us a lot of good as a corporate endorsement. But they were so slow in coming through, and when it came to the crunch they were nit-picking about what would be said in the press release. That's the interesting thing because they're so phenomenally successful and yet we found them like a bunch of government bureaucrats. You can't get them to do anything, and everything takes nineteen signatures. They had a fantastic opportunity with us because they weren't going to pay anything and we were going to give them a royalty, which we were willing to do just for the marketing value. But in the end we thought, this is ridiculous. We don't want to get bogged down with them going forward, so who needs them?"

Cowpland was annoyed, but it wasn't like him to give up hope. He claimed to have a line on two other prospective customers, one of which, Sybase Inc. of Emeryville, California, was the world's third-largest producer of database software. "Sybase is absolutely in love with jBridge—they want to be able to promote it with their database applications," he said. "They actually called us because one of their developers heard what we were doing and said, 'This is just what we want.' So they came up here for a couple of meetings and now we're in the final stages of a contract. It's a sweetheart deal, but we don't mind that because they would become almost our showcase. So here's the endorsement we want but it's a much better endorsement, because what we will do is give them a small royalty, like five dollars per seat, and they'll pay us like a million bucks as an up-front payment." On June 17, Corel announced a licensing agreement with Sybase to develop and deliver Java-based applications to Sybase customers using jBridge technology. The two companies set a target date for commercial release of the product in late 1998.

The other potential deal, Cowpland said, was with a Texas-based division of IBM that manufactures and sells network computers. The details hadn't been worked out, but there was talk of possibly bundling jBridge with future shipments of Big Blue's NC. "There's a meeting on Monday in Austin. I was going to go down but they advised us that their executive vice-president couldn't make it, and they don't want me to go until he goes. IBM is like that, you know."

There it was again: that ridiculous obsession on the part of big, strait-laced companies with protocol and chain of command. Cowpland had been fighting it since his days as a young engineer in the 1960s, but he just couldn't seem to get away from it. Indeed, given Corel's increasing emphasis on the corporate software market as opposed to retail sales, he was likely to encounter it even more in the future. Such was the price of innovation. He understood it, but that didn't mean he had to like it.

Suddenly Cowpland's face brightened as he pondered the huge opportunities that lay—he was convinced—just around the next bend. "This is the most exciting development ever," he said. "In fact, even internally people are saying this is as exciting as the release of DRAW 1. When that came out, we hit the bull's-eye, and this is just like that. This is the bull's-eye."

Less than two months after that conversation, Cowpland threw Corel into another unexpected ninety-degree turn. On June 24, 1998, the company told analysts that it was shutting down its engineering centre in Orem, Utah, phasing out 530 jobs and transferring all research and development work on the WordPerfect office suite to Ottawa. "First and foremost, we're doing this because it's the right business decision," Don Sylvester said. "It's important for us to maximize our operational efficiencies and effectiveness by consolidating our research and development into one space."

In addition, Cowpland had decided to abandon plans to spin off Corel Computer as a separate company. Almost exactly a year after it had been set up, Corel Computer was being folded back into the main company. The man Cowpland had picked to run it, Eid Eid, was out of a job. His second-in-command, Ron McNab, would henceforth oversee all work on the network computer in his new role as a vice-president of Corel Corp. and general manager of the Corel Computer division.

Another casualty of the reorganization was Paul Skillen, who had spent two years as the senior executive in charge of WordPerfect. All of a sudden, Cowpland had decided that Skillen was too much of a nice guy, too undemanding, for a company as fast-moving and dynamic as Corel. "He's a very popular, lovable guy and extremely intelligent, but if I examine his track record it's not there," Cowpland said. "Some people end up winning, other people don't."

It seemed a rather harsh judgment considering that Cowpland had stood by Skillen for six years and had personally chosen him to run the Utah operation. But Cowpland was keen to deflect responsibility for the removal of both Eid Eid and Paul Skillen. It wasn't so much his doing, he said, but the will of Corel's new "executive leadership team" (ELT), a ten-member group of senior managers that was created on the advice of consultants from the Tanev Group. Eid and Skillen had been members of the ELT, but according to Cowpland the rest of the executives held a separate meeting and voted to ask for their resignations.

"The funny thing is, it may look like something I did, but in reality I'm responding to what the team knows is right," he said. "The good thing about the ELT concept is that it formalizes what the team leader believes is the case but others don't necessarily know is the case. And by formalizing it, they share responsibility and it takes away the blame game." Cowpland's choice of words was illuminating. He had never liked being seen as the bad guy when it came time to get rid of somebody. Now, instead of delegating unpleasant tasks to some young, ambitious hatchet man, he had the executive leadership team.

With Skillen gone, the responsibility for jBridge was handed to Derek Burney, a veteran Corel engineer who was rejoining the company after a nine-month stint in the Ottawa office of International Microcomputer Software Inc., a California company that in September 1997 had purchased eight of Corel's consumer CD-ROM titles.

It was while talking to Burney, Cowpland said, that he came to the decision to shut down the Utah engineering facility. "I was trying to persuade him to return and run jBridge for us because I could sense that we had a leader here. So I asked him what he would think if we closed Orem—would that be a huge burden? He said, 'If you do that, all of the engineers in Ottawa will be giving each other high fives.' I thought, that's great, because it just seemed to make more sense to consolidate everything under one roof. When everybody's within walking distance of all the senior executives, it's so much more efficient." After talking it over with Burney, he put the idea to the ELT. Not surprisingly, the other team members decided that Cowpland's idea was brilliant.

In addition to being more efficient, the mothballing of Corel's Utah operations would also save money. Although the company was planning to hire 150 additional employees in Ottawa to carry on the WordPerfect work, its overall payroll expenses were expected to fall by $33 million annually, with the first savings showing up in the final quarter of 1998. Coincidence or not, the figure almost exactly matched the rate at which Corel was then losing money. In the second quarter of the year, the company reported an $8.3-million shortfall on sales of $63 million; losses in the third quarter totalled $7.8 million, after a one-time charge of $15.9 million arising from the Utah shutdown. Thus, if everything else remained the same and the cuts produced the anticipated savings, the company could expect to be making money by early 1999. A sustained comeback, however, would require that it squeeze more revenue out of its existing stable of products—highly unlikely, given the intense competition and pressure for price cuts in both the graphics and office-software markets— or pray that one or more of its new products took off.

By the fall of 1998, the pressure on Corel was intense. Two and a half years had passed since the company had succumbed to the siren song of Java, and still Corel did not have a single revenue-generating Java-based product. Of the several in the pipeline, the one that seemed most promising, jBridge, was not scheduled for release until the end of 1998, and few people inside or outside the company were going to be surprised if it took longer than that. In public, Cowpland continued to preach the revolutionary impact of Java, but privately, he was exasperated by the length of time it was taking to introduce new products. He assigned most of the blame to Sun Microsystems, which had fallen more than a year behind schedule in releasing Java 1.2—an improved and, it was hoped, more stable version of the programming language. "Sun did a great job of hyping Java, but it's always late," Cowpland complained. "People like us suffer the consequences because they're always slipping their schedules like crazy."

The delays were bad enough, but on top of that Cowpland was beginning to wonder if it really made sense for Corel to try to get out from under the shadow of one software giant, Microsoft, only to align itself with another, Sun. "If you want to become an official Sun developer you've got to pay about $350,000, which is more than even Microsoft charges. It's still better to have two big companies rather than one, but the fact that Sun has their paws all over it and is so damn grabby isn't good."

Amid all the problems, there was one encouraging development.

On June 29, Corel finally began taking orders for its first network computer, newly branded the NetWinder, at prices ranging from $699 to $869 (US), depending on the size of hard drive. The first machine, the Linux-based NetWinder DM (for "development machine"), was designed to be used by software developers for the creation of customized applications. Down the road, Corel planned to introduce two other versions based on the Linux operating system: the NetWinder WS, specially configured for use as a Web server, and the NetWinder LC, which was envisioned as a compact alternative to the conventional desktop. "Interest is very high, but realistically the market segment is small at this point," Corel spokesman Oliver Bendzsa acknowledged. "There are always going to be challenges trying to grow from hundreds of units to millions."

That much was obvious. But as the summer progressed, the mood around Corel became noticeably brighter. Six months earlier, Pat Beirne had worried that there wouldn't be a market for Corel's new computer. Now, after numerous conversations with prospective customers and outside developers, he was brimming with excitement. "I was walking down the hall a couple of days ago and there was an argument between one of the product managers and one of the guys from marketing about how soon we can get a shipment of these things out the door," he said toward the end of July. "Honestly, I haven't heard that kind of conversation here for a couple of years. I really believe we're on the edge of something big here. We've done a good job of designing a computer that people want, and it's selling itself."

Was Linux the big wave Cowpland and Corel had been waiting for? Maybe it was and maybe it wasn't, but for the moment it was unquestionably the best opportunity out there. And at least within the Linux development community, Corel had acquired a reputation as a progressive, forward-thinking company. At a time when many industry professionals—and even several senior executives of the company—were skeptical about Corel's ability to pull out of its financial downturn, Linux newsletters and Web sites were full of praise for its decision to clamber aboard the open-source software bandwagon. Linux supporters were also heartened by Corel's introduction of a Linux version of WordPerfect, and its declared intention to produce a full office suite. "It's a huge win for the Linux user community to have the endorsement of a company with the profile and marketing strength of Corel," says Bob Young, CEO of Red Hat Software Inc. of Raleigh, North Carolina, the leading commercial Linux distributor. Adds Young: "There's no sure thing here, but Corel knows it has to break out of its current business model and it's showing that it has a vision. And everyone is pulling for an alternative to Microsoft."

If nothing else, Linux gave Mike Cowpland cause to dream again. With Mitel and again with CorelDRAW, he had twice hit the high technology jackpot, only to squander most of his gains by repeatedly raising the stakes. A sensible gambler would have scooped up his winnings and left the table, but Cowpland wasn't interested in being sensible. He wanted excitement, not predictability. He took chances, and if they didn't always pay off—well, that only made it more interesting.

As for what lay ahead, Cowpland certainly didn't pretend to have it all figured out. In an interview in the early summer of 1998, he spoke of the company's future as resting on three pillars. The first consisted of CorelDRAW and WordPerfect, two old standbys from which he hoped to continue wringing dollars for as long as possible. The second pillar represented Corel's new Linux and Java products. "We're not exactly sure which ones will be the big hits," he confessed, "but we have our net spread pretty wide." Finally, there would be "products we haven't even thought of yet."

"Take a look at a company like Hewlett-Packard," Cowpland said. "Two thirds of their products didn't even exist three years ago. In high tech you basically have to be in the right space with an agile team and you go where the demand is. As long as you have your team dynamically tuned, you're going to come up with those winning products."

It wasn't quite that easy, of course. Back in the early days of Corel, the personal computer industry was a much simpler place, a kind of digital Wild West in which all sorts of energetic new companies were able to ride in and stake claims. Corel rose to become a major player at a time when companies like Microsoft were far less powerful, when it was still possible for a software application created by a team of four young engineers in Ottawa to attract a standing ovation from a Texas convention hall packed with computer hobbyists. By 1998, it was a very different world.

On the other hand, as Cowpland likes to say, he has hit the bull's-eye twice before. Who's to say he can't do it again?

Acknowledgments

M any people contributed to this book, and I am immensely grateful to each and every one. First, I want to offer my appreciation to Mike Cowpland. I approached him with the idea of writing this book in July 1997; over the following year I interviewed him seven times in his office and his home, for a total of 20 hours. He gave me everything I asked for by way of information and access, never seeking to exercise control over the project and never asking to read the manuscript before publication. A journalist cannot ask for more.

My thanks as well to Marlen Cowpland, an entertaining interview subject and a charming host. Among the many other relatives and friends of Mike Cowpland who offered insights, I especially want to thank his father, Ronald, his brother, Geoffrey, and his daughter, Paula. Darlene Cowpland, his first wife, generously invited me into her home and endured my questions with patience and grace.

The list of current and former Corel employees to whom I am indebted is far too long to include here in its entirety, but I would like to pay special thanks to Arlen Bartsch, Paul Bodnoff, Mark Charlesworth, Fiona Rochester Hennessy, Trevor McGuire and Susan Wimmer. Paul Chehowski maintains a Web site for ex-Corel staff, which made the job of tracking people down far easier than would otherwise have been the case. Aili Kurtis was unstinting in her support and proved to be a valuable source of archival material. Pat Beirne was generous with his time and more tolerant of my technical questions than I had a right to expect.

This book could not have been written without the support and forbearance of my friends, colleagues and mentors at Maclean's, including Geoff Stevens and Bob Levin. Above all I want to thank Bob Lewis, my boss. For 14 years he has guided my efforts and put up with my idiosyncracies. He is a superb role model and I am lucky to know him.

Meg Masters, my editor at Penguin Books Canada, was a pleasure to deal with from beginning to end. I am grateful to Meg and to Catherine Marjoribanks for polishing my manuscript, and to Cynthia Good, the publisher of Penguin Books Canada, for entrusting this project to me in the first place. Thanks also to Susan James, Cathy MacLean, Scott Sellers, Jasmine Zohar and Laura Brady. My agent, Bruce Westwood, helped to get the ball rolling. Toward the end of the project, I was privileged to receive the advice of Len Glickman, of the law firm Cassels Brock & Blackwell. My friends Paul Kaihla and Bruce Wallace are faithful and invaluable sources of support, comradeship and inspiration.

Outside of my own family, no one is more deserving of my appreciation than Jennifer Wells, a dear friend and my former colleague at Maclean's. It was Jennifer who introduced me to Penguin, and it was Jennifer who, on several occasions when I was lost in the thicket of my own words, guided me to a clearing. That she did so while completing her own, epic book on the Bre-X gold mystery will surprise no one who has ever had the pleasure of knowing her.

This book is dedicated to my wife, Kathy, the love of my life. All through the research and writing of the manuscript, she offered support, encouragement and solace. Then, mere weeks from completion, she gave birth to Alexandra, a sister for Ariel and Benjamin. I'm still not sure about the book, but about Alex there can be no doubt. Kathy, you make it all worthwhile.

Index